Roberts Brothers

**Where is the City?**

Roberts Brothers

**Where is the City?**

ISBN/EAN: 9783741163319

Manufactured in Europe, USA, Canada, Australia, Japa

Cover: Foto ©Andreas Hilbeck / pixelio.de

Manufactured and distributed by brebook publishing software (www.brebook.com)

Roberts Brothers

**Where is the City?**

# WHERE IS THE CITY?

BOSTON
ROBERTS BROTHERS.
1868.

Entered, according to Act of Congress, in the year 1868, by
ROBERTS BROTHERS,
In the Clerk's Office of the District Court of the District of Massachusetts.

# CONTENTS.

## INTRODUCTION.

## AMONG THE BAPTISTS.

### CHAPTER I.
A Baptist Layman, . . . . . . . 1

### CHAPTER II.
Sketch of the Baptist Minister's Sermon, . . . 9

### CHAPTER III.
The Baptism by Immersion, . . . . 16

### CHAPTER IV.
Restricted Communion, . . . . . . 22

### CHAPTER V.
Conversation with a Baptist Divine, . . . . 31

### CHAPTER VI.
Baptist Society for Religious Inquiry, . . . 40

### CHAPTER VII.
Four Faces, . . . . . . . . 47

## AMONG THE CONGREGATIONALISTS.

### CHAPTER I.
In a Congregational Sunday School, . . . 51

## CONTENTS.

### CHAPTER II.
In a Congregational Sunday School, continued, . 57

### CHAPTER III.
The Baptism by Aspersion, . . . . . . 70

### CHAPTER IV.
Talk with Congregational Clergymen, . . . 77

# AMONG THE METHODISTS.

### CHAPTER I.
The Methodist Prayer Meeting, . . . . . 97

### CHAPTER II.
Cyprian Cutting's Call, . . . . . . 110

### CHAPTER III.
Methodist Doctrine, . . . . . . . 114

### CHAPTER IV.
The Fold of Flocks, . . . . . . . 119

### CHAPTER V.
An Old Man's Opinion of Methodism, . . . 134

### CHAPTER VI.
The Methodist Annual Conference, . . . . 140

# AMONG THE EPISCOPALIANS.

### CHAPTER I.
The Episcopal Ordination, . . . . . . 151

### CHAPTER II.
Episcopal Doctrine, . . . . . . . 159

### CHAPTER III.
Luminous Points of Episcopacy, . . . . . 162

### CHAPTER IV.
Another Opinion, . . . . . . . . 177

## AMONG THE QUAKERS.

### CHAPTER I.
Friends' Meeting, . . . . . . . . 181

### CHAPTER II.
Further Observations, . . . . . . . 186

## AMONG THE SWEDENBORGIANS.

### CHAPTER I.
Conversation with a Swedenborgian, . . . . 195

### CHAPTER II.
Conversation Continued, . . . . . . 208

### CHAPTER III.
Who was Emanuel Swedenborg? . . . . 213

### CHAPTER IV.
Concluding conversation, . . . . . . 218

## AMONG THE SPIRITUALISTS.

### CHAPTER I.
A Sitting with a Spiritual Medium, . . . . 227

### CHAPTER II.
More Advice, . . . . . . . . 237

### CHAPTER III.
Talk with a Spiritualist, . . . . . . 243

### CHAPTER IV.
A Spiritual Trajectory, . . . . . . 253

## AMONG THE UNIVERSALISTS.

### CHAPTER I.
The Universalist Sermon, . . . . . . 259

## CHAPTER II.
Conversation with a Universalist, . . . . . 273

## CHAPTER III.
Second Sermon, . . . . . . . . 286

## CHAPTER IV.
Three Months Later, . . . . . . . 298

# AMONG THE UNITARIANS.

## CHAPTER I.
Preliminary Observations, . . . . . . 303

## CHAPTER II.
Conversation, . . . . . . . . 310

## CHAPTER III.
The Practical Sermon, . . . . . . . 331

# FINDING THE CITY.

A Letter, . . . . . . . . . 345
The Reply, . . . . . . . . . 345
Conclusion, . . . . . . . . . 348

# INTRODUCTION.

ISRAEL KNIGHT opened his Bible at Ezekiel 48 : 35, reading, —

"'And the name of the city from that day shall be, *The Lord is there.*"

Closing the book, he reflected. At length he said, "O! that I might find the city with that name!"

This figure was not marked upon his mind at the bidding of the ideal pencil of a new impulse; it was there as is the print of palms upon stone. Nature, which is one of the names of God, had graven it. It is natural for every soul, soon or late, to utter this aspiration. Whether the accidents are sublime, or trifling, or terribly adverse, the immortal sometimes looks upward. He yearns for the repose which is absolute.

Israel Knight had come to this recognition. The figure before him was beautiful; but more than this, the fact, that — *Somewhere, there is a church, a peculiar people whose name is rightly,* "*The Lord is there.*" Being a youth who lacked a little of his majority, he addressed to his guardian the following:

"Respected Sir:—

"I hope I am a Christian. As I have had but little experience, and have examined few books except those used in my classes, I am undecided what Church I had better select, with which to connect myself.

"Please advise me upon this important subject, and oblige
Yours obediently,
Israel Knight."

He received this reply:—

"My Dear Young Friend:—

"I hope you are a true disciple of Christ. He that doeth His will shall know of the doctrine. Love the Lord your God with all your heart, and your neighbor as yourself, and you will find the truth.

"An old man like myself sees through different spectacles from those used by young eyes. God is good. He gives wisdom to all who seek it with a humble mind. Therefore, look for yourself; but my advice is — *look on all sides before you cleave to any*.

"Be cautious about starting to make your jar, lest, like the one you found in Horace, as the wheel goes round, it turns out an insignificant pitcher.
Yours truly,
Ephraim Stearns."

Our inquirer was now as much in obscurity as before, only it was clear that a work was before him, which no one else could do. "Shall I have recourse to a religious cyclopædia?" he asked himself. Then he thought of the words "books as affected, are as men," and concluded to adopt the most inartificial course for the present. Knowing that business was soon to call him to a distant part of the State, he determined to keep the special object in recollection.

# THE WAY TO THE CITY.

---

"This (my way) is the way, walk ye in it, when ye turn to the right hand, and when ye turn to the left."
THE SECTARY.

---

"When he that is a fool walketh by the way, his wisdom faileth him, and he saith to every one that he is a fool."
ECCL. 10: 3.

---

"And yet I show unto you a more excellent way. Though I speak with the tongues of men and of angels, and have not charity, I am become as sounding brass, or a tinkling cymbal."
PAUL TO THE CORINTHIANS.

# AMONG THE BAPTISTS.

## CHAPTER I.

#### A BAPTIST LAYMAN.

Israel read the New Testament with interest. He thought he had great advantage in being able to study the sacred words in the unadulterated Greek. Besides the Greek Testament which he used in college, he owned one, in which had been written by his father's hand copious marginal notes in Latin and English. This copy was old enough to have on its title page: "Londini, Excudebat A. Lemington: Impensis J. F. & C. Lemington. MDCLVI."

By the time he had arrived at the village of his temporary destination, he had examined into the third chapter of the Gospel by Matthew. It will be seen that he travelled leisurely over the ground. At the eleventh verse of this chapter he stopped short, for here was a note in the paternal handwriting: "*In* water, *upon* repentance. Or, according to the paraphrase of Grotius, 'upon that profession of repentance which you make.'" In his English version, he found this verse to read, "I, indeed, baptize you with water unto repentance."

It was now Sunday morning. Having arrived at the hotel late on the previous evening, he was at breakfast when the church-bell of the village began to ring. He asked his landlord what people worshipped there.

"We are almost all Baptists hereabouts," answered that individual; "we've had a great revival lately, and there's going to be some twenty souls baptized to-day. Better go and see them."

"Yes," said Israel with a new interest; "I shall gladly embrace this opportunity." He thought that his coming hither at that time was providential, and repeated to himself, "For he that hath mercy on them shall lead them, even by the springs of water shall he guide them." Is. 49 : 10. He did not yet see that all events are providential. "You have witnessed such important occasions as baptizings before?" continued the man.

"No, sir," replied Israel; "having spent nearly all my life in school, I have seen but little of the various forms and customs of the world."

"Folks dead, mostly, perhaps?"

"Yes, I can adopt the language of the inspired prophet — 'Behold I was left alone!' I have, however, a good guardian."

"Property, I presume, for him to look after? Well, I hope you will make up your mind to cast your lot in with us Baptists. We're a great people, sir, and we date back to the Lord Jesus himself, who was the true founder of our denomination. That, you know, is what no other sect in Christendom can begin to boast of."

"To whom do the Congregationalists refer, as their founder?" asked Israel.

"Not to the Lord," answered the man, shaking his

head oracularly; "they're always talking about Circumcision and the Covenant. I don't know which of the two they take for their forefather. There never was a set of people more deluded than they are, unless it is the Catholics. *They* beat all for that."

"The Roman Catholics, do you mean?" interposed the young man, quietly.

"Of course, sir," answered the landlord with an air of irritation.

"They refer to Christ as their founder, though we Protestants believe that there has been in some of their data, a falling away from the apostolic faith and practice. We certainly decline to acknowledge the '*Datum apud Sanctum Petrum*,'" added Israel, who had not yet put away the attempts at pedantry, which are the folly of nearly all newly-emancipated collegians.

"O, as to that, you see, sir," said the landlord in an uncertain way — "Ah! what was I about to say? Yes, all the sects try to get straight descent from the Lord of Hosts; but, sir," (striking on the table by way of emphasis), "not one of them have a grain of truth in 'em, only what they fetch round from us Baptists. You know that place where it says, 'If you don't follow my words, you will be cast into the fire and burned,' or something like."

"Do you believe that all who are not Baptists will share that fate?" now asked Israel, dropping his fork and looking fixedly at his host.

"I wouldn't go bail for them," answered the man; then continued in a tone of greater seriousness, — "Young man, if you want to be on the safe side, you'd better make up your mind at once. I think after you have seen them baptized to-day, you will be wholly of my mind."

"I have had friends, of other denominations, whom I highly regard for their goodness," said Israel; "now, these are either going to be saved after death, or they are not. Certain it is that not one of them has been baptized by immersion. But perhaps you believe in a purgatorial state," he added, "in which these people will be disciplined for their delinquency, while the Baptists will go immediately to Heaven?"

"No, none of that. I believe in two places after death, and *only* two," answered the landlord.

"Very well. To which shall these good Christians who have not been baptized like yourself, go?"

"I've got a book," said the man moving uneasily in his chair, "which I want you to read. It is written by one of our most famous Baptist ministers, and explains all this much clearer than I can. You see I am a plain man, and not a D. D."

"And I already have a book which was written by several very plain men, who took their degree directly from the great Head of the church. It is the New Testament, sir. I do not find there denunciations upon any sect; but the requisitions for salvation are boldly stated to be summed up in faith in the Lord Jesus Christ."

"Believe and be *baptized*," said the man, "and thou shalt be saved."

"It does not read, however, that he that believeth not *and is not baptized* shall be damned. The persons to whom I have referred have been baptized, though not in the way which you believe to be right."

"At all events," said the landlord, "I am just as certain as I am of anything in this world, that we Baptists will receive a great reward, in the next life, for our following our Master into the river Jordan."

"Then you must hold to different states of happiness hereafter?"

"There's one glory of the sun, we read;— that glory will belong to our people, while those who may be Christians, but who have lived all their days in daring disobedience to the divine command, will shine about like a star that's almost gone out. But, then there's a mighty host of them that will be cast into outer darkness with other wretched wrong-doers. I can't say but all who have not been baptized, and who know better, will share this dreadful fate."

"Perhaps they will," responded Israel with a deep sigh, as he remembered his father's note in the Greek testament; "but I am rejoiced that it is not left for me to decide."

"I have no doubt," said the man, "that all real Baptists will be among those who, Christ promised, shall set on thrones, and judge the world. O! it will be a blessed day; yes, a most glorious day, when all the kingdoms of the earth shall wail at the triumphs of the truth which they have despised."

Israel had now finished his breakfast. As he rose to leave the table, the landlord said to him, "The more you read the Bible, the more you will see that the Baptists are the only ones who are right." In various forms, he repeated this assertion till Israel had nearly ascended the stairs which led to his room. "The bell will ring again at half-past ten, and if you like, I will take you along and give you a seat in my pew," he called after him.

Israel thanked him, and disappeared.

At the ringing of the second bell for church, the landlord found many things to engross his attention, until it was nearly time for the people to cease going.

"Shall we not be late at church?" asked Israel, when they were fairly started, and had yet some rods to walk.

"All right, sir," answered the man, while he looked slyly at his guest. "You must know it isn't every day that I have a stranger like yourself to bring with me into church."

"To me tardiness seems disrespectful to the officiating clergyman, and also to the place and the sacred object of our meeting," said Israel.

"Undoubtedly; but then our minister knows me, and he knows, too, I suppose, that I'm one of his heaviest payers. 'Money answereth all things' you see."

"It does not answer a good conscience, I believe," said Israel, in a lower voice.

"O! as to that, '*Baptism* is the answering of a good conscience,' Paul says. I attended to that important matter, years ago," added the man with new solemnity.

They gained their seats in season to hear the prayer after the singing. Israel called home his wandering thoughts as well as he could, till he succeeded in fastening his attention. It took him longer to do this, as, following the manner of those around him, he remained in an upright, sitting posture, with his eyes unclosed. Unusual unction accompanied this prayer, and Israel received it, to keep with him ever after.

Not that it was always present in his memory; but its influence remained. The rain falls upon the plot of ground; it dries, and is seen no more; but a fructification remains, which shall repeat itself in endless growths.

Would you know the reason why this prayer was remembered? It was short. It was glowing with feeling. It had color, shape, sweetness, the strength of true reverence for the Unknown God! Not a word was wasted; not one misplaced. The minister had come to the attainment of this Fine Art in Religion, as a genius arrives at excellence in any department of effort, by dint of patient labor. All true genius must have an inspiration. In this case, superadded to the labor was the Unspeakable Gift.

In the earlier periods of his ministerial career, he had often indulged himself in roundly-worded and excursive prayers. He seemed to be striving to obey the injunction of the mournful prophet,—"In the beginning of the watches (or exercises) pour out thy heart like water before the face of the Lord." But he made a mistake and poured out his head. Hence, much was as if spilled on the ground, and could never be gathered up. What remained on the surface was not clear. It mirrored neither the image of God nor man. Had he poured out his heart, it would have been otherwise.

One day, he made a discovery, which, though important, is generally missed by men of his profession.

This was, that, while he was at prayer in the sanctuary, some persons dreamed. The circumstances attending the event were ludicrous, but they entered his soul as though they had been sublime. He pondered the matter. Then, he knew, if some slept, others, whose temperament forbade this lapse from the dignity of the august occasion, would "endure the hour" by considering many subjects foreign to those in which he strove to lead.

There was an error somewhere. Further pondering convinced him of the difficulty, even as men learned by the ass Nauplias what was the matter with their vines. By gnawing them, the creature taught the art of pruning. These stupid people gnawed into his sensibilities, but they showed him how to prune their excessive manifestation.

After this, the minister had no more trouble with sleepers while he prayed.

As Israel listened, his mind expanded towards the speaker, and he felt a sensation of need. When one mind is attracted by another human mind, a want is created to supply a vacuity, — as a rise of the water of the sea at any place, in what is called a tide, produces a depression at another. The attraction of the infinite mind can alone give any impression of supply. But this is never complete in the natural life. Hence, it is written — "I shall be satisfied when I awake in thy likeness."

At present, Israel regarded truth as a palpable reality which he was about to grasp.

## CHAPTER II.

#### SKETCH OF THE BAPTIST MINISTER'S SERMON.

"My text this morning," announced the preacher, "is found in Isaiah, fifty-fifth chapter, twelfth and thirteenth verses, — 'For ye shall go out with joy and be led forth with peace: the mountains and the hills shall break forth before you into singing, and all the trees of the field shall clap their hands. Instead of the thorn shall come up the fir-tree, and instead of the brier shall come up the myrtle tree: and it shall be to the Lord for a name, for an everlasting sign that shall not be cut off.'"

This sermon had two general heads.

*First* — The persons to whom this promise applies.

*Second* — The harmonious relation of the heart of the true disciple with the external world.

Growing out of the first division of the subject was: —

1. The persons who will go out with joy and be led forth with peace are those who keep the divine commandments. "If ye love me, keep my commandments." John 14: 15. "If ye keep my commandments, ye shall abide in my love." John 15: 10. The Holy Spirit, in his office of Comforter, abides with those who love God, so that they are enabled to rejoice under all circumstances.

2. What are the divine commandments and how are they kept? The first sermon which Jesus preached, after his preparation by the temptations, had for a text — *Repent*. His first public act touching himself, as he had no need of repentance, was *baptism*.

The word of John the Baptist was also *Repent ye*.

All need repentance, and this should be the first work of the soul who seeks for God.

John's next act of ministry was the administration of the ordinance of baptism. He baptized Christ by immersion. Hence, baptism by immersion is not less obligatory than repentance. All other modes of baptism are desecrations of the sacred rite. He who said, "I am the way, the truth, and the life," pronounced those who climbed into the fold by any other way, thieves and robbers.

"If there is one soul in my congregation to-day," continued the minister, "who doubts about immersion being the scriptural rite of baptism in profession of faith, or who thinks that another mode will answer a good conscience just as well as the true one, let me inquire, in the words of another, 'if there is not improbability that the just, wise, and merciful Saviour would enjoin upon His disciples the observance of a rite the nature of which could not be determined with any certainty, or at least not without great difficulty. With all the resources of the most copious language in the world at His disposal, it is utterly incredible that He should have selected, to designate the act by which He requires all His followers to profess their faith in Him, a word so vague, or so ambiguous, as to make it impossible for them to understand precisely what He would have them do. The supposition would, in fact, be highly dishonorable and very insulting to Him. If He could have wished to express His requirement by a word which would be equally applicable to several quite different acts, such as sprinkling, pouring, and immersion, it may well be doubted whether He could have found such a word in the Greek language or in any other; but we are bound to believe He could not have wished any such thing. What we have to do, then, is to ascertain as exactly as possible what word He would have used had He spoken in the English language.

"When the meaning of any word which often occurs in the Scriptures is called in question, it is to be ascertained by a collection and comparison of all the passages. That is the true meaning which gives a consistent sense in all the various relations and connections in which the word is used. The scriptural meaning of the Greek words for *baptize* and *baptism* is that which best agrees with *all* that is said about the rite in the New Testament, without any forced interpretation or elaborate explanation. That is the true sense of the words which naturally and obviously explains the expressions, 'going down into the water,' 'coming up out of the water,' 'being baptized in water, in the Jordan, into Christ;' which shows that the abundance of water in Ænon was the reason why John chose that place for the scene of his baptism; which exhibits the resemblance between our baptism and a burial and resurrection; which makes it pertinent to call the overwhelming sufferings of Christ a baptism; which accounts for the fact that *persons* are always *said* to be baptized, the *element* never. If sprinkling meets all these requirements, that is the true scriptural baptism. If pouring meets all these requirements, that is the true scriptural baptism. If nothing but immersion meets all these requirements, then immersion, and nothing else, is the true scriptural baptism. The last particular named, though not so commonly noticed as some of the others, seems to us perfectly decisive of the whole question. If baptism meant sprinkling, then we should at least *sometimes* read that water was baptized upon persons. If baptism meant pouring, then we should of course *always* read that water was baptized upon persons. But if baptism means immersion, then we should always read that persons were baptized in water. We never do find either of the first two expressions; we always do find this last expression. Could the scriptural proof be more complete? We never even read, in the original inspired text, that persons were baptized *with* water; it is always *in*, or *into*, the element. The preposition is indeed sometimes omitted, but as no other preposition is ever used, we are not at liberty to supply any other.

"The best judges are not those who write controversially, on either side, but the most learned and impartial lexicographers, commentators, historians, and antiquarians, of all ages, sects, and nations. And among these there is a remarkable unanimity in declaring that immersion is the primary meaning of the Greek word, and a very general agreement in affirming that it is the *only* meaning. Exclude all *partisan* testimonies, on both sides, and the question ceases at once to be debatable. Where is the church historian, of any scholarly reputation, who disputes that for more than a thousand years immersion was the only regular baptism throughout the Christian world, other and more convenient applications of water being allowed only in cases of sickness or infirmity, and avowedly as substitutes for the primitive rite? Is not the uniform and persistent testimony and practice of all to whom the Greek language is vernacular, of itself a demonstration of the meaning of the word? The Greek language has been the common speech of millions in every age since the New Testament was written; and all these, with one voice, declare, and have always declared, that the word means only to immerse; they all practise, and have always practised immersion; they all refuse, and have always refused, to admit the validity of any baptism but immersion.

"Just as, in consulting the Scriptures, the true sense is that which harmonizes and reconciles all the passages which speak of baptism, so also, in consulting the human authorities, the true verdict is that in which there is a general agreement of competent witnesses. And immersion is the only point in which the suffrages of scholars in regard to the meaning of the Greek word unite and are agreed."

(Israel afterwards found these "words of another" in a paper among the files of the organ of the Baptist Church in New England.)

"Now!" exclaimed the clergyman, striking the pulpit desk emphatically, "I challenge any one in the whole world, learned or unlearned, to find a set of arguments that can match these, which I have just read to you."

"They are remarkably clear," responded Israel to himself, "and I don't see but I must submit to their practical conclusion."

The speaker now hastened to the consideration of his last general division, viz: the relation of the mind, when properly exercised, with nature. Nature was but another name here for all the external world. Everywhere and under all circumstances, the willing and the obedient eat the good of the land, in their souls. Examples of this were cited. Among the most forcible was the great Baptist, John Bunyan. In prison, when expecting separation from his beloved family by an ignominious death, he wrote, "I have been able to laugh at destruction, and to fear neither the horse nor his rider. I have had sweet sights of the forgiveness of my sins in this place, and of my body with Jesus in another world." * * *

"I have often thought," said the speaker, "that the happiest people in the world were the faithful Baptists; and perhaps the brightest of their earthly moments, save those which close their mortal career, are when they follow their Saviour into the watery grave, and are buried with Him in baptism. The reason of this is, that they are the beloved and protected of Heaven. The clouds seem to part over their heads, and we can almost catch the words,— 'These are my beloved ones in whom I am well pleased.' * * *

"I never knew of the least physical injury to come upon a subject of baptism in consequence of the reception of the holy rite, although I have seen the fragile form of delicate woman moving through the water with piles of newly-cut ice on either hand, and beneath the inclement skies of midwinter, while the chill of an approaching storm filled all the air. Yes! that same woman, when deep within the icy wave, broke forth in a melodious strain of sacred song!

"All you," he concluded, "who are about to complete the obedience to the requirements of your Saviour, by the acts of this day, will prove the truth of this sublime and beautiful promise—'For ye shall go out with joy and be led forth with peace: the mountains and the hills shall break forth before you into singing, and all the trees of the field shall clap their hands. Instead of the thorn shall come up the fir-tree, and instead of the brier shall come up the myrtle-tree: and it shall be to the Lord for a name, for an everlasting sign that shall not be cut off.' This name is the true disciple, and this everlasting sign is baptism by immersion."

## CHAPTER III.

#### THE BAPTISM BY IMMERSION.

At the close of the sermon, the minister announced that the ordinance of baptism would be administered in the usual place, at half-past twelve o'clock.

Israel followed his new guide out of the crowded house. "We will make haste," he said, "that we may get a good place at the water, for you to see and hear." The place of baptism was called at a convenient distance from the church, yet it required a brisk walk of some ten minutes.

It was about the middle of June, and, but for the warmth, one of the "perfect days" of the loveliest period of the year. After walking some distance upon a retired street, they struck off from the ordinary route within a range of broad and beautiful pasturage, where was only an irregular path which had been made by the cows and sheep on their daily goings and returnings.

Fresh from a thickly populated place, Israel was more than pleased with the prospect which was now unfolding before him. Afar off could be discerned the soft outline of the distant hills, which seemed asleep in the purpled haze of the summer noon. In nearer view, here and there upon the undulating stretch of lands, he discerned the white farm-houses, half embosomed in the abundant foliage of the trees. These, likewise, looked slumberous, as if the Sabbath calm held them in a dreamy pause.

They soon came to a dilapidated fence of ancient looking design in irregular stones, half hidden by hedges of wild roses, blackberry and sweetbrier. Within this enclosure the herd had ceased to graze, and were lying down in the grateful shadows of several maple-trees and slender silver birches. The sheep, a little scared at the intrusion, moved away softly over the grass, but soon stopped and seemed half satisfied.

"There," said the landlord, as they suddenly made an angle around a slight declivity, "you see our Crystal Lake, where we baptize."

Israel looked. He surveyed the new and beautiful picture in a protracted gaze. Somewhat of an artist by nature, and slightly such by cultivation, his soul drank in the scene with silent delight. Down the hill, a little to the left, was a sheet of water clear as crystal, and reflecting the green banks with the occasional trees, in wonderful distinctness. A fantastic willow whose trunk was wound fast with a large grape-vine, had grown over the water, so that its long, graceful streamers touched the surface with every slight motion of the breeze. Near this a bridge had once been started to span the narrowest portion of the water. A new road in another direction had interrupted the enterprise, so that now there was only a picturesque path built out a little way, and gradually losing its shining sands in the water.

A large stone, which was designed as one of the supports of the railing, the landlord showed Israel for

a resting-place, while his rotund and ample figure
served as a shelter from the surges of the rapidly increasing crowd of spectators. From this point a clear
view of the baptism was obtainable.

Israel thanked his guide, and folding his arms,
yielded to the tide of emotion which began to rise in
his soul.

Although the groups of men, women, and children
were plentiful on the bank for some distance, and all
along the lower paths about the water, they showed a
respectful regard for the occasion, by a quiet demeanor
and a stillness broken only by low murmurs of conversation; or away on the farther bank, by the fall of a
pebble from the hand of some curiously disposed
urchin. But even these ceased, when the last of the
procession made its appearance along the path which
led to the shore, near the position occupied by
Israel.

"Here come the minister and the candidates, with
the deacons and a few other members of the church,"
whispered the landlord.

The minister and each of the candidates, who were
nineteen in number, wore a long black robe, in the
lower hem of which were small pieces of lead. They
walked in couples, the men leading. The minister
stood a little apart on the bank, with his back to the
water, and uncovering his head (which example was
followed by all the male members of the church
present), he began to read aloud from a hymn-book.
After which many voices sang the hymn.

The sound of plaintive song upon the water is ever
tenderly true to the highest impulses of our souls. As

we listen, we hear more than the human strain; a legend of the angels falls from Heaven, and dissolves our ordinary thought into a tenuity of awe. Then, there are pictures. We seem nearer the eternal realities than we were a moment before this singing, by years of time. We wonder that our hope paints not the roughness of everyday life with an immortal splendor; for the ethers, in the calm sky above us, seem strangely transparent. Almost we pierce the veil.

Israel heard this sacred melody, while his eyes rested upon the clear water which nearly touched his feet — heard this song going up from full and consecrated hearts — and he prayed. Unconsciously, he said in his heart, "Mother! help thy erring, struggling boy to come *the right way* to thee, who art now in the presence of the Infinite Christ!"

The mother whom he called dead was near in his thought, and he felt that he had but to put forth his hand, to touch her white robe. He heard not the prayer which followed the singing, nor did he hear any of the remarks upon the nature and obligation of the ordinance that came after the prayer.

A moment there was a perfect silence. This recalled Israel, and he saw the minister first go down alone into the water, then return, take one of the men by the hand, and then again slowly walk into the water. As they went, the clear, impressive voice of the minister spoke: "These were the words of the Lord — 'Whosoever shall confess me before men, him shall the Son of Man also confess before the angels of God.' And thus said one of his disciples — 'See, here is water, what doth hinder? If thou believest with all thine heart, thou mayest be baptized.'"

When they had gone into the water to the usual depth, they stopped; then placing himself on the left of the candidate, the minister said, —

"I baptize you in the name of the Father, and of the Son, and of the Holy Ghost," meanwhile gently drawing him backward beneath the water, and bringing him up again, then saying "Amen." As soon as this was done, the choir on the bank commenced to sing: —

> "Sacred spirit, breathing o'er us,
>   Thy sweet influence may we know;
> Open paths of light before us,
>   And thy peace on us bestow.
>     By thee guided,
>     Up to glory may we go."

Israel observed that the intelligent and tranquil face of the baptized person wore an expression of devout elevation, as though the conscious seal of divine approbation rested on him. Something of this expression was apparent on each of the other persons who received the ordinance. Especially did the faces of the women sweetly mirror the repose of satisfaction which seemed to possess their souls. Some of these were quite young, and as the choir sung, —

> "Down to the hallowed grave we go,
>   Obedient to thy word;
> 'Tis thus the world around shall know
>   We're buried with the Lord:
> 'Tis thus we bid its pomps adieu,
>   And boldly venture in;
> O may we rise to life anew,
>   And only die to sin;"

Israel wondered if their coming lives would verify this sublime prophecy. The reflecting mind cannot shut out these unbidden speculations, even in the most solemn moments of experience. But the disciplined spirit remembers the words, "Charity never faileth," and is hushed. The young man did not know by word or life this beautiful and holy mystery of Christian charity or love; therefore he thought many unquiet things at the suggestion of the Adversary, who is always present among the gatherings of the sons of God.

When the last one had received the administration of the ordinance, and was coming up out of the water, these words were sung with an impressiveness which moved all hearts: —

> "'Tis done; the great transaction's done;
> I am my Lord's and he is mine:
> He drew me and I followed on,
> Rejoiced to own the call divine.
>
> High heaven, that hears the solemn vow,
> That vow renewed shall daily hear,
> 'Till in life's latest hour I bow,
> And bless in death a bond so dear."

"Lord! it is done as thou hast commanded, and yet there is room!" exclaimed the minister. He then closed the exercises with a short prayer and the benediction.

## CHAPTER IV.

#### RESTRICTED COMMUNION.

In the afternoon, the pastor of the church was assisted by another minister of his own denomination, whom he introduced to the audience as the Reverend Doctor Elias of the next city. It appeared afterwards that he had been invited to preach on that occasion, in order to effectually remove certain conscientious scruples of some of the leading Baptists of that church, in regard to the conditions of reception to Christian fellowship at the Lord's Supper.

This man had a concrete expression upon his countenance, as though fixed in the long-continued habit of close investigation of abstract subjects and peculiar persons. But in all denominations, persons who study much upon one subject and upon one point of that subject are inclined to wear this look. One of its peculiarities is, that it comprehends objects in an opposite position from the reality. This is not unlike the operation of the burning-glass. All the sun's rays which fall on its surface are collected by the refraction of the glass into a single point. Whatever the object exposed to such a glass, it presents the image of it instead of the object itself. And this image is inverted.

The theme of Doctor Elias, on this occasion, was

based upon the words found in Colossians 11: 8. "Beware lest any man spoil you . . . after the tradition of men, after the rudiments of the world, and not after Christ." Also, Hebrews 13: 10. "We have an altar, whereof they have no right to eat which serve the tabernacle.".

The tradition of men and rudiments of the world were infant baptism and the baptism of believers by aspersion. Those who served the tabernacle, that is the Jewish rites in this manner, had no right to eat at the altar which was commemorative of Christ's sufferings and death; they were not after-him, in their open disobedience to his commands and indifference to his example. We ought, therefore, to go not after them, nor receive them to our Christian fellowship. The scriptural terms of admission of persons to the Lord's Supper were:—

*First* — Confession of faith in Christ as their Saviour from the consequences of sin.

*Second* — The public profession of their faith by baptism, (which signified immersion, no other mode of receiving this ordinance being admitted to be baptism.)

*Third* — Faithful membership of a Baptist Church.

After the consideration of the first division of the subject, much in the way that is usual for expounders of the Scripture in what are called Calvinistic churches, Dr. Elias proceeded to expend the force of his argument upon the subject commonly called Close Communion.

In the opening and unfolding of this portion of his theme, the preacher clearly acquitted himself of any violation of the first dictum in the formal logical rules of controversy, viz: "The terms in which the question in debate is expressed, and the precise point at issue, should be so clearly defined, that there could be no misunderstanding respecting them."

The "precise point" with the Doctor was, — That Baptist believers, who alone are of Christ, should commune *only* with Baptist believers. His terms were cut clean with a sharp knife; his point as plain to be seen as that of the letter V made by certain wild birds in their semi-annual migrations. But like this shape of the bird-flight, there appeared some disjointed links in his chain of argument. All who defend this doctrine do not openly take the position that believers baptized by immersion are alone of Christ; they admit that others may be of Him, though an awkward arrangement is necessarily effected with being of Christ, and living in what they think is open disobedience to his commands respecting baptism.

This man, however, acknowledged no such difficulty, since he maintained that there are three that bear witness of Christ on earth, "the spirit, and the water, and the blood: and these three agree in one." Faith in Christ in respect to the water was equally essential as faith in Him in respect to the spirit and the blood; and he that believeth not God, hath made Him a liar, because he believeth not the record that God gave of his Son. The eternal life contained in this record included baptism as much as repentance and faith in the atoning blood. Therefore he that rejected one as it stood in God's own record, rejected all. Such persons deserved rejection by all who possessed the threefold witness in themselves.

To substantiate this ground-position he asserted that none but Baptists should be admitted to the sacrament of the Lord's Supper.

1. From the nature of the ordinance.

One of the most ancient terms given to this sacrament was *eucharist*, from a Greek word, signifying a giving of thanks. The object of this act of thanksgiving was the death of Christ. It was sometimes called the Sacrifice among the primitive Christians, because it took the place of the paschal lamb, which clearly foreshadowed the atonement made by the divine sacrifice.

(Here reflected Israel. If the institution of the Lord's Supper took the place of the Jewish passover, why may it not be true that baptism in like manner succeeded the rite of circumcision?)

"This shows," continued the Doctor, "that the sacrament of the Lord's Supper is a commemoration of the sufferings and death of Christ, by those who have obediently entered His visible church, and so have a right to the altar."

2. From the express teachings of Scripture. "I would they were even cut off which trouble you," writes Paul to the Galatians. Again to Titus he says, "A man that is a heretic, after the first and second admonition reject." Any opinion that is contrary to the teaching of the Bible is heresy; the term *heretic* signifies also one who causes division or schism in the church. Those who hold erroneous opinions are sure to endeavor to teach them to others; hence schism. The opposers of baptism (he signified immersion) were schismatics or heretics.

"Now I beseech you, brethren, mark them which cause divisions and offences, contrary to the doctrine which ye have learned, and avoid them." Rom. 16 : 17. All who do not hold to the Baptist or Bible doctrines have departed from the faith, and so cause divisions and offences, and, as one has said, "they are the party who are responsible for all the divisions resulting from that departure."

"Can two walk together except they be agreed." Amos 3 : 3.

"Now I beseech you, brethren, by the name of our Lord Jesus Christ, that ye all speak the same thing, and that there be no division among you ; but that ye be perfectly joined together in the same mind, and in the same judgment. . . . Is Christ divided?" 1 Cor. 1 : 10, 13.

"I here quote," said the speaker, "from an able exposition of our views upon this important subject.* 'It is not difficult to see how they can live in peace together in the same community (Baptists and Pædobaptists), and mutually esteem and love each other, and have much cordial and delightful communion and co-operation, while they abide in separate ecclesiastical organizations, and each understands the other's liberty, and respects the other's conscience, and expects the other to maintain and propagate his peculiar views by all honorable and Christian meth-

---

* Scriptural Terms of Admission to The Lord's Supper, By Rev. A. N. Arnold, D. D.

It would appear that this clergyman was otherwise partially indebted to the same authority in this discourse, — a custom not peculiar to any denomination of preachers.

ods; though even then the difference that requires their separation must seem to both parties a serious evil; but how they are to live and work harmoniously together in one church fellowship, and under one church law, is in theory a mystery past finding out, and in practice certainly a problem yet unsolved. The things about which they differ are matters that particularly and vitally affect church relations. If they are peaceably united in those relations, it can only be on the condition that one of the parties shall consent to see, without protest, what they regard as a pernicious human invention, constantly performed in the church as a divine rite; and that the other party shall consent to see, without protest, what they regard as a sacred parental duty, systematically neglected. . . . Happily there is too much of conscience in both parties to permit a peaceable and lasting union on such unchristian terms. Yes, happily; for so long as our present difference of views continues, it would be a disgrace to us both if we could be cordially united in church relations.'"

"Buy the truth and sell it not." Prov. 23: 23. If we have bought the truth at the price of Christ's own blood, we may not sell it for a mess of pottage, like the Jewish rite of circumcision, which tradition and worldly rudiment is perpetuated in the rite of infant sprinkling.

"Whatsoever is not of faith, is sin." Rom. 14: 23. If we have not fellowship of faith with others, an attempt to establish church fellowship is a violation of right. "Endeavor to keep the unity of the Spirit in the bond of peace. There is one body and one Spirit, even as

ye are called in one hope of your calling; one Lord,
one faith, one *baptism*, one God and Father of all."
Eph. 4 : 5.

It is shown what are this faith and this baptism,
inasmuch as the Lord in his commission to his disciples, associates *teaching* with baptism, and confines
the reception of baptism to those who were so
instructed. This excludes those who are sprinkled in
infancy. The exclusion of infant membership of his
church is also apparent from his instruction to Nicodemus, that the new birth of the Spirit was indispensable. All his teachings clearly pointed to a spiritual
kingdom on earth, and bore no resemblance to that in
which parents and children, in the united church and
state, composed the Jewish theocracy.

"Finally," said the speaker, "the utter futility of
any attempt at church fraternization with other bodies
called evangelical, is made apparent, when we consider that such a step would at once annul our influence against specious errors of faith and practice, and
so effectually destroy our barriers, that there would
appear no need of the perpetuation of Baptist
Churches as separate ecclesiastical organizations."

("Othello's occupation would be gone," irreverently
thought Israel at this juncture.)

"And, my beloved brethren, if any of you labor
under trouble respecting the inconsistency of close
communion on earth and free communion in Heaven,
banish the burden by the assurance that if you keep
the ordinances as they were delivered unto you,
(1 Cor. 11 : 2,) you shall have praise in that great day
when every man's work shall be manifest, while he

that knew his master's will and did it not, shall be beaten with many stripes."

("He believes in purgatory," said Israel.)

"No, my brethren, you will not be asked to commune with the Pædobaptists in Heaven! At the marriage supper of the Lamb and his church there, none will be admitted who have not on the wedding-garment. Or, if we admit that Pædobaptists will go to Heaven, we reply to the charge against us of inconsistency here, that we have nothing to do with the institutes and policy of that pure and perfect world. We leave such adjustments to Him who is Lord of the heavens and the earth. It is enough for each one here to see to it that he walks in the strait and narrow way; that he is really after Christ and not of false prophets, and that he departs not after vain traditions.

"Can each of you within the sound of my voice, from your inmost heart, say, 'I am after Christ, and I am willing to show my discipleship at His altar, by keeping His commandments and following his example?' And does He say, '*Thou art mine*, and thou hast a right to eat at my altar?'"

The foregoing is the substance of what Israel remembered of this sermon; but here is not half of the kernel which Dr. Elias found within the shell of his text.

At the conclusion of this discourse the persons who that day had been baptized, with one or two others recommended from a sister church, came forward in the aisle near the pulpit, and received from the pastor the right hand of fellowship of that church. In this act, among other things specified, the mutual watch-care of the church and the new members was severally promised.

(Israel wondered if this watchcare extended from the church to derelictions which are covered with wealth, real or reputed.)

Singing and prayer succeeded. An invitation to "members of sister churches in good and regular standing" to partake of the Lord's Supper (which was about to be celebrated) was extended, and the congregation was dismissed.

## CHAPTER V.

**CONVERSATION WITH A BAPTIST DIVINE.**

The next morning, Israel took the same train of cars as did the Reverend Doctor Elias. Owing to a slight detention, they were at the depot a half hour together. Apparently together, for Dr. Elias was alone among strangers in public places like a depot — except on rare occasions. His thought went after no one, because it was not worth while; no one went after him, for it would seem to cost too much.

A rare occasion, however, now transpired. While he waited, like a statue prisoned in the tower of Pharos, Israel beheld the august man, and longed to look into him as in a mirror, not for the gratification of an aimless curiosity, but to see the reflection of himself, or rather his thought with the spectre of this man's thought just behind it, that he might gauge, compare, deduce, possibly come to a conclusion. But the idea appalled him. At the very moment when he sighed that there were no self-moving seats which would place him at the side of the profound clergyman, as Homer says Vulcan had constructed for the gods in council, his eye fell upon an object lying upon the solid gravel near the lumbering vehicle that had brought the clergyman and himself, together with an old lady and two little girls, to the station. At first he thought it was a pocket book, dropped by some one of his fellow travellers; but it proved to be more valuable than any pocket book. On opening the shining morocco cover, Israel descried something which impressed him as much as though he had found a sword made by Azalzel.

It was the manuscript of the sermon which he had heard yesterday from Dr. Elias. It contained a sword of the Spirit. His first impulse was to keep it under a compulsory loan, until he had read it at his leisure. For the moment he was discretive, departing from his habitual mood; but remembering himself, he approached the reverend gentleman, and, slightly touching his hat, said:

"Allow me, sir, to restore what I think is your property."

Dr. Elias took the book with some surprise, replying rather awkwardly, "Yes, it is mine. How came you with it? I thought I had it with me."

Israel told him how he had found it, adding after a pause, "I heard the sermon yesterday, and I was tempted to keep it long enough for a review."

"Ah," said Dr. Elias, with a wan smile, "are you a resident of this place?"

"No, sir, I am without a home either in the world or the church."

The keen, searching eye of the clergyman now rested fully upon Israel, while he continued: "The words of Jesus were, 'If any man thirst, let him come unto me and drink.'"

Israel struck straight into his train of thought, and answered in a low, reverent voice, "Where shall I find him?"

"With those disciples who do his will. In your own heart, also, if you are one of these."

"Who are those that do his will?"

"They who believe, and," he added slowly, "who are baptized."

"I have thought somewhat of these things," proceeded Israel, "but they are not clear. I would take the right way, did I but know it."

"You say you heard me yesterday. What did I preach that you could not understand?" now asked the doctor.

"Thank you for the opportunity to state some of the difficulties, sir. And yet, they are not sufficiently arranged in my memory to give in a manner satisfactory to myself."

"Never mind that," said the divine, waving his gloved hand. "What is one of the difficulties?"

"It occurred to me, when you spoke of the Lord's Supper being a continuation of the feast of the paschal lamb, that infant baptism might also be derived from the rite of circumcision."

"It might, did not a difficulty arise when we remember that *only males were the subjects of this rite*. You will find in the fifteenth chapter of the Acts, that when there was a dissension among the people touching circumcision, the apostles abrogated the rite, but made no mention of baptism in any form."

"If I remember rightly," continued Israel, "in the following chapter, it says that Lydia was baptized *and her household*. It appears that the Lord opened her heart to believe the teaching of the apostles, but nothing is said of her household, only that they were baptized."

"Lydia," said Dr. Elias, emphatically, "was one of a number of women who made and sold garments of a purple color much valued in that time. Had she been a wife and mother, some allusion would have been made to her husband and children."

"But 'her household' implies the children. She might have been a widow," persisted Israel.

"You will observe in the verse preceding the statement of her conversion and the baptism, that it reads, 'And on the Sabbath we went out of the city by the river side, where prayer was wont to be made.' This river was the Strymon, and the place might be translated a 'proseuche,' which was a place enclosed with stones in a grove or under a tree, where prayer was allowed by law. 'And we sat down,' the text reads, 'and spake unto the women which resorted thither.' These women were probably the members of Lydia's household, and assisted her in her occupation. The brethren also met there, as we find in the fortieth verse."

Israel was silent.

"You will further notice they were by the *river's side*, which adds strength to the supposition of immersion," the Doctor continued.

"It seems to me," said Israel, after a short pause in the conversation, "from what you said in your sermon, of Christ's kingdom being a spiritual one on earth, that baptism should be held in such a spiritual sense, as a sign of a change in the heart which may be called miraculous, that the *mode* of its administration may be regarded of minor importance. The thing signified is the event rather than the sign, so that persons may consult their choice and convenience in the manner of being baptized. I suppose that the Hystopedes or Eunomians, who baptized in the manner indicated by their name, were just as sincere as the Valentinians, who used oil with their water in baptism; and these, too, were as sincere as the Baptists of to-day. They all signify a spiritual birth into the new spiritual life, as I apprehend."

"We have no right," here spoke Dr. Elias very gravely, "to follow vain traditions and the rudiments of the world. Our pattern is Christ. He was baptized in the river in the manner of immersion. 'See,' said God to Moses, 'that thou doest all things after the pattern showed thee in the mount.'"

"Excuse me, sir," answered Israel, "but I am reminded by your allusion to Moses and his pattern, that when he had spoken to all the people according to the law, he took the blood of calves and of goats, with water, and scarlet wool, and hyssops, and *sprinkled* both the book and *all the people*, saying, 'This is the blood of the testament which God hath enjoined unto you.'"

"That was typical of the sacrifice of Christ which was to be offered to bear the sins of many — a shadow of good things to come," answered the doctor.

"Yes sir, a figure of the true, as it is expressed in Hebrews, and, as I think also, a true figure."

"It was the first testament dedicated with blood, signifying the new testament of the Great Atoning Sacrifice."

"A testament is without force except the testator be dead. If the thing signified was perfected only after the event, the sign was likewise equally sealed at that time. Hence, if the blood and the water were transubstantiated, or to use a less objectionable word, transmitted in the great events of the life of our Lord, why may we not believe that the manner of applying it by sprinkling from the hyssop and the scarlet wool, was none the less given among the pattern of things showed in the mount?"

"Simply because Christ was baptized, not sprinkled; and he left an express command touching this ordinance."

"But may not some of his commandments require modification for different persons and different places of the world? For instance, in a climate like ours, would it not be agreeable to him to practise a mode of baptism less inconvenient than immersion in a river or other body of water?"

"Our baptisteries which we use meet all the demands of this exigency. I have one in my own church in the city," said the doctor.

"It strikes me," observed Israel abstractedly, "that when you modify the pattern of Christ so far as to use a large bowl in the church for baptisms, there is not a very long step to the small one. Pardon! but I can't help thinking of the strain at a gnat and the swallowing of a camel."

"And I am reminded of the words 'If thine eye be evil, thy whole body shall be full of darkness,'" returned the doctor.

"Baptism as I saw it administered yesterday," continued Israel, " is a most impressive spectacle to me. That, truly, seems like following Christ ; but a baptism in a baptistery would be to me little short of profanation of the beautiful and holy Scriptural rite. Besides, it violates the law of fitness. It is inelegant and not cleanly."

"Not at all," said Dr. Elias, moving uneasily, and finally looking anxiously for the arrival of the train; "baptisteries are of great antiquity; as early as the time of Clovis, we read of them. They serve most forcibly to illustrate our willingness to follow the example and commands of Christ respecting immersion."

"I know they have antiquity in their support, but I thought that 'tradition' and the 'rudiments' of the world were of no account against the example of Christ, however respectable or ancient they may appear," quietly answered the youth.

"Our baptisteries," renewed the doctor, while he consulted his watch, " do not interfere with immersion. We challenge the world to show our disobedience to the commands of our Saviour."

."I remember," answered Israel, "that Christ left on record this command : 'If I then, your Lord and Master, have washed your feet, ye also ought to wash one another's feet.' Why are you not equally obedient in this regard?"

"That act," said the doctor, "was symbolical of any deed of Christian kindness which involves personal sacrifice ; it was not an ordinance, to be observed like baptism."

"An ordinance," returned Israel, "we know, is a

rule for observance. No rule to be observed was uttered by our Lord more oracularly than this. He added, 'For I have given you an example, that ye should do as I have done to you.'"

"It was not understood by his disciples as of literal significance," said Dr. Elias.

"I am not inclined to think so," said Israel, "for when Paul recommends a widow to be assisted by the Church, he mentions as one qualification, 'if she have washed the saints' feet.' (1 Tim. 5: 10.) His language evidently was intended in the literal meaning, for he accompanies the words with others of equally practical import."

"But we find no account of the early Christian Church observing the practice as a necessary obligation, and as a testimonial of faith," said the doctor.

"In every age of the Church," persisted Israel, "has this example of Christ been imitated by some of his disciples. To this day, it is observed at least by the Roman Catholics in time of Lent, in Rome, and also by the Moravians, or Church of the United Brethren. If you Baptists place such stress upon your implicit obedience to the commands and example of Christ, the omission of this rite is unaccountable."

The whistle of the approaching train being distinctly heard, Dr. Elias said, "Young man, beware what use you make of the light you have received."

"To be frank," replied Israel, "I am, at present, inclined to think in accordance with the views of the Baptists; I have offered my objections to you, by your leave, with the object of obtaining information.

But I shall come to no practical decision until I have examined more thoroughly."

"We invite the utmost investigation of our doctrines — since they are founded on the Word of God, which cannot be broken," returned the doctor.

## CHAPTER VI.

#### BAPTIST SOCIETY FOR RELIGIOUS INQUIRY.

SOME time after the conversation in the preceding chapter, Israel Knight, being a resident of a New England city, and an attendant at one of the leading Baptist churches, accepted the invitation of some of the young men of that society to be present at their meeting for religious inquiry. It happened that, at the first session which Israel attended, the topic for that evening was the History of the Rise and Progress of the Baptists. The digest of the lengthy manuscript, for the most part compiled from reliable authorities,* was as follows : —

The Baptists came from Christ, who was immersed in the river Jordan by John the immerser. From the Greek word, of which baptism is but the English form, we do not call immersion a *mode* of baptism, but it is baptism itself. Hence, it is incorrect to say that a person is baptized, unless he has been immersed. The Baptists instituted the baptism of *believers* as the fit subjects for the ordinance, in the examples of baptism found in the New Testament, without one exception.

Until the third century, when infant baptism first

* Among these should be cited Rev. Dr. Cox, the English historian of the Baptists.

began to be practised, immersion was the only baptismal rite of the Church. During the Dark Ages, when almost every species of error gained a foothold in the churches, infant sprinkling took the place of baptism in a majority of cases; but even then, we find evidences of the pure rite being administered. Before Augustine visited the ancient British church, they did not baptize infants. The ancient Catholics, so called, the old English Episcopal Church, and the Greek, and Arminian Churches baptized by immersion. In the eleventh century Bruno and Berengarius were opponents of any form of baptism but immersion. Their example was followed by the Waldenses, the Lollards, and the Wickliffites. The first Lollard or Baptist martyr in England was Sir William Sawtre, in the year 1401.

From the accounts of the public disputations upon infant baptism, at an early period of the Reformation, in Zurich, Bale and Berne, we derive sufficient evidence of another existing form in those places.

The Baptists were principally located in Holland during the latter years of the reign of Elizabeth in England, on account of persecutions received from the Court of the High Commission. A Baptist church of English refugees was founded at Amsterdam, about this time, by Mr. Smyth, who had previously been a clergyman of the Church of England and then a Brownist dissenter. But before this there were Baptists among the Anabaptists, though they did not form a separate church. After the death of Mr. Smyth, in 1608, Mr. Helwisse took charge of this church, and soon returned to England with his congregation. In 1620 these Baptists made a memorial to Parliament, in which they disclaimed all connection with the Anabaptists. From their avowal of doctrine it appears that they were General Baptists, or Arminians. Thirteen years later, Mr. Spilsbury established what is called the Particular, or Calvinistic, Baptist Church, in London; and being careful to have no connection with the Arminian branch of the Baptists, they sent over one of their number to Holland to receive baptism, and return with authority to administer it to them.

At the time of Charles the First, the Baptists received much persecution from the Presbyterians.

In 1653, under Cromwell, there appeared Mr. Barebone, a Baptist minister of much influence in both church and state. From his name the Short Parliament of Cromwell was called Praise-God-Barebone's Parliament.

In 1661, owing to the disloyalty of certain divisions of the Baptists for some years previous, an address containing a disavowal of Anabaptist principles was presented to the king of England by the Particular Baptists. At this time and afterwards, till the Revolution in 1688, they suffered persecution from efforts made to restore them, with all other dissenters, to the established church. The year following the legal toleration, delegates from more than a hundred churches met in London, and published the profession of faith known as the Century Confession.

In 1639, Roger Williams established the first Baptist church in America. It was in Providence, Rhode Island. Their early history in New England shows that they suffered much from persecution, and were at one time banished from Massachusetts. A Baptist church was founded in Charlestown, Mass., in 1665. And in the first half of this century, nine out of the seventeen American Baptist churches were in New England.

Among the eminent men of the denomination in England are the names of Gale, Carson, Gill, the Rylands, the Stennetts, Pearce, Fuller, Ward, Carey, Hughes, Foster, Hall, and more recently, Spurgeon.

Dr. Gill wrote a commentary on the Bible in nine volumes, folio, and was the author of other valuable works. Robert Hall is said to have been the greatest preacher that England has ever produced. His books take high rank among standard theological works. The same is true of the works of Foster.

In our own land, the first name dear to every Baptist heart is ROGER WILLIAMS. Not only in the eyes of all our denomination, but of all the sects of our land, is this name precious as that of the pioneer of true liberty of conscience. The polity of the churches founded by him gave to Thomas Jefferson the idea of a republican form of government, expressed in the Declaration of Independence. Truly has Dr. Channing said of Roger Williams, "Venerable confessor in the cause of freedom and truth! May his name be precious and immortal! May his spirit never die in the community which he founded!"

The Baptists have the honor of being foremost in missionary enterprises. In 1792 the Particular Baptists of England founded the first missionary society, and sent Carey, Thomas, and Marshman to India, where their labors were crowned with wonderful success.

The rise of our numerous home and foreign missionary societies, we trace, under God, to the celebrated appeal sent to the American Baptists by Dr. Judson and Rev. L. Rice, in 1814. These men were proselytes to our church from the Pædobaptists, all in consequence of reading and studying the New Testament. . . . . (Then followed long, statistical accounts of the contributions of the Baptist churches of the United States and Foreign Missions, and likewise other benevolent objects.)

In conclusion, all must become Baptists before the temporal kingdom of Christ can be established on earth.

After this, other sects were treated. A summary of some of this treatment, Israel entered in his notebook, as follows: —

The Congregationalists have no divine authority for doctrines, distinctive from the Baptists. They are, however, very respectable as a denomination in both latent and active power.

The Methodists, like all who are in the secondary, procellous, stage of development, are pleased to be heard rather than closely seen; consequently, by way of caution, the adage reversing this process applies. Their usages, for the most part, are not what refined Baptists can approve. The rapid propagation of the sect is easily accounted for, when we consider the class for which its polity is adapted, and how little is required formally to adopt it. John Wesley was a very good man, but he is vastly overrated by the people who profess to make Christ their leader and head.

The Protestant Episcopal Church is but one short remove from the Roman Catholics. It has afforded a good asylum for the ambitious and disaffected ministers of our own fold, and also for some of our sentimental females.

The Quakers, as they were, could teach some of us many valuable lessons, especially our women, upon the subject of fine clothes. They are to be commended for their poor attempts at proselytism.

The Unitarians and Universalists are of antichrist. We leave them to the Searcher of Hearts, meanwhile uttering our solemn protest against their doctrines and practice.

Emanuel Swedenborg was insane, and all his followers are deluded enthusiasts.

The father of Spiritualism is the father of lies.

Israel also entered into his book, "What I gather from the Baptists, that others think of them: —

In general, we are regarded as remarkable for purity of doctrine, and we hope, not less for practice.

In particular, John Calvin held us in great respect. If it had not been for our freedom of opinion, he would have become one, it is manifest, from his words: —

"The word *baptize* signifies to immerse, and the rite of Immersion was observed by the ancient church; and from these words it may be inferred that baptism was administered by plunging the whole body under water."—*Obs. on John* 3:23.

"In England, of late years, I ever thought the parson baptizing his own fingers rather than the child." — *Selden.*

"We grant that baptism (in the primitive times) was by washing the whole body." — *Baxter on Matt.* 3 : 6.

"The custom of the ancient churches was not sprinkling but immersion." — *Bishop Taylor.*

"The person baptized went down into the water, and was, as it were, buried under it." — *Bishop Pearce.*

"'Buried with him in baptism!' It seems the part of candor to confess that here is an allusion to the manner of baptizing by immersion, as most usual in those early times." — *Doddridge.*

"Christ commanded us to be baptized, by which word it is certain immersion is signified." — *Beza.*

"Anciently, those who were baptized, were immersed and buried in the water," &c. &c. — *Tillotson.*

"Mary Welsh, aged eleven days, was baptized according to the first church, and the rule of the Church of England, by immersion." — *Wesley.*

"I could wish that such as are to be baptized should be completely immersed into water, according to the meaning of the word and the signification of the ordinance." — *Martin Luther.*

## CHAPTER VII.

#### FOUR FACES.

ABOUT this time, our young investigator received the following letter from his guardian: —

"Then you are about to become a Baptist, because, you say, their view of the ordinance of baptism is the only correct one according to the New Testament!

"What do you mean by being a Baptist? There are, as I presume you know, at least nine different divisions of this sect in our own country; viz., Regular Baptists, Freewill Baptists, Six-Principle Baptists, Disciples or Campbellites, Seventh-Day Baptists, Winnebrenarians, Anti-Mission Baptists, Christians and Dunkers — in all, comprising about one million and a half members. If you mean a Regular Baptist, are you sure that you fully endorse their views upon other points of doctrine, as this one of immersion? Have you looked on all sides of this, at present, your favorite denomination? Remember that the wrong side of every sect, you best get from the opposition. No observation and inference are so industriously faithful as this.

"You have doubtless noticed already four faces, at least, to the Regular Baptists. This development will appear in every sect; like the cherubim of

Ezekiel's vision. (Ez. 1: 10.) 'The face of a man, the face of a lion, the face of an ox, and the face of an eagle, have they all.'

"The first indicates humanity in the image of the Divine. Under this face range many of the Baptists. These are moved by the spirit of charity. They love, they forgive, they endure. Whoever has the friendship of one of them, has a friend who turns not as he goes.

"The second, or lion-face, includes another class not less certain in their identity. Proud and haughty scorner is his name. The representative man of them deals in proud wrath. He has intelligence like the lion, — a nobility which is selfish, tyrannous. He demands the lion's share. He thinks his roar is terrible; nevertheless a mouse can deliver him. His ideas project his own royalty into the next life. This face, likewise, have the Baptists. It covereth more and more disciples, every day, with the increase of worldly prosperity.

"The third is that of the burden-drawer.

"These are obedient, patient, faithful, laborious. They serve the will of the others.

"The last comprises enterprise, aggressive and progressive. These fly. They soar alone, yet they are not without an eyrie which is near the clouds, and is a divine compensation for their work of isolated result. They plan and carry missions. They build churches and schools where else would be a desert. They adventure royally. They attempt the millennium.

"Israel! look out for the lion. The less you see him

in any denomination, the better it is for the nonce. He roars in the pulpit, in the newspaper, and in the sacraments.

Truly Yours,<br>
Ephraim Stearns."

# AMONG THE CONGREGATIONALISTS.

## CHAPTER I.

#### IN A CONGREGATIONAL SUNDAY SCHOOL.

"THERE must be a right road to the city with that name of names," reflected Israel Knight, "and possibly I shall find it here."

He was among the young men's class of an Orthodox Congregational Sunday school, in the city.

The subject of the lesson was Baptism. The teacher was an elderly clergyman, who resided in that parish, and preached only occasionally, by reason of impaired health. His manner was genial. He invited free discussion, as a teacher will, who understands his theme, and is not afraid of its foundations.

Israel had a good deal of curiosity to observe what could be said on a subject which now, he fully believed, had only one well-defended side.

"Suppose one of you takes the Baptists' position of this question, and see how many good sharp shots you can make at us," said the teacher, glancing about the young men. "We'll endeavor to heal our wounds as best we may," he added.

"There is one here among us," remarked a leading member of the class, "whom, though a stranger to all but myself, I beg leave to introduce as inclined to discussion upon this 'exact science' of baptism. Fresh from Baptist teachings, I hope he will favor us with light from his stand-point."

"Yes," said the teacher, looking at Israel, "we invite you, sir, to state any objections to our view which may occur. By so doing you will best help us to find our own fortifications."

"I am not a Baptist," replied Israel, somewhat embarrassed by these words, "though I confess that their principal arguments upon their mode of baptism seem to me unanswerable."

"For instance, state the first root of the difficulty, if you please."

"The origin of baptism, as an example for Christians, or, in other words, of Christian baptism, was the baptism of Christ by John in the river Jordan; was it not?" asked Israel.

"I hold 'Christian baptism' to be an unimportant term," replied the teacher; "since Christ was baptized, not to found a rite, but to observe one long established. He did not say of his baptism, as of the sacrament of the Lord's Supper, 'This do in remembrance of me,' but 'Suffer it to be so now, for thus it becometh us to fulfil all righteousness,' signifying the necessity of answering an established law of practice. He also said that he came not to destroy the law and the prophets, but to fulfil them. The spirit of this rite under different figures is seen throughout the dispensations which preceded Christ.

"In the first age of the world is the covenant between God and Adam, the article of which was, to have and to hold every tree in the garden for food, save the fruit of the tree of knowledge of good and evil. Abstinence from this fruit was the sacramental seal of the covenant. After this covenant, or baptism into the will of God, man was known by a name distinct from his kind. He was called Adam. This covenant being broken on the part of man, God in his goodness did not forsake him, but manifested his first covenant of grace in a new form, under certain conditions, promising him the sustenance of life. The sacrament of this covenant was the offering of the firstlings of the flock by man unto the Lord, and its acceptance. This prefigured the sacrifice of Christ, and may properly be called the first covenant, with its attending sacrament, between God and fallen man.

"In the second age of the world, the event which prefigured salvation through faith in Christ is best described by the Apostle Peter, 'In the days of Noah while the Ark was a preparing, wherein few, that is, eight souls were saved by water. The like figure, whereunto, even baptism, doth now also save us.' (1. Pet. 3 : 20.)

"God's covenant with man was here renewed to Noah and to his seed after him. In the cloud which should bring a baptism upon the earth, was the bow or sign of his promise of salvation from destruction.

"In the third age of the world, again did God covenant with man through Abram. He was promised to be a father of many nations. His name was pronounced to be Abraham. 'And I will establish my covenant between me and thee, and thy seed after thee, in their generations, for an everlasting covenant, to be a God unto thee and to thy seed after thee.'

"The seal of this sublime promise was the rite of

circumcision, which was also a like figure to baptism, typical of salvation through faith."

Here Israel asked to interrupt the teacher, and said: "Since it was only the male child who was required to receive this rite, how can it be made to answer in correspondence to baptism, which is the profession of faith by all believers, or by the responsible for the irresponsible, whether male or female."

"Before the birth of Christ," answered the clergyman, "woman was considered, like Eve, to be one flesh with man, — bone of his bones, and flesh of his flesh. But when Christ came, born of a woman, her sex took on a new importance, and assumed a distinct personality."

"Eve," said Israel, "was a wife, and I supposed the identity of sexual bone and flesh to have referred solely to this relation of life. By whom were the single women represented before the descendants of Mary?"

"By their fathers and brothers," promptly replied the teacher. "The rite of circumcision," he went on, "like baptism, was a figure of Christ's death. In that death the man, and not the mother, suffered. And although it may be truly said that no being, male or female, other than Christ himself, endured the penalties of man's transgression on the cross, it is equally plain that Christ's human nature, united with the divine, endured the agonies of the Passion. This nature belonged to man peculiarly, while in general it embraced all mankind.

"From this I derive the idea that it is far easier for woman to experience the birth into the new life or the regeneration, than for man. Throughout Christendom it will be found that women are far more numerous among the followers of the Master, than men. This is one of the compensations in the Infinite Plan, for the curse she received at the Fall."

Some of the members of the class exchanged glances of incredulity; but Israel, unconsciously adopting the expression of a work in the French language, which he had lately translated, said, in a low voice, "*Vous avez raison.*"

"It appeared," now spoke one of the young men of the class, "that when Moses asked Pharaoh that they might go and serve the Lord, and Pharaoh said, Who are they that shall go? Moses said, We will go with our young and with our old, with our sons and with our daughters, with our flocks and with our herds will we go: for we must hold a feast unto the Lord. Not so, answered Pharaoh; go now ye that are men, and serve the Lord. It seemed, then, that Moses and Aaron made some account of the daughters as well as the sons, in distinctive enumeration."

"That," said the teacher, "was with reference to the event, which was one of joy — a feast not of suffering. The benefits of circumcision as a ceremonial observance accrued equally to the female as to the male."

"In all mention of the ancient Church, the promise includes the seed of the Father of believers," observed another.

"What evidence," asked Israel, "do we find in the New Testament of any change taking effect in the state of woman after the incarnation of Christ?"

"Turn to 1 Cor. 7 : 14" said he, "and there you

learn that the believing wife of an unbelieving husband makes the children holy, or members of the Church, and partakers of the covenant of grace. If she be a true believer, she will avail herself of the benefits of the Abrahamic covenant to the children of believers, which is promised to be everlasting. She will be faithful to instruct her children in the faith, and bring them to the participation of its sacramental fruits, in answer to the seal which she caused to be placed upon them in their infancy."

"We infer, then, that the coming of Christ, not only effected the scheme of Redemption of the human family, but preeminently redeemed the condition of woman," remarked a member.

"The fourth age of the world brings us to the Passover," the teacher resumed. "Upon the fourteenth day of the first month, which was the fourth of May, Monday evening with us, did this event take place. (Ex. 12: 11.) Here we find that the paschal lamb was to be for every house, unless the household be too little for the lamb, in which case, the neighbor was to unite, according to the number of souls.

"Not long after this, we read of a baptism of the chosen people by God himself: 'Moreover, brethren, I would not that ye should be ignorant, how that all our fathers were under the cloud, and all passed through the sea; and were all baptized unto Moses, in the cloud and in the sea.' And yet they all walked upon dry land in the midst of the sea. You will here mark that God must have baptized children as well as the heads of families; but more of this hereafter," he concluded, for the bell announcing the close of the exercises rung.

## CHAPTER II.

IN A CONGREGATIONAL SUNDAY SCHOOL, CONTINUED.

On the following Sabbath, the subject for their lesson being continued, the teacher said, "Perhaps I have already said enough to satisfy you that the baptism of Christ was in obedience to the old law pertaining to the covenant of God with the faithful children of Abraham."

"It is not clear to me," said Israel, "what connection exists between the Old and the New dispensations; or, rather, what evidence is found in the New Testament of the transmission of the benefits of the Abrahamic covenant and the ancient laws given to God's people."

"In Gal. 3: 24, we read: 'Wherefore the law was our schoolmaster to bring us unto Christ, that we might be justified by faith.' And again: 'Christ is the end of the law for righteousness to every one that believeth.' Hence, in this dispensation they baptized in the name of the Father, and of the Son, and of the Holy Ghost.

"Turn to the second chapter of Acts, thirty-eighth and thirty-ninth verses: 'Then Peter said unto them, Repent, and be baptized every one of you in the name of Jesus Christ, for the remission of sins, and ye shall receive the gift of the Holy Ghost. For the promise is unto you and to your children, and to all that are afar off, even as many as the Lord our God shall call.'

"Here is the most impressive allusion to the promise made to Abraham — to be a God unto him and to his seed after him. *To you and to your children*, says Peter. He also exhorts every one of them to repent and be baptized. As his hearers were composed of representatives of many nations, this strictly verifies the promise to Abraham, 'Thou shalt be a father of many nations.'

"You will here notice that this was the opening event of what is called the Christian dispensation; it was based by the apostle upon the Promise. In Paul's epistle to the Romans, fourth chapter and sixteenth verse, we find these words: 'Therefore it is of faith, that it might be by grace; to the end the promise might be sure to all the seed: not to that only which is of the law, but to that also which is of the faith of Abraham, who is the father of us all, (as it is written, I have made thee a father of many nations.')

"These words alone, without the aid of further testimony of the writings of the apostles, clearly show the transmission of the blessings of the exceeding great and precious promise included in the covenant with Abraham, to the disciples of the new dispensation."

"Granting this," said Israel, "I cannot see but that immersion is the example of baptism under the Christian dispensation, and its subjects only believers."

"Looking at one point at a time, we next consider the mode of baptism," continued the teacher.

"You must be aware that the Greek word for the

English word 'baptize' can faithfully be rendered 'baptize,' 'wash,' 'drown,' 'sprinkle,' 'dip,' 'plunge,' 'overwhelm.' The only way that remains to us to determine which meaning of the word *baptizo* was intended to be used, as instructing the true method of interpretation, is a comparison of all the passages in the Bible which use this word. This, certainly, will be admitted as honesty in sacred hermeneutics.

"We have already seen that the baptism of the Israelites in the cloud and in the sea could not have signified to immerse. This points clearly to a spiritual or internal baptism, as does also that passage in Rom. 6: 3, 4, 'Know ye not that so many of us as were baptized into Jesus Christ, were baptized into his death? Therefore we are buried with him by baptism, into death.' The apostle also says, 'Know ye not that as many of us as were baptized into Jesus Christ, were baptized into his death?' That these figures cannot teach in a literal sense or prove a baptism by immersion, is evident from all the doctrine of the context. The 'buried with him by baptism' no more points to a literal immersion than does that kindred passage: 'Knowing this, that our old man is crucified with him, that the body of sin might be destroyed,' point to a literal crucifixion of the disciple. If it were literal, and the burial really taught the mode of baptism, the figure should be supported still further by putting on something according to the words: 'For as many of you as have been baptized into Christ have *put on* Christ.' Or yet, the literal sense equally impresses into its service the words, 'In whom also ye are circumcised with the circumcision made without hands, in *putting off* the body of the sins of the flesh.' Here, something should be put off.

"The unfairness of using these passages as instructive of the mode of baptism is too clear to require much comment. 'God is a spirit, and they that worship him should worship him in spirit and in truth.' 'The wind bloweth where it listeth, and thou hearest the sound thereof, but canst not tell whence it cometh or whither it goeth; so is every one that is born of the spirit.' Every type pertaining to Christ, received by his disciples, should be used in the spiritual sense. We have no right to make any likeness of his burial more than of his death.

"Again, we find the fulfilment of the promise to the disciples that they should be baptized with the Holy Ghost, signified in the Day of Pentecost by the act of *pouring out.*

"The baptism of the cups, and pots, and brazen vessels, and tables, alluded to in Mark 7: 4, is more clearly illustrated in Numbers 19: 18 — 'And a clean person shall take hyssop, and dip it in the water, and sprinkle it upon the tent, and upon all the vessels, and upon the persons that were there,' etc."

"But what means that passage in Hebrews 10: 22 — Having our hearts sprinkled from an evil conscience and our bodies washed with pure water?" inquired Israel. "Does not the washing here signify something more than the act of aspersion?"

"As in the cases already mentioned, let us compare the passages where the word *wash* is used," said the teacher.

"In the Old Testament, when Moses washed Aaron

and his sons, according to the command of God, before all the congregation, the whole body could not have been intended.

"In John 13: 8, 9, 10, we read, 'Jesus answered him, If I wash thee not, thou hast no part with me. Simon Peter saith unto him, Lord, not my feet only, but also my hands and my head. Jesus saith to him, He that is washed needeth not save to wash his feet, but is clean every whit.' By a similar rule of interpretation we understand his words in Matt. 26: 12, 'For in that she hath poured the ointment *on my body*,' when in a previous verse it is distinctly stated, 'There came unto him a woman with an alabaster box of very precious ointment, and poured it *on his head*.'"

"Except ye be born of water and of the spirit," continued another member of the class — "does not 'born of water' foreshow baptism by immersion?"

"No more," answered the teacher, "than do the words 'born of the spirit' indicate absolute perfection of regeneration. If you accept one horn of the dilemma in a literal and complete figure, you must equally accept the other and become a Perfectionist, than which nothing is more absurd. Indeed I regard this verse as containing one of the strongest arguments in favor of a partial baptism of the person, as also the kindred one, 'He who shall come after me shall baptize you with the Holy Ghost and with fire.' This baptism of the Holy Ghost in no wise was a complete immersion of the spirits of men into union with the Divine Spirit."

"But why is it that John is stated to have baptized in the river Jordan, also that, when Jesus was baptized, he went up straightway out of the water?" now asked Israel.

"Yes, and likewise Philip and the Eunuch went down both into the water, and they came up out of the water," added another of the students.

"And they baptized in Enon because there was much water there," pursued a third.

"Now he is surely out and quite lost," reflected Israel triumphantly.

"Both you and I have studied the Greek sufficiently to know that all those words which in English place the persons engaged in the rite of baptism *in* the water, also the coming *out* of the water, etc., could just as easily and honestly be rendered by other prepositions. A laborious investigator\* of this part of translation has taken pains to furnish the following statement, which, thinking it might be useful as well as curious to you, I have brought with me to-day: —

"'The Greek word in those places translated *in* is *en*. The word expressing Jesus went up *out* of the water, is *apo*. The word expressing Philip and the Eunuch went down *into* the water, is *eis*. The word expressing they went *out of* the water, is *ek*.

"'I have examined those prepositions in all those five books, how they are translated in every place where they are used. There are, of all that I have examined, 2859. *En* is used 1033 times, of which 47 are rendered in adverbs. In 25 cases the sense is

---

\* Rev. Ebenezer Chaplin. From this author the teacher derived many of his arguments, which appear in this and the foregoing chapter.

involved in other words, so that there is no distinct word in English answering to *en* in the Greek. The rest, 964, are rendered in English prepositions, seventeen different ways; viz., *in, by, with, among, within, for, under, at, through, on, before, unto, into, of, to, about, over.* It is translated *in* more than all the rest. But it is rendered *at* 53 times, *by* 44, *with* 42, *among* 45, *on* 30. The rest are less, as 10, 7, etc.

"'The word *apo* I have found used 423 times in those five books; 6 are rendered adverbs, 11 are involved. The rest, 406, are rendered in English prepositions, 13 different ways. It is translated *from* 235 times, all the rest 172; so that *from* is many more than all the rest.

"'The word *eis* is used in those first five books of the New Testament 955 times; 17 are rendered adverbs, 36 are involved. The rest, 902, are rendered in English prepositions, seventeen different ways. It is rendered *into* 388, *to* 138, *unto* 97, *in* 86, *on* 45, *for* 23, *at* 18, *against* 18; the rest are less, as 10, 8, etc.

"'*Ek* is found 446 times in the same books; 4 are rendered adverbs, 6 are involved. The remainder, 435, are rendered in English prepositions, thirteen different ways. It is rendered *of* 191, *from* 102, *out of* 77, *on* 30, *with* 17.'"

"How are we to arrive at a certainty respecting the translation of any passage, if the original words can be rendered in so many ways?" asked one present, who had no acquaintance with any language but his own.

"Only by the obvious sense of the word in connection with the spirit of kindred passages," replied the teacher. After a moment's pause, he continued, " In those countries, the multitudes who gathered for baptism could only be accommodated near the water. This was necessary for the comfort of themselves and their beasts. As they were a nomadic people, and being in the wilderness, vessels were not convenient. In Mark, we find it stated that John began to baptize in the wilderness. In John, it reads, 'These things were done in Bethabara beyond Jordan, where John was baptizing.'

"Likewise, in the case of Philip and the Eunuch, it will be noticed that recourse to water by the wayside was a necessity. But here the translators have not been faithful to their own rules. In connection with the baptism of Christ, the word rendered 'out of the water' is '*apo*,' while in this position, the word having the same translation is '*ek*.'

"It is just as true to say that they went *by* or *from* the water as *out of* it.

"The case of baptism in Enon is explained likewise by reference to the original, where it reads, 'for there were *many waters* there.' These numerous springs, or waters, would accommodate the multitudes who flocked to the baptism of John."

"That he could not have immersed so many, is evident from the multitudes who received the rite. This also appears in connection with the baptism at the Day of Pentecost, when three thousand were added to the Church in one day. It would have been impossible to have immersed so many.

"In regard to your other point of difficulty, respecting believers being the only proper subjects of baptism," continued the clergyman, "here I must again insist upon the spiritual meaning of the outward act. The baptism of infants who have not arrived at sufficient age to participate in the act of faith themselves, is always in the faith of one or more responsible believers."

"Since Christ was circumcised in his infancy," said Israel, " and if baptism came in the room of circumcision, why was it necessary for him to be baptized upon his own responsibility? Or rather, if children are now sprinkled in the room of circumcision, why should they not again be baptized upon profession of their faith, after the pattern of Christ?"

"It reads, 'Except a man be born of water and of the spirit, he cannot enter the kingdom of God.' The birth of water is mentioned first, as coming in the divine order, before the birth of the spirit. It is certain that Christ's baptism, though accompanied by water, was a spiritual one, for the heavens being opened, the Spirit of God descended like a dove, and lighted upon him. From this event commenced his divine career among men."

"But why was he circumcised, if the first act of his baptism, namely, that of water, was typical of that rite?" pursued Israel.

"While subject unto his parents, he deported himself like a natural child, and was subject to the natural rite; but when he assumed his divine mission, he instituted the spiritual nature of the natural baptism. Hence, the special spiritual manifestation from heaven.

Israel looked as though not perfectly satisfied, but he forbore to follow his questions in that line of difficulty. His next words were: "The Baptists assert, as I think with good reason, that there is not a single instance of infant baptism in the Scriptures."

"We also assert, with no less confidence, that the children of proselytes to the faith of the Gospel were baptized, with their parents, by the apostles," answered the teacher.

"But you will hardly venture to claim an explicit mention of a case of the baptism of a child," continued Israel, smiling triumphantly.

"That there is no mention of the baptism of one of the twelve apostles is no argument against the validity or universality of baptism in the apostolic churches. Or yet is it any proof of their being under no necessity for regeneration, because no relation of the conversion of any of the twelve is found, other than their being called or chosen, and accepting their commission by the external act. It is rather a proof of the universality of the custom of infant baptism, and not less of its approval by Christ; else, he would have somewhere brought his condemnation upon it. On the contrary, the Saviour decidedly manifested his gracious love of children by taking them in his arms and blessing them. Observe, he never baptized adults; but he deigned to perform this act of condescension, and taught the ambitious disciples to receive the little child in his name. One of the evangelists says that Jesus called a little child unto him, and set him in the midst of them, and said, Verily I say unto you, except ye be converted and become *as little children*, ye shall not enter into the kingdom of heaven.

"From this, we have a right to infer that Christ considered the little child a more meet disciple of his kingdom than any of his adult followers. And lest this humble pattern should be undervalued, he adds, 'Take heed that ye despise not one of these little ones: for I say unto you, that in heaven their angels do always behold the face of my Father which is in heaven.'

"For myself," he continued, "were I the veriest believer of the Baptist doctrines, I should not dare despise, or in any wise underrate, the baptism of an infant, were there no other portion of Holy Writ in proof of the membership of children of the Christian Church."

"If there were as clear evidence of the baptism of children as of their blessing and reception to Christ's favor, it would be more satisfactory to me," said Israel. "I have thought these passages inculcated a lesson of humility to all Christians, however eminent, rather than the obligation of the administration of a rite to children — like those other words of Christ, 'Whosoever will be greatest among you, let him be as the younger.'"

"We do find, however," said the teacher, "that Lydia and her household were baptized, although no mention is made of any but herself being a believer;— 'whose heart the Lord opened, that she attended unto the things which were spoken of Paul.' After their baptism, she said, 'If ye have judged *me* to be faithful to the Lord (not *us*), come into my house and abide there.' Here it appears that she bore the responsibility of the faith of all her household. Had all of these been adults and capable of an independent act of faith, she, a woman of those days, would not have used this language. The household of Stephanas was also baptized. Paul said unto the jailer, 'Believe on the Lord Jesus Christ, and thou shalt be saved, and thine house.' As he had then seen only the jailer, he could not have known whether his household included any children too young to understand the faith he afterwards preached to them. The condition of the salvation of his household was only his own faith."

"If you bring out so much stress upon the faith of parents and heads of families, where is the encouragement for the children of the evil and untoward generation?" inquired a member of the class.

"St. Paul to the Ephesians answers your question," said the teacher, "in the second chapter, eleventh, twelfth and thirteenth verses: 'Wherefore remember, that ye being in time past Gentiles in the flesh, who are called Uncircumcision by that which is called the Circumcision in the flesh made by hands, that at that time ye were without Christ, being aliens from the commonwealth of Israel, and strangers from the covenants of promise, having no hope, and without God in the world: but now in Christ Jesus ye who sometimes were far off are made nigh *by the blood of Christ.*'"

"I remember being present at the funeral of an infant, at which a minister of your communion officiated," spoke Israel, "and that, in his address to the mourners, he offered the consolation of the safety of their departed one, *since it was the child of baptized believers.* It occurred to me then, ought there to be any doubt respecting the salvation of an infant of the unbaptized unbelievers. May I ask your opinion upon this question?"

"It is not for me or any other to pronounce who is safe and who is not," answered the clergyman; "yet we are permitted, with all saints, to search the Scriptures for the grounds of our faith. Paul says, 'For this cause I bow my knees unto the Father of our Lord Jesus Christ, of whom the whole family in heaven and earth is named.' Christ died for all, that all *through him* might be saved. All are therefore safe who do not refuse to accept the provisions of the efficacy of his death — the salvation through him. The infant cannot choose nor refuse. He is therefore safe, as a member of the whole family of God. I do not recognize any distinction between the infants of the Circumcision or the Uncircumcision — the church or the world. But I am only an individual, not the exponent of the whole of my church."

Here the session ended.

## CHAPTER III.

### THE BAPTISM BY ASPERSION.

THAT afternoon, in the church, Israel witnessed the baptism of children. After the ordinary preliminary exercises, the minister descended the pulpit steps and stood near the table, on which was a small silver basin containing water. A father and mother came forward, the former holding an infant of months, while the mother led a little boy, of apparently three years.

These persons were of a sober countenance, and had an expression of undoubting belief in the act in which they were engaging. They seemed to realize the peculiar blessings of the Abrahamic covenant. The curse contained in the words, "Whatsoever is not of faith is sin," was causeless to them in this baptism.

The infant wore a long dress of white cashmere, wrought heavily with white silk; the little boy, a blue coat, much braided. The first reminded Israel of the cherub of cunning work in the Tabernacle; the other, of Hannah's child, who appeared in the temple in a new coat.

And as of old did God promise to meet His people and commune with them from above the mercy-seat, and between the cherubim which are upon the ark of the testimony, now did His presence appear to come between these children and meet their parents with all in that congregation who, in like manner, believed.

The officiating clergyman, who looked like a reverend man of wisdom, addressed a few words to the parents upon their duty and obligation as persons responsible for the Christian nurture of their children — the current of which words was somewhat marred by the ripple of wailing made by the babe. These discords faithfully represented the earthy element in every mundane scene, however heavenly and beautiful.

Israel said to himself, "The baby has been eating from the dish at the feast of Clodius, which was made of the costliest singing-birds."

The minister took the infant in his own arms, and having exchanged words with the father in a low voice, placed water upon the forehead of the babe and said, "Harriet Newell Payson, I baptize you into the name of the Father, and of the Son, and of the Holy Ghost."

The little boy was then baptized by the name of Edwards Theodore. Israel noticed that he was very fair, with light, delicate locks falling upon his waxen neck. His unquestioning blue eyes looked like myrtle blossoms. He seemed like a young ear of corn which ripens among the white mulberry shades of Padua.

Until this moment, he had not observed from his position another scene, in the background of this picture. There now drew near a woman advanced in years, into whose bruised hand the Lord had put the cup of trembling. She wore deep mourning, though it was poor and rusty; she had outlived many of her kindred, and the last one who had gone hence was the only son, the staff of her declining years. He had starved to death at Andersonville.

Was it any marvel that her head was bowed, her eyes often filling with tears and her motions wavering? "Afflicted and drunken, but not with wine!" Even yet, she heard the words which had said to her soul, "Bow down, that we may go over."

But why is she here?

She leads a boy of seven or eight summers, or rather winters — her only grandson, — the remnant of the dead hope — the living answer to the Lord's question, "By whom shall I comfort thee?"

Precious lamb of the pitying Saviour's fold! Angels shall feed thee! ministering ones shall walk at thy side!

The boy has an old face, almost severe in its lines of thought and woe. Life has already taught him the lessons of sternest design, sharpest finish.

He knows what it is to be hungry, to be very cold, to weep such tears as they keep in Vendome, imprisoned in a crystal phial, because the Saviour shed them, as tradition teaches. He grows in a shadow — not of the white mulberry-trees of sunny lands, but of the sighing pines and hemlocks laden with the ice of midwinter. But through their branches he sees the same stars in the heavens that shine over the mulberry-trees.

Praise God!

The minister speaks words of consolation and aspiration to the poor old grandmother, and words of advice and encouragement to her boy — as though they were regnant ones, clothed in shining raiment. Then he tenderly baptizes the child, not only into the Triune Name, but into that of the martyred parent of Andersonville. Many eyes fill with tears. The grandmother covers her face. But the boy moves not. His dark, speaking eyes, "like the eyes of those who can see the dead," look down at the feet of the minister, while the long lashes quiver a little upon the brown, gaunt cheek.

It is certain that he takes into his soul every word uttered on that solemn occasion. His long head will suffer no shade of the shifting scene to escape. Very plain is the poor boy, but he is dowered. His father would have been a man of books as well as of deeds, had he lived, for the mother had doled out the last of her substance to help him on in his student career, and after. He had helped himself likewise, so that it wanted but a little time for him to have found a place which would have repaid all the efforts with interest.

Now there was only this child. He was consecrated to God publicly to-day, privately from the hour of his birth, when the mother had uttered a prayer for him and died, — when the father had sent afar off his latest thought from the edges of the lucid intervals of frantic starvation, — when the grandmother had taken the child to her heart, — from the earliest moment to the present.

There was now, like a coming breath of joy of the witnessing angels of heaven over these children of Zion, — an awakening of the organ. A strain of ineffable tenderness, a Christ-like compassion, then an exultant pæan filled all that house of God, — and died away as does the south wind over an Oriental garden of spices — *the* garden, typical of the Church; — then the voice of the minister was heard in prayer.

The prayer arose higher, as he talked with the Divine Ones, on wings of the fire of the Holy Ghost.

He prayed to God.

Christ interceded. And the people listened, some to pray, others to fear, yet others to wonder.

Israel said to himself, "How amiable are thy tabernacles, O Lord of Hosts!"

That evening, he read with new appreciation the following words, found in a book entitled "Elim, or Hymns of Holy Refreshment:" —

### CHRIST AND THE LITTLE ONES.

"The Master has come over Jordan,"
 Said Hannah, the mother, one day;
"Is healing the people who throng Him
 With a touch of His finger, they say.

"And now I shall carry the children, —
 Little Rachel, and Samuel, and John;
I shall carry the baby, Esther,
 For the Lord to look upon."

The father looked at her kindly,
 But he shook his head and smiled;
"Now who but a doting mother
 Would think of a thing so wild!

"If the children were tortured by demons,
　　Or dying of fever, 'twere well;
Or had they the taint of the leper,
　　Like many in Israel."

"Nay, do not hinder me, Nathan,
　　I feel such a burden of care;
If I carry it to the Master,
　　Perhaps I shall leave it there.

"If He lay his hand on the children,
　　My heart will be lighter, I know;
For a blessing forever and ever
　　Will follow them as they go."

So over the hills of Judah,
　　Along by the vine-rows green,
With Esther asleep on her bosom,
　　And Rachel her brothers between;

'Mong the people who hung on His teaching,
　　Or waited His touch and His word,
Through the row of proud Pharisees listening,
　　She pressed to the feet of the Lord.

"Now why shouldst thou hinder the Master,"
　　Said Peter, "with children like these?
Seest not how from morning till evening
　　He teacheth, and healeth disease?"

Then Christ said, "Forbid not the children,
　　Permit them to come unto me;"
And He took in His arms little Esther,
　　And Rachel He set on His knee;

And the heavy heart of the mother
　　Was lifted all earth-care above,
As He laid His hand on the brothers,
　　And blest them with tenderest love;

As He said of the babes in His bosom,
 "Of such are the kingdom of heaven;"
And strength for all duty and trial,
 That hour to her spirit was given.

## CHAPTER IV.

**TALK WITH CONGREGATIONAL CLERGYMEN.**

THE next day, Israel called at the study of the clergyman whose ministrations he had attended for some Sundays previous.

This minister was a leading one of the city of Israel's present residence, a graduate of Yale College and of Andover Theological Seminary, a man of ancient and honorable ancestry, (as is very desirable for a representative of a sect which lays its finger reverently upon covenants extending back to Adam,) and a fair exponent of the right wing of Congregationalism, in that section.

The left wing of that sect has ministers of another type; leaders of people are these also, but a different class. A hearer would not know precisely who these are or what they believe, not even after examining their own record. But the left wing preachers are always in the high enjoyment of popularity.

The Reverend Charles Ingersoll was not a Doctor of Divinity. Had he been a minister of either of two or three other sects, his reputation would have secured a thrice dubbing of the human-divine degree; but this denomination is much more conservative in the bestowment of their honors than some others. He was none the less a man to be revered.

He received Israel with urbanity, yet with a certain formality and reservation of confidence that often characterize these persons with strangers.

After some circumlocution, the difficulty in hand transpired.

"Until recently," said Israel, "I have thought of uniting with the Baptists, inferring from the instruction received from them, that they and they only, were right; accident brought me among your people, of which I was glad, as I had been recommended to examine more than one side of a question so vital to one's interest as the church with which to unite."

The clergyman levelled his eye upon Israel, with the expression which a man wears who believes in high Calvinism, with a low estimate of such questions as Woman's Rights and the rights of all unprivileged classes.

"If I may trouble you to assist me a little in my investigations, sir, I shall be thankful," continued Israel.

"What can I do for you?" asked Mr. Ingersoll, very quietly and with a half-suppressed smile.

Israel noticed this look, and felt that he was not "appreciated," as certain sensitive and half-sustained people say; but he had too much breadth of calibre, too deep a sense of the magnitude of the work in which he was engaged, to wholly abandon himself to this painful consciousness. A young man with a sincere purpose carries a power with him, not to be vanquished in any slight encounter, provided this good seed has been sown on the soil of common sense.

"Then you have thought of uniting with the Baptists?" spoke the clergyman.

"To listen only to their words of themselves and their authority, as also of others and their authority, a youth like myself might easily be persuaded that way," replied Israel.

"What did they teach you about us?" continued the clergyman, extending his hand upon the open book before him with a certain indescribable decision.

"That you had no authority in the Bible for your mode of baptism, and for the baptism of children who were not believers. But this point has been considered by my Sunday School teacher, in the school connected with your church. That the practice of your sect in this regard dates back but a short time, comparatively into antiquity, the only regular baptism throughout the Christian world for more than a thousand years being immersion, and that " —

"Stay," here spoke Mr. Ingersoll; "let us pause to consider this objection, before passing to others."

He took down a book from his library, and opening it, said, "Irenæus, Bishop of Lyons, who was a disciple of Polycarp (who was a disciple of John the Evangelist), and, as some believe, was born before the death of the latter, has left these words." He read, "Christ came to save all persons through himself — all, I say, who through him are regenerated unto God; infants and little ones, and children and youth, and the aged. Therefore he passed through the several stages of life, being made an infant for infants, that he might sanctify infants; and for little ones, a little one, to sanctify them of that age."

Next, from another book, he read as follows: "Listen to Tertullian. 'According to the condition, disposition, and age of each, the delay of baptism is peculiarly advantageous, especially in the case of little children (*parvulos*). Why should the godfathers be brought into danger? For they may fail by death to fulfil their promises, or through the perverseness of the child. Our Lord indeed says, Forbid them not to come unto me. Let them come, then, when of adult age. Let them come when they can learn; when they are taught *why* they come. Let them become Christians when they shall have learned Christ. Why hasten that innocent age to the forgiveness of sins?'

"Tertullian was born about 160, at Carthage. His career was less than a century of the apostolic age. Yet you will notice that he speaks of infant baptism as a prevailing custom of the churches. If it was contrary to the authority of Scripture and the customs of the early Church, why did he not bring these statements as arguments against it? It is certain, from his words, that the practice of infant baptism was a general one in his day, and he does not allude to it as an innovation, or as contrary to the teachings of Christ."

"It seems hardly possible," here commented Israel, "that, with such facts as these upon the common page of history, persons who profess to be reliable critics of the present day can boldly utter such statements as those to which I have referred respecting the origin of infant sprinkling."

"Let us turn to Origen," said the minister. "He,

as you may remember, was born in 185, at Alexandria. He was a man of profound learning, studied philosophy under Ammonius, and theology under Clemens Alexandrinus. He travelled extensively, so that he was acquainted with the churches in every country. These are his words: 'Little children are baptized agreeably to the usage of the Church; the Church received it as a tradition from the Apostles that baptism should be administered to children.' According to Eusebius, Origen received this instruction from his pious ancestry, who of the second or third generation from him must have been contemporaries with the Apostles.

"We learn also from history," continued Mr. Ingersoll, "that in the time of Cyprian, who was converted to Christianity about A. D. 246, and afterwards became Bishop of Carthage, that there arose a query in the African churches whether a child might be baptized before the eighth day or not."

He opened a book to this item, and read, "'Fidus, a country bishop, referred the inquiry to a council of sixty-six bishops, convened under Cyprian, A. D. 253, for their opinion. To this inquiry they reply at length, delivering it as their unanimous opinion that baptism may, with propriety, be administered at any time previous to the eighth day.'

"If the practice was altogether wrong, why was not some objection raised on an occasion so favorable for the adjustment of difficulties as a council of bishops? On the contrary, the practice was not only defended, but left as a rite which was obligatory," said the minister.

"St. Augustine, who spent the greater part of his life in controversy, and whose works form eleven folio volumes, has left many passages to show that this rite was a common and established usage of the Church. His words are: 'The custom of our mother-church, in baptizing little children, is by no means to be disregarded, nor accounted as in any measure superfluous. Neither, indeed, is it to be regarded as any other than an apostolical tradition.' Of this, he also writes, '*Quod universa tenet ecclesia nec conciliis institutum, sed semper retentum.*'

"This ancient father was born in 354. So much, and more, may be cited in reply to the Baptist accusation of the lack of antiquity of our peculiar rite."

"Here," observed Israel, "the homely saying is verified: 'One story is good till another is told.'"

"There is nothing in regard to these things like reading for yourself, and not trusting to the statements of any man," said the clergyman.

At this juncture a low knock upon the door arrested the conversation. The servant showed in a gentleman whom Mr. Ingersoll introduced to Israel as the Rev. Mr. O'Hara, pastor of the third Orthodox Congregational Church of that city.

The Reverend O'Hara was a man of the left wing of Congregationalism, as at present represented in America, and especially in its flourishing parishes. He was considered a great orator, a good fellow in the common acceptation of that term, and a decidedly rising man, not only in his profession, but in the general ways and means of getting ahead in this world.

His record as to antecedents of piety and education was rather mystical. People of limited culture thought he used "splendid language," and was "a most interesting preacher." Conversions, according to the standard of the strictest of his sect, were very rare under his ministrations, though he was not without a record of revivals.

As he drew crowded houses, like any "star," he was not meddled with by the more conservative. But they thought he was rather coarse, and that it was strange he came to be a Congregationalist. Some of these privately sniffed "a man of straw" under his coat; but all great geniuses have their enemies. By degrees, the topic of that morning came to Mr. O'Hara's knowledge, and the conversation was resumed.

"The Baptists," said he, "are a sect who are very peculiar. They have no liberal ideas. In fact, they remind one of the ram of Daniel's vision. That ram, you know, had two horns, and the two horns were high; but one was higher than the other, and the higher came up last. These two horns of the Baptist ram are *immersion* and *close communion*."

"Which is the higher horn?" asked Mr. Ingersoll.

"O, close communion, among our American Baptists," he answered, laughing heartily, while he used his knife industriously upon his finger nails.

"Their arguments upon this point of their belief are quite formidable," remarked Israel.

"Formidable as the ram's horn. With this, and

dipping all over, they push in all directions, and think themselves very great."

"Let me see," said Mr. Ingersoll, "I don't exactly remember the history of that beast of the prophet's vision." He opened the Bible on the table before him.

"I can tell you," continued O'Hara, tipping back his chair and elevating his hands; "there came along a goat from the West, — the West has always been a great place for conquerors, you see, — and he saw the ram with the two horns standing before the river, — there you have the water Baptists again, — and he pitched into him, in the fury of his power, with his one horn (which is infant sprinkling), and busted the ram all up into nobody, breaking his two horns, cracking his skull, and casting him down to the ground."

Israel laughed, though not heartily. Mr. Ingersoll hardly smiled, while he continued examining the Bible. At length he said quietly, "You dispose of your Baptist brethren rather summarily."

"Not a whit more than they dispose of us. To hear them preach about the errors of people who do not dip, and of their own righteousness in keeping the commandments in their big basins of baptisteries while they sanctimoniously exclude all others from their sacrament-table, you would think that 'filthy rags ought to rise ten per cent, so as to bring down the price of all kinds of paper used for certificates of church membership."

"I must say, that I have thought the Baptists far more careful about their terms of communion on the ground of immersion than they are of morality," said Mr. Ingersoll.

"They know full well that the moment they let down their bars of communion, they make void their law in regard to dipping, and their existence in this country is at an end. Besides, it is in conformity to their likes and dislikes, to draw such small cords around their little, narrow, contracted folds. If their people were more enlightened, they could not keep them penned up in that shape, like simple sheep," Mr. O'Hara continued, while he took several new positions for his feet and hands.

"There is no Scripture authority for their doctrine of close communion," said Mr. Ingersoll, addressing himself now to Israel; "on the contrary, many words of our Saviour go to inculcate the unity and fellowship of all his disciples of all his folds."

"That is too evident to need any proof," said O'Hara; "nobody but descendants of the Anabaptists, who used to run about the streets of Munster naked, would think of setting up any such ridiculous doctrine as close communion of those who have been all over in the water, in one particular little sect, — as though they were the infallible Church of God."

"But they have many names of which to boast among their sect," said Israel, "notwithstanding their cousinship to the Anabaptists."

"O yes, what sect has not? There was old Roger Williams, a turn-coat from the Church of England and also from Congregationalism. He it was [this he said very emphatically] *who refused to hold communion with the Church of Boston because they would not make a confession of guilt for having communed with the Episcopal Church while they were in England.* A beautiful man was he to start close communion in America! Very consistent were his professions of toleration to all religions!"

"But he is quoted by the Baptists and also by others, as the pioneer of the system of pure religious toleration," said Israel.

"Persons with such a limited knowledge of history as those prove themselves to be, who make such grave falsities respecting the origin of infant baptism, may be pardoned for a parallel inaccuracy respecting the originator of religious toleration," said O'Hara. "Mackintosh says," he went on, "'The government of Cromwell made as near approach to general toleration as public prejudice would endure; and Sir Henry Vane, an *Independent*, was probably the first who laid down with perfect precision the inviolable rights of conscience, and the exemption of religion from all civil authority.' But Roger Williams has an undisputed claim as the originator of a free form of baptism; in that he got Ezekiel Holyman, a man who had not been baptized, to dip him all over, that he might start the Baptists in Rhode Island. The man's name answered his conscience as a qualified administrator of the ordinance, I conclude. Roger Williams probably supplied Tom Jefferson with his notions of a republican government about as much as did another Baptist minister, who sent him, when President, an enormous cheese made by his parishioners in Cheshire, supply him with opinions in astronomy."

Israel no longer wondered that this man was heard by the crowds.

"Some have supposed," said Mr. Ingersoll, "that the Baptist Church of Holland, composed of English refugees, was perpetuated by means of their minister, Mr. Smyth, having baptized himself. This, however, is denied by some authorities."

"Likewise," continued O'Hara, "they should follow the usage of the Dark Ages, and have the church bell baptized, that it might drive demons out of the air in thundery weather."

"They would not allow us Congregationalists so much antiquity as a church bell in the Dark Ages," said Mr. Ingersoll.

"Antiquity?" repeated Mr. O'Hara, "what superior claim can the Baptists put forth to that, as a separate church organization? There is no account of such a church until the seventeenth century. And the American Baptists owe their origin to the man whom we have just contemplated!"

"May I inquire," now spoke Israel, "at what time the Congregationalists date their origin as a sect?"

"As a separate denomination of Christians," said Mr. Ingersoll, with renewed dignity, "we refer our foundation to John Robinson, in 1602. He was the pastor of an Independent church in the north of England. Before that time, Robinson belonged to the Brownists, who, at first, were disciples of Robert Brown, the first originator of the principles of Independency, or Congregationalism. As Brown afterwards recanted and returned to the Church of England, these people looked to Mr. Robinson as their leader. His followers were not wholly like the Brownists, having more moderation in their opinions and method in their church government. Some authorities state that the first Independent or Congregational church in England was established in 1616, by a Mr. Jacob; but these call Mr. Robinson the real founder of the sect. While in England, this Church received much persecution."

"Yes," interposed Mr. O'Hara, "our people have had their share of baptism in the enemy's fire."

"Which, I suppose, "said Israel, "means that they were aspersed or sprinkled with the cleansing element of opposing ire, while the Baptists received similar purification by a larger measure."

"You will have the goodness to remember that we use figures and shadows as such, and by them mean the higher and truer element of thought," returned Mr. O'Hara, laughing.

"He does not mean that those early Independents were wholly destroyed or completely burned in the persecuting fire, as a people, though this actually took place in individual instances," remarked Mr. Ingersoll.

"As a people they got their garments pretty well singed — that is all," said Mr. O'Hara.

"Independency then inculcated the doctrine of the absolute right of each church to govern itself, 'that regenerated men in church fellowship should be left unfettered, and that Christianity was a question between God and man.' In 1620, the younger members of Mr. Robinson's church came to Plymouth in New England. Here, they strove to avoid the evils of extreme Independency as well as Prelacy; and they early established a Congregational form of government, disclaiming the title of Independent. The words of Samuel Mather about this are: 'The churches of New England are Congregational. They do not approve the name of Independent, and are abhorrent from such principles of Independency as would keep them from giving an account of their matters to members of neighboring churches regularly demanding it of them.'

"The Puritan Church was stimulated to seek emancipation from the errors into which they might have been insensibly drawn, by the remarkable counsel of Mr. Robinson in his Fast Sermon, which was preached to his people a short time before their departure for America."

Mr. Ingersoll now opened an ancient-looking volume, and said, "Here is an extract from that memorable sermon: 'Brethren, we are now quickly to part from one another, and whether I may ever live to see your faith on earth any more, the God of heaven only knows; but whether the Lord hath appointed that or not, I charge you before God and his blessed angels, that you follow me no farther than you have seen me follow the Lord Jesus Christ. If God reveal anything to you, by any other instrument of his, be as ready to receive it as ever you were to receive any truth by my ministry; for I am verily persuaded — I am very confident, that the Lord has more truth yet to break forth out of his holy word.'"

"Very sensible that," here interposed Mr. O'Hara, who had been charged by his ministerial brethren with heresy upon some of the points of the creed of his church. But this deflection was mostly kept concealed in the ministers' meetings.

"He must have referred, at least by a kind of presentiment, to the Confession of Faith issued by the Congregational churches in 1680, entitled 'The Cambridge and Saybrook Platforms,'" said Mr. Ingersoll.

"Or," said Mr. O'Hara, "it might have been to the half-way Covenant of 1657, which taught, 'That it was the duty of those who came to the years of discretion, baptized in their infancy, to own the Covenant. And if they understood the grounds of religion, and were not scandalous, and solemnly owned the Covenant, giving up themselves and their children to the Lord, baptism might not be denied to their children.'"

This he said to offset the construction of Mr. Ingersoll upon the words of John Robinson. Mr. Ingersoll was known to be very strict in his view of the necessity of a clear evidence of regeneration as one of the qualifications for church membership.

"To continue with the words of Mr. Robinson," said Mr. Ingersoll, while the other minister applied his knife with new vigor to the sole of his elevated boot, "'I must also advise you to abandon, avoid, and shake off the name of Brownist. It is a mere nickname, and a brand for the making religion, and the professors of it, odious to the Christian world.'"

Mr. Ingersoll was an honest man; and if he had been asked what he had omitted in this letter between the two paragraphs which he read, he would have given it. As it was, he deemed it the part of wisdom to read no more. It remained for Israel to hear the missing and most remarkable portion from the lips of one who believed less with John Calvin than did Mr. Ingersoll.

"Who do you consider your most eminent divines?" asked Israel.

"There are John Cotton, Increase and Cotton Mather, Thomas Hooker, Hopkins, the two Edwardses (father and son), Bellamy, Smalley, Dwight— among the earlier writers upon our faith; while among the later, it would be almost invidious to endeavor to institute a suitable comparison of talent in the array of so many eminent names as we have.

"We consider our sect to be foremost in the educational ranks," continued Mr. Ingersoll; "we have founded the majority of colleges in New England alone, two theological seminaries, and many excellent academies. Our missionary operations are also second to those of no other sect."

"I do not think I fully understand the articles of your creed, which are necessary to be endorsed in order to become one of your number," here spoke Israel.

"Our churches do not all have the same creed," said Mr. O'Hara.

"How is that?" asked Israel, somewhat astonished; "are you not all consociated upon terms of fraternal action and fellowship?"

"O, yes; we fellowship each other upon essential points of faith. Each church has a right to make or alter its own creed, however, while other churches can withdraw their fellowship, if they please. Some of our churches have some modifications of the views of Calvin, Hopkins, Emmons, or other standard," said Mr. O'Hara, looking significantly at his fellow-laborer.

"I have often heard of Calvinism and Calvinistic churches," said Israel with much simplicity of manner; "but I never exactly knew what were the articles of that faith; I have heard that the vital points might be summed up under the names of predestination, particular redemption, total depravity, effectual calling, and final perseverance. I confess that I do not understand the full import of these formidable names."

"Nor do I," said Mr. O'Hara, drily; "that is to say, I do not understand them as John Calvin did. You have heard of the 'Five Points' of Calvinism? Let me repeat them to you, *verbatim*."

"Had we not better give this young man some explanation of these terms in theology, in order to prepare his mind for the reception of truth which, otherwise, might be objectionable?" now asked Mr. Ingersoll, with a slight loss of his usual poise.

"I object to any private interpretations of a public creed," said Mr. O'Hara; "if the creed is sound and kind, as we say of a good family horse, it will carry us through to the better country, safely and surely; but if not, why then let it fall to the place where it belongs, which is under the bridge."

"But then," persisted Mr. Ingersoll, moving uneasily, "there is a difference in the manner of expressing the same truth."

"Here you have it," said Mr. O'Hara, beginning with the first word of the "Five Points," and not stopping till he came to the last. It was, in abbreviation, like this:—

I. "That God hath chosen a certain number of the fallen race of Adam, in Christ, before the foundation of the world, unto eternal glory, according to His immutable purpose, and of His free grace and love, without the least foresight of faith, good works, or any conditions performed by the creature, and that the rest of mankind He was pleased to pass by, and ordain to dishonor and wrath, for their sins, to the praise of His vindictive justice.

II. "That though the death of Christ be a most perfect sacrifice and satisfaction for sins of infinite value, and abundantly sufficient to expiate the sins of the whole world; and though, on this ground, the Gospel is to be preached to all mankind indiscriminately; yet it was the will of God, that Christ, by the blood of the cross, should efficaciously redeem all those, and those only, who were from eternity elected to salvation and given to him by the Father.

III. "That mankind are totally depraved in consequence of the fall of the first man, who, being their public head, his sins involved the corruption of all his posterity; and which corruption extends over the whole soul, and renders it unable to turn to God, or to do anything truly good, and exposes it to His righteous displeasure, both in this world and that which is to come.

IV. "That all whom God hath predestinated unto eternal life, He is pleased in his appointed time effectually to call by his word and spirit out of that state of sin and death in which they were by nature, to grace and salvation by Jesus Christ.

V. "That those whom God has effectually called and sanctified by His spirit, shall never finally fall from a state of grace. That true believers may fall

partially, and would fall totally and finally, but for
the mercy and faithfulness of God, who helpeth the
feet of His saints; also, that he who bestoweth the
grace of perseverance, bestoweth it by means of
reading and hearing the word, meditation, exhorta-
tions, threatenings and promises; but that none of these
things imply the possibility of a believer's falling from
a state of justification."

"Calvin likewise taught the doctrine of the Trinity,"
said Mr. Ingersoll; "the three equal persons in the
Godhead, in one nature, and that Jesus Christ had
two natures."

"Also," said Mr. O'Hara, emphatically, "that the
happiness of the righteous and the misery of the
impenitent commenced directly at death, and was
endless."

"Is this, then, the belief of what are called Calvinistic churches, including Baptists?" asked Israel.

"Substantially," answered Mr. Ingersoll, "and
there is Scripture, varied and sufficient in proof of all
these periods of belief."

"We do not all interpret Scripture alike," said Mr.
O'Hara. "I am the pastor of an Evangelical Congregational church, so called; but our creed is so worded,
that, while we are 'guilty of all' these doctrines, we
'offend in none,' I believe."

"The offence of the Cross hath not yet ceased
among those who are faithful to its doctrines," here
spoke Mr. Ingersoll, very gravely.

Israel now rose to leave. He thanked both the
clergymen for their instruction. Mr. O'Hara said,
"If you make up your mind that you must be im-

mersed, and yet wish for a more liberal scope of church membership than the Baptist, you can come to me and I will willingly do it."

"I would *not* do it," said Mr. Ingersoll, "for I do not believe it is necessary."

"Neither do I," said Mr. O'Hara, laughing, "but then, 'conscience not of thine own, but of the other.' If we are liberal, we must show our liberality, and not be so narrow-souled as the Baptists. I declare it is truly laughable," he went on, "to see them so calm in their sublime egotism, as though God made the universe on purpose for them, all except hell, which is for their enemies. They make one think of the Congoes, who say that all the world was made by hands of angels, except their own country, which was constructed by the Supreme himself, who took great pains to make them very black, and was so well pleased with the model man, that he smoothed him over the face, and therefrom his nose and that of all his posterity became flat."

"I do not comprehend your figure," said Mr. Ingersoll.

"Never mind," said Mr. O'Hara, "perhaps I do not comprehend it myself."

On retiring from this conference, Israel had many thoughts. Of one thing he was sure — that he could not join a church with a Calvinistic creed, until he had, at least, examined farther.

# AMONG THE METHODISTS.

## CHAPTER I.

#### THE METHODIST PRAYER-MEETING.

Not long after Israel Knight's conversation with the Congregational clergyman, he was walking, early one evening, in company with a young man of his acquaintance, on one of the less frequented streets of the city. Their attention was arrested by strange, and, as he thought, unearthly sounds, which seemed to issue from a row of lighted windows in the basement of a building near them.

"Persons in distress," said Israel, in a tone of sympathetic excitement.

His companion laughed. "Look up and see where you are," he said.

Israel obeyed the suggestion, and discovered that the building was a plain-looking church. His eye fell again upon the lighted windows, and at the moment his ear took in a prolonged sound which seemed composed of pain and exultation, all concentrated in the word "*Glory!*"

Next he heard the word "*Hallelujah!*" in an equally remarkable outburst of vocal power.

"Who are they? What is it?" now asked Israel of his friend.

"Don't you know? Is it possible that you do not understand the mysteries of a real Methodist prayer-meeting?" returned his friend, taking him by the arm and turning down the walk which led to those windows.

"I know nothing of them," said Israel, in a tone of awe, for he perceived that "the combat deepened" every moment. Sounds as of pounding now accompanied strong cries and hollow groans. "Can we obtain admittance?"

"Certainly; the core of their doctrine is, 'Whosoever will, may come and partake freely.' They deal in a free salvation."

They passed into the outer hall, and seeing other persons waiting about the door, paused there till the favorable moment for entrance. Soon one of the persons within broke out into singing, "I'm glad salvation's free, salvation's free for you and me;" and all who had been on their knees rose to their seats, while our friends moved in. A person who sat near arose and showed Israel, with his friend, to seats in full view of the preacher's desk.

Israel listened to the many voices in this singing, and saw the expression of the faces of some of the foremost who sat in conspicuous seats, which seemed fully committed to the manner and time of the work, and he thought "This is what is meant by 'singing lustily.'" As the song went on, some one broke out with the exclamation, "Praise God." This was followed by several voices crying similar ejaculations, till the singing was borne down and stopped.

A person at the desk, who seemed to be the leader of the meeting, now arose, and standing still a moment, looked around in a wild and intense way upon the audience, then said a few words expressive of his hope that they should have a good meeting that night — such a meeting as they never had enjoyed before in their lives. Souls were to be converted by scores, if they only had faith, and were willing to come up to the work of the Lord; but if the drowsy, stupid church members were going to hold back, as they so often did, — just like great leaden cogs on the wheels of the car of salvation, — they might as well give it up, first as last, and bid farewell to the miserable wretches in that audience who were now swiftly on their way to the pit of damnation. He concluded by calling upon every soul in that congregation who had put himself or herself in the Lord's ranks over against those of the devil, and was willing to keep there by going to work mightily for the Master, to come forward on the front seats around the stand, and consecrate themselves anew to the Lord.

For a moment there was a breathless silence, then each began to look at his neighbor, to see who was going to move and who was not.

"Clear the seats!" now cried the leader, waving his arms on either hand; "clear the track for the progress of the car of salvation! We are going to have a mighty time to-night — a glorious warming-up here. Now while we sing, all who love our Lord Jesus, and are willing to stir themselves for him, come around here."

He then began to sing, while a movement commenced throughout the house.

When the vacated seats were all filled, and others stood near who seemed to belong to that company, the leader said, "Now, sister Atkins, we will join with you in prayer. We want every one here in these seats to give himself or herself up anew to the Master. Right here, and just now, expect a blessing. Every one kneel; every one pray now, while the sister calls upon the Lord to fit us up for a glorious work here to-night. Let every soul in this house, saint or sinner, get down on their knees."

As Israel did not think this injunction to kneel included him, he remained in his position. But he saw the eyes of this man fixed searchingly upon him from above the chair where he knelt with his face to the audience.

No sooner had the sister began to pray, than voices from every direction broke out with loud ejaculations, so that it was difficult to catch only broken sentences of her petition. These were accompanied by other loud noises made by their hands. The strong cries of "Just now, Lord!" "O, come right here, Jesus!" "Yes, yes, that's what we want." "Amen!" "Come Lord, come right down now and work like thyself!" "Amen!" "Hallelujah!" "Glory!" "Glory to God!" bore down the minor key of the woman's voice, so that it seemed it would have been equally well if she had but commenced praying, and ended when these cries ceased.

No sooner had the weaker voice died out, than there was a momentary lull, succeeded by a roar like the outbreak of waters at the removal of their strongholds.

A stentorian brother now led the mighty current like the afflicted Job when he cried, "Am I a sea, or a whale * * * ?"

Israel knew not whether to be amused or disgusted. He caught the eye of his companion, who smiled. The contagious glance caused him to turn away to gather new self-control.

The next time he looked towards the leader, he saw his searching eye levelled like an arrow of reproof upon him. In confusion he dropped his head upon the bench before him.

These things continued for a short time, when all were bidden to rise and sing.

The singing concluded, the leader said, "Now all who have got a blessing and are willing to work for the Master to-night, rise right up and show your colors for the Lord." Most of the persons on the front seats arose, but a few remaining in their positions, he seemed possessed with a spirit of rebuke, and said, "O ye stupid Christians! who have a name to live, while you are just dead in trespasses and sins, — what, think you, is to be your portion? You are all like woodchucks in your holes. Nothing will ever bark you out but the dog of persecution. You need to be called to straits from the enemy, like the Christians of old, in order to be willing to run and not be weary, to walk and not faint. Here are souls around us to-night going right on to hell, and you a-setting there so stupid and careless! I see the precious souls of young men here, who are now laughing at us. [Here he gave a terrible look at Israel.] And there are young women, too, right on the flowery borders of perdition. Yes, brethren and sisters, there is work here for us to do to-night. How can you keep your seats one precious moment of time, while the arch adversary is busy in our very midst!"

"Now," said he, "clear these seats again; we are going to have all up here who desire to save their souls and want to be prayed into the kingdom to-night. Brethren and sisters, go forth among the congregation and compel them to come in and sup with us at the marriage-supper of the Lamb."

He then struck up another tune, while certain ones moved among the crowd, and invited them to go forward for prayers.

The leader looked again at Israel and his companion, who did not seem inclined to move. "Young men there, near that middle pillar," he cried at length, while the singing went on, "Come up here to the altar and get religion to-night. You'll never have a better time than this."

Several now turned and looked at them with an expression of commiseration for their hardness of heart.

"What shall we do?" asked Israel's companion of him, in a low voice. "If we stay out here, they will set us down for burglars or escaped convicts. We shall be branded in the face of all the people, and our characters will be gone forever. Let us escape at the door before it grows worse."

"No," said Israel. "Let us go forward. It will not hurt us to be prayed for."

"But are you sincere?" asked his friend.

"I am," answered Israel." "It has just occurred to me that the fault may be in me, and not in them."

They went forward, while the leader cried,

"Hallelujah, two more have decided to go with us in the glorious way, to-night."

Soon after, the leader knelt, calling upon every soul of them to do likewise, and began to pray for the spirit to come down.

A portion of the prayer was directed in the behalf of those two stranger young men in their midst, especially that one whose proud spirit had refused to kneel when he first came in among them. Israel knew that all those people were praying for him. He was not angry. No; the feeling of gratitude began gradually to rise within his heart.

"These good people are in earnest for the salvation of my soul," he said to himself; "although I have believed I was a Christian before, I feel now that I am not like these. Perhaps I have been deceived."

"Search him, strip him, O Lord!" spoke the leader; "strip him naked of all his filthy rags of self-righteousness and put on him a clean white robe."

At this juncture, a clear, sweet voice commenced to sing something about "palms of victory" and "white robes," "clean robes," and the prayers ceased, though all remained on their knees.

Tears filled Israel's eyes. "Surely," thought he, "they are unselfish to take so much heed for an entire stranger. This must be, truly, an apostolical faith and practice as new to me as it is beautiful."

Now some one bent over him and whispered, "Friend, do you feel better? Have you got religion?"

"I don't know," said Israel, "I thought I had sometime ago; but I have not been enough in earnest, I fear."

"He wishes to feel more the terrible weight of his salvation," said the leader aloud, and renewed his strong supplication to that effect, until another voice cried out, "I know it is all right with him now. Let us praise God. He has got the victory. Shout, brother!"

The audience became seated, and after the singing of another verse, those who felt that they had obtained salvation were requested to rise. Several stood, but Israel was not among them.

"How is this?" asked the leader, looking at Israel, "can you not give God the glory for your salvation? Speak! speak a word for the Master, and tell us what he has done for your soul. If you hold your peace, the spirit may leave you, and you may be silent in the cause forever."

Israel now arose, and looking down very modestly, said that he felt new convictions of his duty to be a more earnest Christian, such as he never had before. He asked their prayers that the will of the Lord might be made plain to him.

His friend looked on him in astonishment, but was silent himself. Many responded fervently "Amen," and "We will pray for you, brother."

Nearly all those who had newly risen "gave in their testimony," as it was called, what the Lord had done for them — these testimonies being often interspersed with singing.

It may be thought unaccountable that Israel had so soon fallen in with a tide which, at first, he was disposed to resist or undervalue. The contradiction is only apparent. A young man with a naturally decided religious temperament, possessed with a conviction that somewhere on the earth the divine presence dwelt with a peculiar people, whose local habitation could be named, "The Lord is here;" such a person, comparatively alone in the world as to kindred and near friends, and disposed to conscientiously discipline himself in a religious way, would easily become affected with the new and strange interest manifested towards him by this fervid, and apparently friendly and humble people. Hitherto, it had not been in his experience to hear the voice of prayer uttered by another in his individual behalf. With the Baptists, he had more than once knelt at their family altar, and no word had gone up for the guest, orphaned and desolate on the threshold of manhood, although they had prayed most kindly for their own beloved ones. The Congregationalists had vouchsafed no such friendly regard as this. Hungering and thirsting after a personal righteousness, he began to have an emotion of partial satisfaction in this new demonstration of strangers towards himself. Although at first he had felt that injustice was done him, yet it was far better for them to think of him, even though the thought was short of what he wished, than not to think of him at all.

"Brother Simond," spoke the leader, when the testimonies from the anxious seat were concluded, "I want you to pray now, and particularly remember our strange brother," looking at Israel, "who so sincerely desires to understand his duty. The Lord has surely sent him among us for his profit to-night. Let us all invoke a special blessing upon him, that he may leave this place, feeling as he never did before. After that, let other of the brethren and sisters pray for all the rest on these seats, that they may be confirmed and strengthened in the faith. Let us all now expect a present blessing."

Brother Simond was unlike some others who had prayed there that night. To the fervor of his religion was added a loving charity, otherwise called by his people "a sweet spirit," which moved upon the hearts of those of a certain temperament with a remarkable power. He was often called a Christian of the St. John stamp. He leaned much upon the Saviour's bosom, and so caught His heavenly spirit. Low and reverent were his tones, unless the tide of his feeling ran uncommonly strong and high, when he grew not loud, but deep and powerful, like a beautiful and full-flowing river of Faith hastening towards the sea of Infinite Compassion.

He it was who now prayed for Israel, and touched his heart by the might of his spirit as never man had done before. Words of Holy Writ, clothed with the seemingly unlimited power of his friendly soul, were on his lips as if they belonged there. The sword of the spirit accompanied them. They cut Israel to the heart. They transfused his nature into contrition and love. He wept.

Before the exercises of that evening had closed, Israel arose unbidden, and asked leave to speak to the people present.

"Speak, brother, and the Lord fill your heart with His Spirit," responded the leader.

"I came in hither," said Israel, "without knowing for what intent the Lord led me. I came with gainsaying, and it seemed to me that your words and ways were strangely erroneous. I confess that I had no part nor lot with you. But God has moved me to feel very differently."

"In answer to the prayer of faith," ejaculated the leader; "but go on, dear brother."

"I think of a truth that the Spirit of the Lord is here," he continued.

"Amen! Glory to God!" cried voices on all sides, while the tears fell from many eyes.

"And, although I have had a hope of a Christian before, I never realized my state as here, around this altar, to-night. I came in to wonder, I fear to despise; but what do I not owe to the grace of God, who opened my eyes, softened my heart, and filled it with love for you all."

"Bless the Lord! Bless God!" cried voices.

"For a long time I have sought for the people whose God was truly the Lord, for the church from among the varied churches of the land, of which it might well be said, as of the city described in Ezekiel, whose name was '*The Lord is there.*' I believe that I now have glimpses of this holy place with the holiest of names. My soul is filled with rejoicing that it sees, though in the dim distance, the spires and turrets of its home — its Christian home!

"My friends! I have no earthly home which is blessed, centred, and filled with the presence of kindred according to the flesh. My parents both died before I well remember. I have been well cared for, but it has been by strangers and hirelings; by good friends, it is true, but not by the blessed ones of home!"

"The Lord bless the dear young brother," was now heard in strong tones of tenderness.

"It seems to me, as I have said," Israel went on, amid tears, "that I am nearing the home of my soul, among true Christian brethren who love the souls of others."

No sooner had he concluded, than they commenced and sang the following beautiful words: —

> "In the Christian's home in glory
>   There remains a land of rest;
> There my Saviour's gone before me,
>   To fulfil my soul's request.
>
> *Chorus:*
>
> "There is rest for the weary,
>   There is rest for the weary,
>   On the other side of Jordan,
>   In the sweet fields of Eden.
> There is rest for the weary,
>   There is rest for you —
> Where the tree of life is blooming,
>   There is rest for you.
>
> "He is fitting up my mansion
>   Which eternally shall stand:
> For my stay shall not be transient
>   In that holy, happy land.
>
> *Chorus:* "There is rest for the weary, etc.
>
> "Sing, O sing, ye heirs of glory;
>   Shout your triumph as you go;
> Zion's gates will open for you,
>   You shall find an entrance through.
>
> *Chorus:* "There is rest for the weary," etc.

Sung, as were these words, by voices which welled up from hearts overflowing with emotion, Israel thought he had a foretaste of heaven.

No sooner was the meeting closed, than numbers of the "brethren" gathered around Israel to offer him their hands, with hearty words of welcome.

The leader took his address, and promised to call on him at an early opportunity.

"Things have taken a different turn to-night from what I expected," said Israel's companion, on the way to their boarding-place.

"Yes," he replied, "it is all very providential."

## CHAPTER II.

#### CYPRIAN CUTTING'S CALL.

THE next morning, before Israel had breakfasted, there was a knock on his door, and the servant told him that a gentleman waited to see him.

"Where is his card?" asked Israel in some surprise at such an unwonted summons.

"O! he told me he did not carry cards to play with, when I asked him, sir; but he said, 'Tell him I have a message from the Lord of Hosts, and it must be delivered without any delay.'"

Israel was about to offer some excuse at this singular request, when a footstep was heard upon the stair. He turned and saw the face of the leader of last night's meeting.

"Halloo there!" said the man; "don't you know your own brother in the Lord? I am a servant of the Almighty; my name is Cyprian Cutting; rightly named, too, for my business is to cut the hearts of sinners with the sword of Gideon, and I cut church members as well, if they lie asleep by the king's highway like snakes a-sunning."

"It seems to me that you are a very strange man for a minister," said Israel, who now showed him into his parlor, and opened a blind to admit the morning light. At this proceeding, the visitor began to sing in a low, sweet voice, "The morning light is breaking," stopping suddenly at the end of the first verse, and saying "I am not a minister yet, brother, though I am a making all the time, these glorious days. I shall soon stand on the heights of Zion, and proclaim a free salvation, in louder tones even than I now do."

"I supposed you were, from the fact of your position last evening," said Israel.

"I only led the meeting in the absence of our preacher. Religion is in a very low state in our church now."

"I thought quite the contrary," said Israel; "it seemed to me there was a remarkable fervor prevailing there."

"O! you ought to have seen us last winter," said Cutting, smiling with an ecstatic joy, "when every single night of the week, scores fell down, cut to the heart; and on Sunday nights we calculated we had done nothing, unless we could count seventy or eighty slain around our altar. O dear! our church members," he sighed, "are such stupid, blind guides! fools of heart, and slow to believe! I have to speak to them just as the Spirit gives me utterance, every once in a little while."

"Do they receive it peaceably?" asked Israel.

"Sometimes; but when I pour it on them the hottest from the fiery furnace of God's love, they squirm, I tell you; and they would turn Brother Cutting out of the church if they could — that's a fact. But they can't fight against the Lord to any good purpose."

"Then you think the Lord speaks through you," continued Israel.

"So long as I do His will to the letter, brother, I have not a doubt of it, and that's the reason I came here so early this morning; it's the early bird that catches the worm, you know. I am after your soul, brother, and I have come to tell you that if you don't come right out and own your Master with us — stand up like a good soldier of the cross and do your duty, you will soon fall into Satan's ranks and be eternally lost."

He fixed his eyes upon those of Israel with a look like a maniac. Yet he was pleasant and genial as the summer morn.

"Let us pray," next spoke Cutting, while he dropped suddenly upon his knees.

A listener would have inferred that he had full faith to the measure of his "soul's request," that "the heavens would bow and come down." To characterize this prayer by the word earnestness, is as scant of the fact as "light" falls short of a description of the sun. It was a practical obedience to the words of the Lord found in Isaiah xli: 21. Produce your cause: bring forth your strong reasons.

The breakfast bell terminated this exercise, but not the interview, for Cutting accepted the invitation to accompany Israel to breakfast, adding that he had not eaten a "full meal" for four days. It soon transpired that Cutting was boarding himself, and in all ways trying to eke out enough to provide the means for an education.

"It must be very hard for you," said Israel.

"Not at all, dear brother, since my Master looks out that I have all I really need. The glorious service *pays*, I assure you." And he smiled as though contemplating a broker's board, on which he had a right to thousands of gold.

In answer to the request of the landlady that he should ask the blessing, he prayed at least five minutes, in which he took occasion to remember every individual around the table, each with an original request, not forgetting to offer a petition that the colored handmaids who wait upon us " may have their souls washed and made white in the cleansing blood of the Lamb." Also, he said in conclusion, " If any of these persons, O Lord, fail of securing admission to Thy kingdom, it will not be the fault of Thy servant who warned them on Tuesday morning, August seventeenth, in the year of our Lord, (here he gave the year,) Amen."

The result of this unprecedented faithfulness to a conviction of duty appeared in a few days, in the form of a new coat, ordered by subscription of those persons there present, for "Mr. Cyprian Cutting — a man among a thousand, who dares to say what he thinks."

## CHAPTER III.

### METHODIST DOCTRINE.

ISRAEL soon became so much interested in what he heard and saw among these Methodists, that he took advice of the minister of this persuasion, whose services he now chiefly attended, as to what books he should read in order to become acquainted more thoroughly with their doctrinal belief. He was told that no stress was laid upon the belief of the laity for membership, provided they loved our Lord Jesus Christ in sincerity, and were striving to live a good life; but that the ministry were strictly required to accept their creed in the fifty-three discourses of John Wesley, and his Notes on the New Testament, all of which is of the "Arminian type."

He was curious to know how the belief of the Arminians could read in distinction from those "Five Points" of Calvinism which he had received with so much reservation of confidence.

He found it to read thus: —

I. That God, from eternity, determined to bestow salvation on those who, he foresaw, would persevere unto the end, and to inflict everlasting punishment on those who should continue in their unbelief, and resist his divine succors; so that election and reprobation are conditional.

II. That Jesus Christ, by his sufferings and death, made an atonement for the sins of all mankind, and of every individual in particular; that, however, none but those who believe in him, can be partakers of his benefits.

III. That mankind are not totally depraved, and that depravity does not come upon them by virtue of Adam's being their federal head.

IV. That the grace of God, which converts men, is not irresistible.

V. That those who are united to Christ by faith may fall from a state of grace, and finally perish.

Upon some of these views he found that those of Wesley appeared to join issue. For instance, in Wesley's own words, he read as follows:—

"*Question.* In what sense is Adam's sin imputed to all mankind?

"*Answer.* In Adam all died, *i. e.*, 1. Our bodies then became mortal. 2. Our souls died, *i. e.* were disunited from God. And hence, 3. We are all born with a sinful, devilish nature; by reason whereof, 4. We are children of wrath, liable to death eternal. (Rom. 5: 18; Eph. 11: 3.)

"*Q.* In what sense is the righteousness of Christ imputed to all mankind, or to believers?

"*A.* We do not find it expressly affirmed in Scripture that God imputes the righteousness of Christ to any, although we do find that faith is imputed for righteousness. That text, 'As by one man's disobedience all men were made sinners, so by the obedience of one all were made righteous,' we conceive, means by the merits of Christ all men are cleared from the guilt of Adam's actual sin."

In addition to what is contained in the creed of Arminius, he found these teachings, also, of Wesley: —

"*Q.* What is implied in being a *perfect Christian?*

"*A.* The loving the Lord our God with all our heart, and with all our mind, and soul, and strength.

"*Q.* Does this imply that all inward sin is taken away?

"*A.* Without doubt; or how could we be said to be saved *from all our uncleanness?*" (Ezek. 36 : 29.)

Of faith, he found the Wesleyan idea to be, " not only a divine evidence or conviction that God was in Christ reconciling the world unto himself, but a sure trust and confidence that Christ died for my sins, that he loved me, and gave himself for me. And the moment a penitent sinner believes this, God pardons and absolves him; and as soon as his pardon or justification is witnessed to him by the Holy Ghost, he is saved."

A standard writer of this connection, Israel found, adds to the foregoing: —

"That comfortable persuasion of God's favor, resulting from the witness of the Holy Spirit, for which the Methodists contend, they distinguish from an assurance of final salvation. It is simply a persuasion of present pardon and acceptance. Without this, say they, we cannot love God, and therefore cannot yield those fruits of righteousness which indicate a state of grace and safety. The induction thus supposes the antecedent ' witness,' as truly as lunar beams give evidence of the power and brightness of the sun. Where the attesting spirit dwells, He produces the graces which are enumerated in Holy Scripture ; and thus arises what has been called [perhaps not very accurately], a 'second witness', to ratify and confirm to us the first.

"Comparing many texts of Holy Scripture which are addressed to those who are 'in Christ,'—and of which the burden is, to urge each to 'cleanse' themselves 'from all filthiness of the flesh and spirit, perfecting holiness in the fear of God,'—the Methodists infer that *in this life* the Christian man may be 'sanctified wholly;' and that his 'whole spirit and soul and body' may 'be preserved blameless unto the coming of our Lord Jesus Christ.'"

"Beautiful doctrine!" exclaimed Israel, as he read the foregoing *substance* of the Methodist belief; "I will search for the evidences of its truth, and if found, it shall be the creed of my heart and the practice of my life!"

He then spent the greater part of weeks and months in exploring the best works of the standard writers of Methodism, occasionally availing himself of conversations with such of the most learned and pious persons of that persuasion as he could meet. Especially was his soul moved and confirmed in this "way of salvation," when he read such books of devout and faithful zeal as the lives of the Wesleys, of Fletcher and his not less saintly wife, of Carvosso, Mrs. Hester Ann Rogers, and others of that procession of true followers of the apostolical faith and practice, who went about doing good everywhere as they had opportunity, asking not, nor expecting reward in this life.

All this was not without its effect upon his own purposes of life. He had caught the holy fire, and air beneath the trees of the forest, newly kindled his interest. He heard the words: —

> "O for a heart to praise my God,
> A heart from sin set free;
> A heart that always feels thy blood,
> So freely spilt for me.
>
> "A heart in every thought renewed,
> And full of love divine;
> Perfect, and right, and pure, and good,
> A copy, Lord, of thine."

Then he came in full view of the scene. He paused a moment to study what he saw.

It had rained heavily during the previous night, so that all the abundant foliage of the giant trees of the old wood, with the gravel paths which led about the grounds, and the white canvas roofs, had been washed, refreshed, and endued as with a smile from the heavens. A gradually rising hill, which formed a kind of natural amphitheatre, was bounded to the extent of a semicircle by the different tents, on each of which was the name of the place of the society which composed its occupants. These tents were very similar in construction and furnishing, except some smaller ones in the rear of the semicircle, which had been put up by private individuals for the use of one family or small sets of persons. Each tent was thickly carpeted with straw; seats extended around the walls, and articles of various kinds, like chests and trunks, were packed away in remote corners. To the rear of each was a cooking-stove, and benches which served for tables and other domestic uses. These composed the kitchens and family rooms of the establishments. The lower base of this amphitheatre was occupied by a roofed house, before which was a stand for the preachers, and from which extended, up to within a short walk from the tents, rows of substantial seats capable of accommodating many hundreds of persons.

Although the sermon for that afternoon was over, they were now partially filled by people who were engaged in a meeting of a more social nature. Hence the singing which he heard on his approach.

Aged men and women, middle-aged persons, children, and even babes, were here to be seen or heard. Hardly a color or a people was not represented in some form.

The words of the divine prophecy — "And Sharon shall be a fold of flocks," came to the memory of Israel, as he stood before the door of the first tent he reached and gazed about him.

Not long did he linger there, for he was attracted by the strong musical tones of a well-known voice in the most violent exhortation to that audience on the seats. It came from among the people and not from the preachers' stand; yet no minister full of years and weighty with the sheaves of precious souls could have spoken with greater authority and earnestness.

Israel moved forward, exchanged a nod with the sheriff in attendance, and took his place among the hearers of that powerful, hortatory address.

"O Cyprian!" he said to himself, "are you never weary in your Master's work? Somewhere about you must be concealed the patent of indefatigable perseverance." All else looked worn with the long day's excitement, and waiting to be renewed by " the cup which cheers but not inebriates," while he was, to appearance, as fresh and heart-full as though just risen from a plunge into the river of life.

His attention soon wandered to the group of faces upon the preachers' stand. Only two or three of as many score were known to him. He read them as he would a page in Hebrew, from right to left, directly the reverse of the vernacular.

Not more than one in fifteen had received a college diploma, and all but two or three of these were bestowed by a university of medium rank. Very few, and these among the younger portion, had studied in a theological seminary. Half of them referred only to an academy of their denomination, which they proudly called EVERSHAM.

All except two, or at the most four of these preachers, had the look which speaks of hidden power to survive all kinds of transformation. This was the result of the cultivation of their peculiar system of itinercracy. They were used to being changed about into shapes in which they would not have recognized themselves, had it not been for their surnames, occasionally pronounced in strong tones by their bishops, at the beck of the presiding elders.

Spallanzani has proved that the snail has the power of reproducing a new head when decapitated; but it should be noticed that the brain of the snail does not reside in its head.

Hopeful, cheerful, satisfied with their sect, looked they all; and how could it be otherwise when Methodism was progressing in its victorious march over this continent, at the rate of five hundred souls a minute, or better yet, of five hundred thousand dollars an hour of lunar time!

Not that Israel Knight thought this, as he gazed at that formidable array of preachers. Far from it. He thought of them only as the most faithful, the most humble, apostolical servants of the true church of Christ; and, as he thought, he sighed that he could not be there, one in their midst.

"I understand that the elders here have asked God to give us at least one hundred conversions for the harvest of this camp-meeting, and how are they going to get them all if they do not bestir themselves more than they have?" cried Cyprian Cutting.

(He had before said, in Israel's hearing, that he had laid out to be the means of converting fifty thousand souls before he left this world).

In a similar strain he went on till the bell rung announcing the time to close.

After supper, and before the time for the evening sermon, Israel was in one of the tents, whither he had been invited by some friends of slight acquaintance who belonged to the society which occupied it.

A class meeting was in progress there. After singing and prayer, a young minister spoke a few words explanatory of his own feelings at that particular time, and invited all present to do likewise. The purport of what he said was that religion never had appeared better to him than it did at that moment. He loved the work in which he was engaged; he loved all his brethren and sisters, and hoped he should meet them all at last in heaven. This was good; but as nearly every one present, in regular succession, gave in a not very dissimilar testimony, Israel began to think that a change, even for the worse, would be a relief. He was about to dismiss this thought as a temptation, when he was asked to speak. The nature of his own private feelings seemed to him too sacred to parade there before all that tent's company. He was not accustomed to such an exhibition of himself, and respectfully asked to be excused.

"Speak, brother," said a friend who sat next him, "speak a word for the Master." He was silent, and looked down heavily upon the straw. Forty-six eyes were fastened on him, and for that moment, Napoleon at St. Helena did not feel more painfully than he did.

"Tell us, young friend," spoke the minister, "just how you feel. Christ is a present Saviour, and he gives a full and free salvation just now, if we ask it. Are you willing to be saved from all your sins?"

Still he answered nothing. If he told them "just how" he felt then, he would have said that their exercise had begun to seem tiresome to him. To tell them of his present views and purposes, he did not deem meet for the time or place. His present sins he reserved for his closet, and not for any human confessional, private or public.

He was then addressed as though he were not one of them, or in other words, not a Christian. They hoped he would soon be made willing to testify for the Master.

This was all in keeping with Methodist estates, or orders of spiritual government. With these estates, the article of *speech* has prime value. Without it, religious character is a paradox, something to be doubted, and to be disciplined. A multitude of sins are covered by Methodist "testimony."

Israel being new to this economy, he did not comprehend it. He began to consider from left to right, — no longer in Hebrew style, but in that of Saxon common sense. He asked himself if these people were right in their judgments, based on premises so slight and insufficient? If they condemned upon such grounds, they might also " save " in like manner. It seemed to him that they put themselves in the place of Christ, hardly less than did the " Vicegerent of Rome."

The singing of one of the beautiful hymns, which these people sing in an almost unequalled style, for the time restored his equanimity, and with it came his confidence, though its wings were no longer plumed.

The evening sermon was upon holiness. Many passages of Scripture were ingeniously quoted to prove the doctrine. The theory was adapted to the comfort of all who were hungering and thirsting after righteousness. Israel listened with reverent attention. Some of it was in this wise : —

* " Christian Perfection or Holiness is that state of grace which excludes all sin from the heart. 'Blessed are the pure in heart.' 'Create in me a clean heart, O God!' 'The blood of Jesus Christ, his Son, cleanseth us from all sin.' 'Being made free from sin, ye have your fruit unto holiness, and the end everlasting life.'

---

* These words on Christian Perfection are taken from a work entitled " *Perfect Love.*"

"The difference between regeneration and sanctification is — The man who is merely regenerated is but partially saved from sin, while the sanctified is *wholly saved*. The regenerated soul does not commit sin, though he is conscious of remaining *inbred sin*. The sanctified soul neither commits sin nor feels any consciousness of remaining inbred sin. In justification, the strong man is *bound;* in sanctification, he is *cast out*.

"The graces of the spirit exist in the entirely sanctified without alloy. The graces in the sanctified are perfect in kind, but limited in degree. Regeneration affords victory over sin subdued; sanctification gives victory over sin exterminated and cast out, so that all the graces of the spirit exist perfect in kind — that is, to the exclusion of their opposites.

"Sanctification does not add any new virtues to the soul. It simply cleanses the soul from all in-dwelling sin, so as to allow the graces implanted in the soul at regeneration to exist without alloy, or without their opposites in the heart.

"The cause of so much prejudice and opposition to the doctrine of holiness among professors of religion is that the doctrine has been misunderstood. It has generally been taken to mean more than was intended, and more than was taught by the standards of the Church.

"We teach absolute perfection in none but God. The brightest, the highest, the sweetest, and the most lovely angel in paradise is not absolutely perfect. In this sense, 'there is none good but one, that is God.'

"We teach no *angelic* perfection in man while he is out of heaven. In this world we must be contented with Christian perfection, which, according to Mr. Wesley, is ' pure love reigning *alone* in the heart and life.'

"The sanctified soul trusts more perfectly and constantly in the *atonement* than any other. He, more than any other man, feels

' Every moment, Lord, I need
The merit of thy death.'

"Christian Perfection does not exclude the possibility of growing in grace. The pure in heart grow faster than any others. There is no standing still in religion or sin. We are either progressing or receding. If we are neglecting present duty, we are backsliding, however great our attainments may have been.

"Christian Perfection does not exclude a liability to temptation. Our holy Saviour was tempted. So long as we are in an unholy world, we may expect to be tempted. It is no sin to be tempted, provided proper caution has been used to avoid the occasions of temptation.

"Christian Perfection does not exclude the possibility of falling away; but it renders it much less probable. We must wait for absolute security until we arrive at heaven. Hence, we are to ' work out our salvation with fear and trembling.'

"No temptation or evil suggestion to the mind becomes sin till it is tolerated. *Sin consists in yielding to temptation.* So long as the soul maintains its integrity, so that temptation finds no *sympathy* within, no sin is committed, and the soul remains unharmed, no matter how protracted or severe the fiery trial may prove.

"Christian Perfection does not make any one perfect in knowledge. Of those sanctified wholly, it may be emphatically said, they 'walk in the light, as he is in the light.' The perfect in love have a more clear apprehension of God, of His presence, and of spiritual things, (other things being equal), than any other.

"Christian Perfection does not exclude the *infirmities* of human nature, — such as slowness of understanding, errors of judgment, mistakes in practice, erratic imaginations, a treacherous memory, etc.

"Holiness may be perfect, and yet be progressive. It is complete in the sanctified soul in *kind*, but limited in *degree*. Perfection in quality does not exclude increase in quantity. The capacities of the soul are progressive, and holiness should increase in a measure corresponding to its increasing capacity. Faith, love, humility, and patience may be perfect in kind, and yet increase in volume and power — in measure."

At the close of this sermon, another preacher arose, and in a few words gave his testimony of the possession of the "Second Blessing," and urging all those present who had this witness, to profess it — laying much stress upon the idea that the blessing of entire sanctification could not be retained without confessing its possession on all suitable occasions. He also cited standard authorities in proof of this.

Israel thought of these words found in Romans 14: 22: "Hast thou faith? Have it to thyself before

God," and wondered what disposition this man would make of them.

One after another, both men and women, young men and young girls, rose before all that numerous audience, and said like this: —

"By faith in the atoning blood of my Saviour, I am saved from all sin, and live now with the Spirit witnessing to my spirit that I am clean."

Or, in these words: "At [a given time] I reckoned myself to be dead unto sin but alive unto God through Jesus Christ our Lord. Praise to the grace which saves."

Israel said to himself: "This may all be true, but how can I reconcile it with the scriptural command, "in lowliness of mind let each esteem the other better than themselves. Look not every man on his own things, but every man also on the things of others." Christ's own account of the Pharisee and the Publican also presented itself at that time.

After this kind of testimony, a short exhortation was given to all present who had the blessing of justification, to seek "just now" the blessing of sanctification. The seats around the altar were cleared while this verse was sung: —

> "Break off the yoke of inbred sin,
> And fully set my spirit free;
> I cannot rest till pure within —
> Till I am wholly lost in thee."

Several short, earnest prayers to the present object were now offered, a few more words from the leader of the occasion spoken, and then it was urged that all who had now obtained the second blessing should rise, and in the fewest words, profess it.

A young girl was one of the first to testify that she was now saved from all sin. Others, in quick succession, followed, till some twenty persons had professed to the new possession.

These words, with other similar ones, were sung in a remarkably solemn manner:—

"The world is overcome by the blood of the Lamb!
My sins are washed away in the blood of the Lamb!
The devil's overcome by the blood of the Lamb!
I've lost the fear of death through the blood of the Lamb!
The martyrs overcame by the blood of the Lamb!
I hope to gain the skies by the blood of the Lamb!"

"If it is really so," reflected Israel, "that these persons have now overcome the world, the flesh and the devil, and have arrived at that heavenly state which was enjoyed by the martyrs and saints of all ages in their hours of death, this must be called the very gate of heaven."

These scenes deeply impressed him. Afterwards, when he had entered the tent whither Cyprian Cutting invited him to tarry for that night, he could not but reflect earnestly upon this, to him, new doctrine. But the scenes which soon transpired around him, the night-worship — the getting ready to lie down upon the straw under a blanket, and with a carpet-bag for a pillow, while nothing but a canvas divided them from the women, who seemed to talk incessantly during their similar process, scarcely interrupted by the cries of infants — drove away these reflections for the present. Every once in a few moments, for hours, Cyprian cried out in stentorian tones, "Glory to God! O, I am on the mount!" Similar sounds were heard also from one of the adjoining tents; and in another, a meeting of the most arousing description was in progress all night.

It is contrary to the rules of the camp-meeting to have meetings in the tents, or other disturbances, after ten o'clock; but on the later nights of the week, this rule, under extraordinary occasions, is sometimes suspended or ignored.

Israel found it impossible for him to shut his eyes in sleep; he therefore arose and went to the tent where the meeting was in progress. Here he perceived that two or three persons lay in the arms of others of their own sex, apparently in a stupor; one of them occasionally rallied sufficiently to shout. On inquiry, he was told that these had passed into that state which is called "losing the strength."

He ventured to ask a man who seemed inclined to talk with him, if there was any spiritual authority for this demonstration; and was referred to the example of Saul of Tarsus, who was on his way to Damascus; to the case of the prophet Daniel, who says when he saw the "great vision," "and there remained no strength in me;" and to John, in the Apocalypse, who saw the one in the midst of the seven golden candlesticks, and "fell at his feet as dead."

"Were not those more extraordinary cases than it is possible for any of these to be?" asked Israel; "Those persons saw Christ himself, or at least his angels, which sufficiently accounts for their remarkable prostration."

"But these," continued the other, "have had revelations, by the power of great faith, here to-night, in answer to prevailing and almost unceasing prayer, as great, comparatively speaking, as the divine ones. Friend! have you ever been converted?" he suddenly asked.

"I trust I have," answered Israel, in a modest tone.

"Then you will understand what I mean," he continued, "when I say that the soul, convicted of its need of the application of the cleansing blood — and truly *seeing itself*, and also having a clearer vision than ever before of the pure and infinitely holy Jesus, *might*, under certain favorable physical circumstances, lose its power of self-control, and to appearance become as dead. We have had a glorious meeting to-night, and Jesus has been right here in our midst, doing wonders, whereof we are glad, and rejoice with exceeding great joy."

"It may be so" answered Israel reverently; "and I would not be one to speak a word or harbor a thought against the possibilities of the work of the Holy Spirit. Yet I remember that when Job saw the Lord, or his angel, it affected him with supreme self-abasement as never before; 'but now mine eye seeth thee, wherefore I abhor myself, and repent in dust and ashes.' Less than ever, did he feel that he was *holy*."

"With the doctrine of holiness," answered the man, "I have not much to do. It may be true and it may not."

"What! then you, sir, are not a Methodist?" asked Israel.

"I've been a member of the Methodist Church since I was fifteen years old. I was converted at a place much like this," he replied.

"I thought all Methodists, that is, all who continue steadfast in the doctrine of the Church, believed and taught Holiness or Christian Perfection," said Israel.

The man shook his head.

"I suppose it's generally thought so," he said, "but not half of our people think much about it any way. Half of those who look into it at all, are ready to offer a reward for the sight of a perfect man or woman, since they never yet have seen one."

"The sermon, certainly, was a good one, which we had this evening on that subject," continued Israel.

"O yes, very good for theory — very good to awaken the people. I guess you are not used to camp-meetings, are you?"

"This is my first attendance," said Israel.

"Like it?" he continued.

"I have not yet made up my mind," said Israel.

At this juncture, the shouting and the singing became so powerfully sonorous, the conversation had to be suspended.

## CHAPTER V.

### AN OLD MAN'S OPINION OF METHODISM.

THE more Israel observed of this people, the more undecided was he what course to pursue respecting them. Some features of their faith and also of their practice commended themselves strongly to his approbation; of certain others he was in doubt; and yet others he wholly disliked.

He wrote to his guardian for advice, and received the following: —

"You ask me my opinion of the Methodists, so called — referring, I conclude, to the largest body of that family in this country. Never was there a more palpable misnomer. A set of doctors of medicine, who lived about a century before Christ, first wore it, for what reason I know not, unless it was that they killed systematically. In the seventeenth century, certain Roman Catholics, who could split a hair between their dogmas and those of the Protestants, were called Methodists.

"In 1729, in England, there arose a 'godly club,' headed by John Wesley, to which this name was finally fixed. You had better hunt up an account of this religious movement, which is considered by the impartial historian one of the most remarkable events that ever happened in the annals of all Christendom. A great deal of its notoriety is derived from the fact of the then existing corruptions of the old Church of England, which furnished a splendid dark background for the new lights and strange shadows of the doings of these people.

"John Wesley was somewhat like Job. He, at first, sat down among the ashes of the mother church, with his three friends for counsellors, and scraped himself of its prevailing sins with the potsherd of self-denial. He then prepared himself by fasting and prayer, with works of charity, for his future mission.

"After a time he took a wife, and he thought she spoke like one of the foolish women, and deported herself still more like a fool, in being jealous of him. But not many women would bear to have their husbands away from them most of the time, in all sorts of places, though preaching, and writing meanwhile the most 'bowel-moving' letters to hosts of women, any more gracefully than did Mrs. Wesley.

"Like Job, also, he lost his old estate in the establishment, but finally came out with great possessions, so that his latter end was blessed of the Lord to the surprise of himself and everybody else.

"John Wesley had executive talent, education, and an indomitable will; but he was narrow, tyrannical, and superstitious. [I use this last word not as infidels employ it, to fling a stone at the rites of true piety, but simply as a Christian does when contemplating erratic bondage to idle and unauthorized fancies].

"In proof that he was narrow, it is only necessary

to refer to his slavish adherence to the Church of England, and his general views of the progress of true religion in the world — as though it were a sin to send out the gospel of a free salvation in any other groove than the old, well-worn one, which he thought cut out by Christ and his apostles.

"That he was tyrannical is clear enough in every chapter of his history. His whole system, though professedly a free, democratic one, is a system of tyranny over the will, the conscience, and the actions, to the most minute degree. His ministers were hampered at every turn by numerous petty rules, which extended even to what they should say in private, and just how long they were to say it. He told them, as a clincher to his long list of 'duties,' that they were to act in all things not according to their own will, but as a son in the gospel, and in union with their brethren — which meant as a son to him and in union with him. Their rules, which were all framed and sealed by himself, he concluded in this manner: 'Remember, a *Methodist preacher is to mind every point, great and small, in the Methodist discipline;* therefore you will need all the grace and all the sense you have, and to have all your wits about you.'

"He taught toryism to his followers who were in America at the time of the Revolution. He was strongly opposed to the independence of the colonies until time and circumstance compelled him to be silent. He believed in keeping people under a monarchy both of state and church — the first to be centred in a king; the last in John Wesley, as a delegated power from the establishment. For well-organized tyranny, the

Wesleyan see is second to no other contemporaneous power.

"That Wesley was superstitious is shown by his heed to apparitions, noises, dreams, and demoniacal possession. It is true that Scripture warrants some belief in these things, but a wise man will remember that 'secret things belong to God,' and be careful how he intermeddles therewith. From this demonstration of himself, though considerably guarded in his own case, has radiated all kinds of fanaticism in his followers.

"It is certain that Wesley did much good. He was an apostle of reform to the ignorant and degraded. God raised him up for a particular era, and for a special purpose. He is entitled to the qualified regard of all good men for what he accomplished.

"Philip Embury, who had been a local preacher in Ireland, was the first to start Methodism in America, in the year 1766. The inauguration of his work originated in this manner: Barbara Heck, a pious Irishwoman in New York, found this Embury one day with a set of other fellows who were playing cards. She threw the pack into the fire, and said to Embury, 'You must preach to us, or we shall all go to hell together, and God will require our blood at your hands.' And this man received her admonition, and began to preach in a private house, afterwards in a rigger's loft.

"From this beginning, Methodism has become a power in our land, eminent for its activity and numerical strength. Like Ephraim, while it was trembling in Israel, it prospered; but as soon as it began to exalt itself in worldly pride, its spiritual power declined. Its present history is strangely inconsistent with its real life. Once it was adorned with humility and self-sacrifice; now it vaunts itself in gold and the tricks of mammon. It is second to no other sect in its aspirations for vain show. Its ministers adorn themselves with gold baubles, use great swelling words about the progress of their sect, and are all athirst for power. They are often unreliable, and treacherous even to each other. No more regard is now paid to Wesley's 'Rules' than to the traditions of Prester John.

"Methodism is adapted to the ignorant and to the worldly wise or managing leaders. It is jealous of 'lay-representation,' of the most liberal education, and of refined culture.

"Its periodicals represent their peculiar style of doing and saying. Take up its leading newspaper and read at random; the editor, who has received catholic culture to an unusual degree, is justly celebrated as one of their prominent men; you will find most undignified and common, often coarse, phrases used by contributors in allusion to subjects of the highest and gravest import.

"The annals of its centenary year attained the culmination of ridiculous folly. The adventures of Don Quixote pale beside the color of its denominational nonsense. False as fair were its continual boasts of what it had achieved and was still doing. Its statements of what it was giving were most like the old riddle of going to St. Ives. An observer, on examining closely into the matter, found that, save the alleged 'subscriptions' and 'pledges,' with a few really magnificent donations advanced, there was but a comparatively small basis for the foundation. In connection with all these vaunts, the name of Wesley was recorded ten times to that of Jesus Christ once. This name of a faulty man is nailed like a horseshoe to all their public edifices and denominational movements. Every tenth baby of them all receives it for his life-dower.

"The round numbers footed up under this name are the crown-diamonds of this people who aspire to royalty. If the anger of the Lord was kindled against David, when he, in his pride, numbered the people; and also against Hezekiah, who displayed unto the Prince of Babylon all that was in his house and in all his dominions, including the silver and gold, what shall this people say, in the time of the Lord's visitation? When Elijah was in the cave of contemplation, he was taught that the Lord was not in the great strong wind, which rent the mountains and brake in pieces the rocks before him; nor was He in the earthquake, nor yet in the fire. The still, small voice spoke the will of the Lord.

Truly yours,<br>
EPHRAIM STEARNS."

## CHAPTER VI.

#### THE METHODIST ANNUAL CONFERENCE.

Not wholly satisfied with the opinions of his guardian, Israel determined to make further observations.

In the following spring he attended the Annual Conference of this people, which, this year, met in one of the inland cities. During this session he kept a journal, extracts from which follow:—

"I had a curiosity to see the Bishop who presided on this occasion, as he has the reputation of being a great man in the Methodist House of Zion. Probably he is better known outside of his own denomination than any other of his colleagues. His appearance is hieroglyphic. It is common-place at the first glance; ugly at the second; but by-and-by he gives one the impression of a man of power. It is, however, the power of a strong man by nature rather than by cultivation. His look reveals a silent but mighty struggle with his destiny, or rather, what with ordinary men under the same circumstances would have been his destiny. His will must have been fire-proof. He governs men and religious bodies by this latent power. Sometime, if not now, he must have been a man of sorrows. You see in his face much that you yourself have endured. Hence his charm over his hearers.

"When he speaks, I am disappointed, even more than when I first saw him. His voice is certainly a tone, superadded to which is a wave of brogue. He is called an orator. My ideas of what constitutes an orator are now all at fault, or else this man is not what he is called. As a presiding officer he is calm, dignified, correct.

"This body of men is a study from my position in the gallery. It includes more stars and comets than did the camp-meeting stand.

"To-day an old friend from this city dropped in upon me accidentally, and volunteered some information. He is not a Methodist, and therefore his views are not altogether reliable respecting this people, but I listened with attention.

"'There,' said he, pointing out a man who sat in one of the front seats, 'is the presiding elder of one of the districts. He is a great operator, and is noted for his long and methodically worded prayers. A good and kind man at heart, withal discreet. He knows enough to be silent when he should. Astute, meditative, but intensely active in the cabinet.'

"What cabinet?" I asked.

"'Don't you know that the presiding bishop and all the elders of a conference are called the cabinet? They lay their heads together and concoct the appointments. But committees from the churches have more than half to do with this business. There is as much pipe-laying about the appointments assigned to the itinerants, as at any political campaign of the same magnitude of interest.'

"'Possible!' I rejoined, 'when only last week I

read in a Methodist paper the devout prayer that the people might receive their preachers as sent to them by the head of the church.'

"'O yes, I dare say. But the head of the church has no more to do with it than with the election of a fence-viewer or councilman. In both and all cases it is providential, or systematically the work of shrewd tactics, just as you regard the science of cause and effect.'

"'Here comes one of the stars of the Conference,' he went on. I looked and saw a man, rotund, sleek, noisy, but not swift.

"My companion continued, 'This is a mesmeric man. All the conditions laid down in the psychological canon are fulfilled in his getting up. He is one who gets on. Unlike the orthodox apostles of the most Christian Church, he speaks to everybody whom he meets — child, maiden, boy, and hoary-haired. Even the lamp-posts of the street receive a blessing from his ample shadow. He is not unctuous, but simply gracious.

"'In result, he wins place and honor from second-rate appointments, for his limited intellectual acquirements forbid his engineering the largest steamers of the line. When I say place and honor, I refer to side issues, as election to political office.

"'He prophesies to the people smooth things with a loud, sonorous voice. It pays, as this thing always will pay. [If ever you take to prophesying, either by word of mouth or pen, remember this and copy Tray. Have no shadows in your pictures of men and their manners, only just enough to bring out the high lights that you lay on with palette-knife. Scumble all your work with a semi-opaque toadyism].'

"'This man, not unlike his predecessor, finds money in the fish's mouth, even when he casts his eloquent eyes officially upon the old specimen suspended in the Hall of Representatives. Brother Bunsen is a comfortable individual. I wish him well. He wishes well to himself. All the people respond, "Amen."'

"I was on the point of remonstrating with my old classmate for his characteristic irreverence, when he gave me an unwarrantable jog, and whispered, 'Behold that youth, just booked for an advanced stride in the orders. Not yet in full blast, he does preaching occasionally by the job. Meantime, he works at teaching, and goes by the title bestowed by his people on all their male teachers and soap-venders — Professor! I should say, all who are not D. D. Mark his carriage. Like a suddenly loosed colt, he bounds up the aisle, tossing his "ambrosial locks" to the right and left, and snuffing the air with a supreme consciousness that his days, being all halcyon, are swifter than a weaver's shuttle. A clerical gymnast is this hero. That is to say, he takes preaching as one takes the bag of beans and dumb-bells, in order to develop the muscles and chest.

"'Mistake him not for a fool. He graduated with honors, and devours books voraciously. Moreover, he has ideas. One of them is, that this world was not made in six days, because, forsooth, it would have taken longer to have conceived the plan and power of Methodism.

"'The plan and power of Methodism have representative-men, as the ostrich has eggs. Himself is one of these eggs. It pips at the Annual Conference. Anon, it will hatch, and lo! a full-fledged, strange ostrich, which shall out-run the north wind. Vulcan, you know, was educated in heaven, and, doubtless, would have always remained there, had he not been kicked out. That kick, however, made him, — as one in the stomach by a co-laborer, — made Sir Isaac Newton. This young man believes in making people. There is power in the toe of his right boot.'

"I should so infer," I replied, laughing, "by the noise of his unusual tramp; but this making people is as dangerous business as working in a powder mill. There is a verse in the Bible that reads something like this: 'He that rolleth a stone, it shall return upon him.' Milton alludes to it, in these words: 'like a devilish engine, back recoils upon himself.'"

"'Hum!'" responded my friend reflectively; "'there is no system without its difficulties. Non-resistance is a system. So is resistance.'" At this juncture an intermission was announced. Several preachers, who appeared to be strangers, crowded about the Bishop, whose manner towards them was unexceptionable.

"No sooner was the recess over, than these ministers were announced to the body by the Bishop. Thereat the whole *posse comitatus* (this phrase being inelegant, I will substitute that of *olla podrida*) arose, thus displaying their Wesleyan good manners. It appeared that the presented persons were representative of other friendly denominations, who had come in to spy out the land, and bring away clusters of — sour grapes, perhaps.

"To-day is Sunday — the great feast-day of the Conference. In the morning, before service, I attend a Love-Feast. The church is crowded. One of the elders presides. About the altar and in the pulpit are other elders, like the six Turkish viziers of Constantinople, who are called viziers of the bench because they have seats in the Divan. Lord Kames, in his 'Elements of Criticism,' teaches that it is fitting for persons in power to have higher seats than the populace. I am glad that any lord has authorized it.

"After prayer and praise, the bread and water are distributed, when begin the speeches. Of these, I remember not many. They are too same to remember. But some stand out like a windmill against the sky of a picture. One woman rises, and with a high, shrill voice, frees her mind, meanwhile emphasizing her rhetoric with an expressive flourish of her muff. She talks like one in a kind of joyful trouble, if such an anomalous idea is admissible. Women, when excited before the audience largely composed of ministers, appear somewhat troubled, but yet sweetly hopeful.

"There are some speeches from the preachers which are strongly touching and even beautiful. Some are fresh from the graves of beloved ones. God help them! One relates a dream. There was poetry in that dream, and truth as well. I would record it here in my note-book, only it strikes me that I should be violating confidence. 'Declare ye it not at Gath.' (Micah 1 : 9.) Young men, scarcely yet out of their foolery, (by this I only allude to the old Italian proverb, 'Men learn to shave on the chin of a fool,') rise and testify. I notice that these are very loud and strong in their voices, purposes, and responses. There are some young ministers, however, who are truly modest and devout in their appearance. Each is, as Saul was, 'a choice young man, and goodly.'

"Matters hasten; the bell strikes for church service. The great bishop will preach to-day. Everybody is expectant.

"I have heard the bishop preach. He *is* a man of power. He made me think, at first, of stupendous summits, of beetling crags, and a Western forest in December. But as he went on, I discovered beneath all 'a fire infolding itself' as in the vision of Ezekiel, not lurid nor yet rose-colored, but amber-gold, as if struck off the sun in the heavens. It warmed and spread until there was a glow in the farthest corner of the house, and in the coldest heart of them all.

"The man lives, and moves, and has his being in this viewless fire. It is lighted by God. Hence his power. I shall remember no more his voice, his look, nor other of the elements. He is a result — a tetrachord or four-sounded soul whose extremes are immutable. By the touch of other minds, the two middle chords sometimes vary; but the beginning and ending of his life-purposes are complete in himself. The man cannot be overruled by state, place, nor human mind; he therefore rules all these.

"Not all preachers are 'ministers of God's word.' But this man is a V. D. M. The Bible is his library; the sacred ccurie, his alma mater; his degree that described in 1 Tim. 3:13.

"The servant is not above his lord, and he is not wiser than that which is written. Hence, the greatness of the man which is great enough to change his mental vectures into chariots of royal purple and gold; and his mien gradually puts on robes of majestical flowing."

* * * * * *

"As the sermon from his lips proceeded, some 'for joy tenderly wept;' others responded in deep, sympathetic tones, yet others became noiseful, possessed with that spirit which shines equally at a dead-wake or a figary, though clothed in an appearance better painted by Milton: —

> 'Earth trembled from her entrails, as again
> In pangs, and Nature gave a second groan.'

Evidently the bishop did not savor this as of true knowledge. Gently was wrought into his speech a rebuke to all excessive demonstrations.

"The storm immediately subsided, and emotion disappeared. The sun came out, and every man looked on his neighbor as though he could smile. The sympathetic silence of true souls is more grateful to a great man than the hoarsest and loudest echoes of meaningless minds.

"There is a character sifting at these Conferences. The name of each member (and by member I mean travelling preacher, so called, as no other belongs to this body,) is read aloud. He retires from the audience room, and the question is asked which involves the sift. If they are really faithful to this line of mark, they do well. A good institution would this prove in other denominations. But how entirely silent are the newspaperial organs of the sect which has a new exile from the Paradise of Innocence! As though silence were a proposition whose demonstration insures the success of oblivion! Thank God! there is a secular press which is emancipated from the serfdom of priestcraft!

"How pleasant must be the sensations of these ministers who wait to hear their appointments read off for the year! A. B., who has been to college, and knows an enthymeme from the syllogism, and the year when rotary pumps were invented, is portioned off to Valley-Hack, which has a church of thirteen paying members, no one of whom owns but three books, viz: the Bible, the Life of John Wesley, and Memoirs of Hester Ann Rogers. A young man of talents is A. B., and under an imprescriptible career would make a fair show of a man; as it is, the service of man-pleasing and stone-rolling will cramp his motions, deaden his energies, and file his teeth so that he will not know himself when forty years old — *unless* he discovers an aptitude for Methodistical sycophancy and sound, in which event he may ultimately be sent to a city charge, which, though greater in numbers and wealth than Valley-Hack, has scarcely more resources of an intellectual nature.

"But even this is not to last more than two or three years consecutively, at the longest. By-and-by he is passed over to the superannuated list, and gets a paltry stipend. What a career for a free man in a free land! What an illustration of the Latin proverb, '*Anguillam cauda tenes!*'"

(The two foregoing notes were pencilled in the note-book by his friend, while Israel was engaged in finding a hymn for an old lady who sat next him.)

# AMONG THE EPISCOPALIANS.

## CHAPTER I.

#### THE EPISCOPAL ORDINATION.

When reading the history of Mr. Wesley's work in England, Israel noticed these words written by him two years before his death: "I declare once more, that I live and die a member of the Church of England, and that none who regard my judgment or advice will ever separate from it."

He had, therefore, considerable curiosity to make some investigations in this faith and practice, before arriving at the decision to which he was constantly aiming. A favorable opportunity for observation was soon presented. A friend of that religious organization invited him to be present on the occasion of the ordination of several presbyters or priests, by the bishop of that diocese.

His Episcopal friend called his attention, with no little enthusiasm, to the superior architecture of their church.

"In all these things, we transmit, as nearly as possible, the most ancient and reverential symbols of the pure church of Christ and his apostles," he said, while he went on to explain to Israel the beauties of the Gothic order, which he believed to have originated from an avenue of over-arching trees. "Doubtless," he continued, "there was such an avenue in the garden of Gethsemane."

"I was taught," said Israel, "that the pointed arch arose from the intersection of semi-circular arches in that Norman style which went before the Gothic."

"You see the circular window above the entrance," his friend continued, without appearing to notice his objection; "that is typical of the silence which should reign in the house of God."

"That is the rose window, which is often called a 'Catharine wheel;' and the name being that of a woman, I can hardly reconcile it with your explanation," said Israel. But to this, likewise, his friend vouchsafed no notice. They were next at the inner church doors.

"These three doors may signify the Word, the Sacraments, and the Ministry in the three orders of Bishops, Priests, and Deacons," he continued, in a low voice.

The "dim, religious light" which came in through the lofty, stained windows, was calculated to remind a student like Israel of many things of which he had read among the annals of the past. He questioned within himself if this partial obscurity was also typical.

His friend had also much to say to him about the chancel and the large window directly in front of the audience seats, on which were represented many symbolical devices. As the day was not Sunday, he took occasion to explain many of the peculiarities of "the church."

"But why do you call your church, '*the* church,'

as though that was the only one?" inquired Israel at length.

"We hold no other ministry to be valid than that which we trace as a direct succession from the apostles, and no place of divine worship to be truly consecrated except by such persons," answered his friend, very gravely.

"Then you believe that other denominations are no more than outside heathen," said Israel.

"They are certainly not 'the church of the Living God, the pillar and ground of the truth;' for they do not receive the truth nor conform to its dictates as taught in the word of God. Their ministry proceeds from themselves, and not from men consecrated by men who could trace their ecclesiastical parentage through Archbishop Sheldon, and on through the English, Italian, and Irish Episcopate, to the apostles themselves, as can our ministers."

"You talk like a Roman Catholic," said Israel.

"The Roman Catholics have the truth with them, the same as we have; only they have become corrupted. If I were on my death-bed, and could not get access to the ministers of my own church, I should not scruple to avail myself of the privilege of their priestly offices," he replied.

"But would you not also permit the attendance of a Baptist, a Congregational, or a Methodist clergyman?" pursued Israel.

His friend shook his head. "No," said he, "not as ministers of God, for that would be lending countenance to error. They are only laymen, made what they claim to be by men like themselves, and in some instances, not so good. Our ministers never permit these unauthorized men to come into their pulpits; neither are they ever found in theirs, more than they would go to any reading or lecture room."

"I think," said Israel, "that there is a divine provision for any man, whereby he may die alone and die well; of this I would avail myself rather than to put my confidence in any arm of flesh."

"People are ignorant," his friend went on, "else they would all be of the Church. They do not know the errors into which they have been blindly led. They do not know that the bishops, priests, and deacons, in an unbroken succession from the apostles, are with us and not with them."

"No; they do not," answered Israel. As the congregation began to gather rapidly, further conversation was suspended.

When there appeared upon that part of the house appropriated to the reading desk or ambo, a priest in a long white robe, who knelt at the pulpit, as also other of these men with the Bishop, Israel gazed attentively and studied carefully.

Throughout the ceremony, as much time as he could spare from the prayer-book, he studied the faces of those men. Recently, he had somewhere read that no man can wholly conceal himself from the eye of one who studies character in the face, and he resolved to profit by the dogma.

Something like this he might have seen: a company of men, who strongly associated with "the church" that important ecclesiastical word "*Living.*" For the sake of this word, which was full of spiritual and temporal consolation, "the church" had won them (with but one or two exceptions) from other Christian folds, which did not offer so many inducements appertaining thereto.

With this word was also associated that other, of scarcely inferior value, — *Power*.

Magical words — "*Living*," "*Power*"! One other they required to complete the perfect three-fold Episcopal charm — viz., "*Infallibility*." Without this, the others were broken, limp, liable to vanish away.

This authorized the look they wore, and which seemed to say, "I am right. All others, save the Roman Catholics, are wrong. We are the only pure Church of Christ and his Apostles. Stand aside, who follow and obey us not."

With a kind of attempt at churchly gust did these men engage in their united service, sometimes in the acme of their chants, casting a sidelong glance down upon the congregation to witness the effect of such concentrated devotion.

All of them chanted on full stomachs. They kept the faith in the succession of a harmless and useful apostolical wine for the sake of that member of the body, not less faithfully than other traditions. It was just as certain in their private *credo* that several flagons accompanied St. Paul to plant Episcopacy in Briton, as that he really went there on that errand.

To many readings, chantings, and prayers, accompanied by gettings up and sittings down, did Israel there listen, but in none was he so much interested as the ordination service. There had been changing of gowns in the adjacent closet, till all were now fixed for the business in hand. Of what took place, he most pondered on the following: —

The Bishop was addressed by the priest who presented the deacons for the office of priest, as " Reverend Father in God."

Among the questions propounded to the candidates by the Bishop were these, with their affirmative answers:

"Will you be diligent in prayers and in reading of the Holy Scriptures, and in such studies as help to the knowledge of the same, *laying aside the study of the world and the flesh?*

"Will you be diligent to frame and fashion your own selves, and your families, according to the doctrine of Christ, and to make both yourselves and them, as much as in you lieth, *wholesome examples and patterns to the flock* of Christ?

"Will you *reverently obey* your chief ministers, unto whom is committed the charge and government over you, following with a glad mind and will their godly admonitions, and *submitting yourselves to their godly judgments?*"

When all the questions pertaining to the ceremony were concluded, several of the presbyters, as also the Bishop, laid their hands simultaneously on the heads of each candidate, while in each case the Bishop repeated: —

"Receive the Holy Ghost for the office and work of a priest in the Church of God, now committed unto thee by the imposition of our hands. *Whose sins thou dost forgive, they are forgiven; and whose sins thou dost retain, they are retained.* And be thou a faithful dispenser of the Word of God, and of his holy sacraments: In the name of the Father, and of the Son, and of the Holy Ghost, Amen."

Then giving to each one a Bible, he added, "Take thou authority to preach the Word of God, and to minister the holy sacraments in the congregation where thou shalt be lawfully appointed thereto."

At the sound of these words, so strange and significant to him, Israel looked around upon the people of that congregation, to see if they were moved.

Innocent youth! he had yet to learn that most people who help to sustain these "authorities" "to remit and to retain sins," are like the ostrich, which swallows bullets scorching hot from the mould, rags, leather, iron, and stone, with unqualified voracity.

Determined not to be hasty or superficial in his observations of this people, Israel followed this service, by attention to the notice of an evening meeting to be held soon thereafter.

At the appointed time he hastened to the chapel. Passing into the entrance room, he hesitated about going within until he had made some observations, unobserved.

What was his surprise to find that the audience room contained the minister with only about a score of women! Although the meeting was a general one, not a "male member" was present. He determined to retain his position of observer instead of participator.

His surprise was greater when he afterwards heard the minister proceed with his exhortation, as it read in a book, in a formal and reverent manner addressing those sisters more than once as " my brethren."

"This," thought Israel, "is formality wrought into folly." He mentioned it to his Episcopal friend, and received this reply: —

"In so doing, the minister showed his faithfulness to the proscribed order of the church. A minister who seeks to please men by the dictates of worldly wisdom, will adapt himself to the prejudices and foibles of his hearers, till his own identity and that of his sect are sacrificed. Such are worthy only of being compared to the celebrated French dramatic writer Gasper Abeille, who had a face of such extraordinary flexibility, that when he was reading a drama or tale, he could vary his features to suit the various characters as effectually as though he had worn a mask to represent each personage. Who has not seen such men among the preachers of the denominations? We had better deserve the imputation of formality, and be true to the truth, than be informal actors conscious of falsehood and deceit."

## CHAPTER II.

#### EPISCOPAL DOCTRINE.

ISRAEL next procured The Book of Common Prayer used by the Protestant Episcopal Church in America, and read it attentively. From all that he there found he inferred that the doctrines of this church materially harmonized with those of other churches called Calvinistic, so far as he instituted a comparison upon a general reading. A more careful examination raised a query respecting the idea of this faith upon regeneration, or qualifications for baptism. Great stress seemed to be laid upon being born of water, as though baptism possessed hidden power to carry with it, when administered by *the* church, the virtue of the new birth. If the subject were thoroughly instructed in the dogmas of the Prayer Book, and received the rites of *the church* in good faith, all was well without any change of heart — any radical regenerating process other than the baptism.

This idea he found from conversation with those who were qualified and authorized to expound the letter of the instruction. It was true that the letter of the doctrine cited as a requisition of persons to be baptized, " Repentance whereby they forsake sin : and faith, whereby they steadfastly believe the promises of

God made to them in that sacrament;" but it also stated it in such a manner as to make easy the interpretation that the "inward spiritual grace" *always accompanied* the "outward visible sign," provided all the ceremonial conditions were fulfilled. Also that infants, regularly baptized, are at the time regenerated by the spirit.

Upon further investigation, he found that the opinions of standard church authorities divide upon these points. "In baptism," says Archbishop Cranmer, "those that come feignedly, and those that come unfeignedly, both be washed with the sacramental water, but both be not washed with the Holy Ghost, and clothed with Christ."

Another authority of this faith (Rev. C. P. Miles) states that "The blessing of regeneration, as shown in the Articles and Prayer Book, is a contingent blessing; it is neither promised nor received *absolutely* in baptism, but promised and affirmed to be received when the administration of the rite is accompanied by prayer and faith." Of the baptism of infants, he also says: "Repentance and faith are demanded as *prerequisites* even in the case of infant baptism. And *before the ordinance is administered*, prayer is enjoined to be offered in behalf of the child. The church here *pleads the promise* of Christ; and *assuming* that the *repentance*, and *faith*, and *prayer* of the parties present are genuine, she praises God, after the child is baptized, for having bestowed, in fulfilment of his promise, the *particular blessing* that was asked. The Church of England, if she errs at all in this matter, errs simply by adopting an expression of charity more extensive than is warranted by the circumstances of her position."

Again, Israel found this statement made by the same prominent Episcopal divine: "The doctrine of baptismal regeneration is held by a large body of English churchmen [it might also have added "and American churchmen"]; but it is also denied by vast numbers both of the clergy and laity."

This difference of opinion among churchmen Israel found to prevail upon nearly all the points of belief to which they subscribe *ex animo*. The subsequent reading of the principal works of the Tractarians or Puseyites confirmed him in this opinion. In these he found stated with unqualified boldness the doctrine of baptismal regeneration, transubstantiation, and other dogmas of the Roman Catholic Church. Indeed, there seemed no difference between this branch of Episcopacy and the followers of the pope, save in name and certain associations. He therefore abandoned the attempt to determine absolutely the real creed of this church as they understood it.

## CHAPTER III.

#### LUMINOUS POINTS OF EPISCOPACY.

For further understanding of this communion of Christians, our inquirer resorted to their history, both in the past and present, with testimonies of churchmen upon mooted questions. In this record from differing stand-points there was much which reminded him of the "Cato" and the "Anti-Cato," — the one written by the Ciceronian friend, the other by the Cæsarian enemy.

As, in the Indian mythology, Mirtlok lies between the two divisions of heaven and hell, he hoped to attain that position for observation, equally distant from either extreme. The following are

#### EXTRACTS FROM HIS NOTE BOOK.

"The Church of England has no real history apart from the Catholic Church, until the sixteenth century, although the Episcopal Church claims for itself independence of the Church of Rome for more than five centuries. After the Saxon invasion in the year 596, the Bishop of Rome, Pope Gregory the Great, sent Augustine with forty of his order to England as missionaries. Augustine founded an abbey at Canterbury, and was the first archbishop in England. His doctrine soon spread throughout Britain.

"The sixth archbishop from Augustine, Theodore, divided the land into parishes, in the seventh century.

"A writer of the English Church observes 'We have now only to regard the Church of England, in common with the churches of the continent in the mediæval ages, as whilst emitting, here and there, an occasional ray of light, yet deeply involved in the corruptions and superstitions of the times.'

"For a long time the Northumbrian church refused to submit to the domination of Rome; but in 664, King Oswy compelled his clergy to submit to Rome, which now held undisputed sway over the whole of England.

"Marsden says that Elfric, one of the latest writers of the Anglo-Saxon church, A. D. 1014, informs us that 'there are seven ecclesiastical orders in the church — ostiary, reader, exorcist, acolyte, subdeacon, deacon, and priest.'

"It was not till the council of Winchester, in 1076, that celibacy was made imperative on the English clergy. (Eadie.)

"Henry the Eighth rebelled from the papal authority, though it had been in part successfully resisted by William the Conqueror. In 1534, the Church of England professed to be free. But this freedom was only nominal, or a transfer of tyrannical power from the pope to the king. It was still the Church of Rome in all but the name. In 1539, parliament passed 'An act for abolishing diversity of opinions.' The death penalty was affixed to the denial of the doctrine of transubstantiation; also to denial of all the other peculiarities of the Romish faith.

"Under the reign of Edward, and still more in that of Elizabeth, the reformation of the church rapidly progressed. From this period it assumed a thoroughly Protestant character. The names of Cranmer, Ridley, Latimer, and Hooper are associated with the reforms from the abuses of popery.

### *Wealth.*

"The English Church, as such, has ever been characterized for a love of political and worldly emolument. In America, the Episcopal church seems to be, for the most part, the church of the wealthy. Their beginning in this country justifies the basis of this supposition; their subsequent history, the complete conclusion.

"The first Episcopalians of the New World, who were men of power in England, settled in Virginia, not for religious freedom, like the Puritans of New England, but for 'purposes of worldly emolument.' As early as 1621, the Virginia company set apart in each of the boroughs an hundred acres of land for a glebe, and two hundred pounds sterling for a standing revenue for a *living*, out of the profits of each parish.

"It has steadily increased in wealth, and at present has centralizations of church properties of immense value. It is exactly suited to accommodate that class of people whose wealth demands preservation from vulgar contact, and yet whose conscience would adhere to the faith which was once delivered to the saints.

This class of persons take 'the church' as the most respectable road to heaven.

### Love of Power.

"This church, like every other composed of men, has displayed in times of prosperity a love of power.

"King James, who believed that Episcopacy was an aid and comfort to monarchy, used to say, 'No bishop, no king.' This sovereign was not alone in this style of argument. He understood the pith of the matter.

"Archbishop Laud was an unqualified tyrant. He hated the Calvinists, and persuaded Charles to make this proclamation at the head of the Articles of Faith: 'We will that all curious search into these things be laid aside, and these disputes be shut up in God's premises, as they be generally set forth to us in Holy Scripture, and the general meaning of the articles according to them.'

"In 1662, the Act of Uniformity was passed — an act worthy of a body of men with pretensions to infallibility, which demanded a total withdrawal of all investigation. By this act, all the ministers in England must declare 'their unfeigned assent and consent to the entire Book of Common Prayer, or be ejected from their livings.' In that year, more than two thousand ministers who refused to subscribe, were made to feel this rod.

"Two years later, the Conventicle Act declared that but five persons above the age of sixteen, besides the family, were to meet for worship.

"Next followed the Corporation Act — 'that no

person shall be chosen into any office of magistracy, or other employment relating to corporations, who shall not, within one year next before such elections, have taken the sacrament of the Lord's Supper according to the rites of the Church of England.'

"The Five Mile Act, in 1665, 'imposed an oath on all non-conformists, binding them to attempt no alteration in either church or state; and provided that all ministers who did not take it, should neither live in, nor come within, five miles of any borough, city, etc.'

"By the Test Act, every person who held any office or trust must receive the sacrament of the Lord's Supper in the Church of England, within three months after his admittance to the office, or be subjected to severe penalties.'

"The Episcopalians of the New World, true to their education, having the power in Virginia, early passed laws to drive all sectaries from their colony. Six years after, a Congregational church of one hundred and one persons was dispersed, and their pastors banished.

"Sir Edmund Andros, a provincial governor of the colony of New England, and a zealous supporter of this faith, in order to build up the Episcopal church, pronounced no marriages valid unless celebrated by the Church of England. The Old South Church in Boston was demanded and used for the Episcopal service, until, in 1688, a church was built, called King's Chapel.

"The same spirit of proscription animates the clerical members of this body at present; and to perpetuate their power, they refuse practical acknowledgment of the validity of the ministry of all the denominations, and call their own branch of the true vine *the Church*. This is likewise evident in the requisition imposed for matriculation to one of their principal colleges in America. In the college statutes is found the following:

"'*Sec.* 1. Matriculation shall consist in signing, in the presence of the president, faculty, and others, the following promise: "I promise to observe the statutes, lawful usages, and customs of this college, and to maintain and defend her rights, privileges, and immunities, at all times and in all places, according to my station and duties in the same."'

"The last clause of the promise is a supplementary offshoot of the laws of this Church in olden time, and should be called the Act of Gag. Whatever indignities a student might suffer from this institution, he must maintain her 'rights' and 'privileges,' and be silent respecting all her errors. Free speech according to the honest conviction, unless favorable to the college, is here totally interdicted.

### *Apostolical Succession.*

"Nothing assists this people so much in retaining their power as constant proclamation of the apostolical succession; yet I find that one of its archdeacons says: 'I deny, my lord, that succession of bishops is an infallible point to know the church by; for there may be a succession of bishops known in a place, and yet there is no church, as at Antioch, and Jerusalem, and in other places where the apostles abode, as well as at Rome. But if you put to the succession of bishops, succession of doctrine withal, as St. Augustine doth, I will grant it to be a good proof for the Catholic Church; but a local succession is nothing available.'

"Bishop Pilkington also taught: 'So stands the succession of the Church: not in mitres, palaces, lands, and lordships, but in teaching true doctrine, and rooting out the contrary.'

"On the other hand, the Puseyites say: 'The fact of the apostolical succession — that is, that our present bishops are the heirs and representatives of the apostles, by the successive transmission of the prerogative of being so — is too notorious to require proof. Every link in the chain is known from St. Peter to our present metropolitan. Can we conceive that this succession has been preserved all over the world, amidst revolutions, through many centuries, for nothing?'

"Another Episcopal divine says: 'The Church of England was founded, probably, in the Apostolic Age, and, it is said, by the labors of St. Paul.'

"Of what real value is such an assertion as this? Probabilities and 'they say' are no authority to the unprejudiced inquirer. If we take such proof as valid, we shall next give credence to the virtue which, 'it is said,' accompanies contact with the bones of a saint, and also the toe of 'His Holiness!'

"Where is the historical *proof* that the Church of England was founded by one or more of the apostles? And if such proof was clear as the noon-day sun, what would it signify for this church more than any other, — since the mission given to the apostles by Christ, was to go into all the world and preach the gospel to every creature.

"When Simon Peter had toiled all night a-fishing, and had caught nothing, he cast his net on the right side of the ship, according to the direction of Jesus, and now 'they were not able to draw it for the multitude of fishes.' In this multitude there must have been more than one kind. This event, which was typical of the salvation of men by the ministry of the Gospel of our Lord and Saviour, proves conclusively that it was never meant by the founders of the Christion Church to inculcate the idea that there was to be included in the Church of God only one kind of believers. Had it been so, it would have been stated what kind of fishes these were, that there might have been motives to perpetuate the succession.

"Likewise does the vision unfolded to Peter, when he saw heaven opened, and a certain vessel descending unto him, wherein were all manner of four-footed beasts of the earth, and wild beasts, and creeping things, and fowls of the air, prove that no one class of men is more favorable in the eyes of God, provided he hath cleansed them, than another. 'Then Peter opened his mouth and said, Of a truth I perceive that God is no respecter of persons; but in every nation he that feareth Him and worketh righteousness, is accepted with Him.' 'And they of the circumcision which believed were astonished, because that on the Gentiles also was poured out the gift of the Holy Ghost.'

"The Church of England, or the Episcopal Church, by arrogating to themselves the possession of 'the Word, the sacraments, and the threefold ministry,' illustrates the claims of monarchists in all ages of the world, — 'We are the men, and wisdom will die with us, unless kept in the authorized channels of succession in both church and state.'

### The Three-fold Ministry.

"Their claim, also, to the ministry as founded by the apostles in a three-fold office of bishops, priests or presbyters and deacons, is not valid.

"The apostles styled themselves by various names. In 1 Tim. 5: 17, they are called elders and laborers. Again they are styled teachers and shepherds. The terms bishops and elders throughout their writings are used without distinctive difference. This is also true of the usage of the ecclesiastical writers who followed the apostles. From the writings of Coleman, I find Chrysostom as saying that 'the elders or presbyters were formerly called bishops and deacons of Christ, and that the bishops were called elders.' Also, Theodoret styles both the elders and bishops watchmen. In another passage, he says that those who were called bishops, evidently held the rank of presbyters and elders. Iræneus, Bishop of Lyons, calls all the bishops who preceded Victor, presbyters. Jerome adds a similar testimony.

"From this and other equally copious and valuable testimony, it is clear to me that the Episcopal church has no warrant for this their assumption of the pure order of a three-fold ministry.

### The Liturgy.

"Another claim of the superiority of *the* church, or its exemption from liabilities to departure from the faith, is its Liturgy. Having found an argument* in its favor, which, though not by any means conclusive, is ingenious, I copy it herein.

"'What, it may be asked, is the *authority* and what is the *utility* of a Liturgy? I hardly need answer that forms of prayer are no new thing. If you ask me where they originated, I answer, in *heaven*. The very first suggestion of a precomposed form of divine service came from God himself. Liturgies are, therefore, no human invention.

"'When the Tabernacle had been erected, and the people gathered into it, God gave to Moses a form of words wherewith he should bless the people when they departed, saying: "The Lord bless thee, and keep thee," etc. When an Israelite brought to the priest "the first fruits," he was required to repeat a certain form of words. Just before the death of Moses, God commanded him to write a song commemorative of God's mercies, which the Israelites and their descendants were required to use. In the time of Christ, the Jews had a Liturgy in their synagogues. In this service he himself joined. He rebuked the Jews for many things, but never for using a Liturgy. He censured them for *formality*, but never for employing forms of prayer. He reproved the Pharisees for their pride, and formality, and long "prayers, which they made, standing at the corners of the streets, to be seen of men." These prayers were made to attract the public attention, and so to win the praise of passers-by, and, therefore, may have been extemporaneous.

* From "Why I am a Churchman," by Rev. G. M. Randall, D. D.

"'The Jews had never been accustomed to other than a *Liturgical* form of worship. When John the Baptist appeared, who was the appointed forerunner of Christ, and whose ministry was not, therefore, of the Jewish economy, while the Christian Church was not yet established, he very naturally prepared a service suited to his peculiar mission. He gave to his disciples a form of prayer.

"'When Christ entered upon His ministry, He continued to attend upon the temple and synagogue service, and sometimes took part in that service. When His disciples came to him, with the request that He would furnish them with a *form of prayer*, as John had done for his disciples, He did not reply to this request that John did that which was indeed allowed in the Jewish service, but was not to be permitted in the more spiritual worship of the Christian Church. So far from this, He immediately framed a form of prayer, gave it to his disciples, and told them to use it. It is not a little remarkable, that this form is taken mainly from the Jewish Liturgy. It is sometimes urged by those who are not accustomed to a Liturgical service, that prayers in a particular form of words cannot come from the heart. When our Saviour was in the garden, on the night of His betrayal, He prayed in the midst of the agonies of that awful hour. Think you the prayer He offered to His Father did not come from His heart? Yet He used a *form!* He prayed three times, using a form of words. Again when hanging on the cross He prayed. Did ever mortal man doubt that the prayer upon the cross came from the heart of that crucified Saviour? And yet that prayer was a form in these words: "My God, my God, why hast thou forsaken me;" a quotation from the twenty-second Psalm. The last sentence that fell from His lips, ere He gave up the ghost, was taken from the thirty-first Psalm: "Father, into thy hands I commend my spirit." Thus the Saviour of the world died with a form of prayer upon His lips.

"'The apostles, like their divine Master, were accustomed to the Liturgical worship of the Jews; they, with Him, attended the temple and the synagogue service. Such was the strength of their attachment to a Liturgy, and so firm the habit of using a form, that on the occasion of the liberation of St. Peter from prison, when their hearts were overflowing with joy, and when, if ever, they would spontaneously express their gratitude, in an extemporaneous thanksgiving, they employed a *form*, "they lifted up their voice to God with one accord, and said," etc. This form has been recorded by St. Luke. It is chiefly from a Psalm of David. We are not then surprised to find the churches which they planted employing forms of prayer in their worship.'"

Much more of this continued able argument Israel would have transcribed, had he not have recalled these words, found in 2 Corinthians, 3: 6: "Who also hath made us able ministers of the new testament; not of the letter, but of the spirit: for *the letter killeth, but the spirit giveth life.*"

Likewise this in Romans 2: 19, 20: "And art confident that thou thyself art a guide of the blind, a light of them which are in darkness, an instructor of the foolish, a teacher of babes, which hast *the form of knowledge, and of the truth in the law,"* etc.

Also 2 Tim. 3 : 5 : "Having a form of godliness, but denying the power thereof; from such turn away."

These words proved to him that the form of godliness and the letter of the law were not accounted by the apostles as of any worth, compared to the true spirit of the gospel of our Lord and Saviour.

### Signs of Power.

"In regard to the authority and utility of their clerical vestments, I have but to remember the words of Christ, in Matt. 23 : 5. 'But all their works they do to be seen of men: they make broad their phylacteries, and enlarge the borders of their garments.'

"I find an Episcopal divine\* has these words upon this point. 'As to the *authority* I have only to say that, God has once, in the Mosaic dispensation, expressed his pleasure in this regard, and He has never annulled that expression of His will.'

"Why did he not cite the particular instance to which he referred as the expression of divine pleasure in this regard?

"Moses took Aaron and his sons, according to the command of God, unto the door of the tabernacle of the congregation, and after washing them with water, he put upon Aaron 'the coat, and girded him with the girdle, and clothed him with the robe, and put the ephod upon him; and he girded him with the curious girdle of the ephod, and bound it unto him therewith.

\* Dr. Randall.

And he put the breastplate upon him: *also* he put in the breastplate, the Urim and Thummim. And he put the mitre upon his head; also upon the mitre, did he put the golden plate, the holy crown.

"'And he poured of the anointing oil upon Aaron's head.'

"'And Moses brought Aaron's sons [here was the succession] and put coats upon them, and girded them with girdles, and put bonnets upon them.'

"If the 'authority' is here derived, why is not the usage of the Episcopal church to clothe their priests according to *all the pattern*, as well as in one or two particulars?

"Why do not these priests don their canonicals in the door, before all the congregation? By what authority can they omit the pouring oil on the head, and likewise dispense with the girdle and bonnet?

### *Repetition of the Creed.*

"The same divine also says: 'At every service we are required to repeat the articles of our belief, in the form of a Creed. The Church has a Creed, because she is the church. There can be no such thing as a Christian Church without a Christian Creed. There are some persons, I am aware, who affect to have no creed. But Christ has effectually settled the practicability of such a theological anomaly. Nobody can go to heaven without a creed. Creed is belief. Christ has said, " *He that* BELIEVETH NOT *shall be damned*."'

"According to the Word of God, the way is so plain, that the wayfaring men, though fools, shall not err therein, the type of which way was the very simple looking of the diseased Israelite at the brazen serpent uplifted in the wilderness. But yet men like Dr. Pusey read the creed of *the* Church with a widely different sense from others who likewise read the same words in high places.

"The authority quoted evidently wishes it to be understood that the creed of 'the church' is the one of which it is true — 'he that believeth not shall be damned.' If we accept the statement, we may learn the fate of those who do not believe in 'one catholic and apostolic church,' 'one baptism for the remission of sins,' and 'the resurrection of the body.'

"The thief on the cross had no idea of this elaborate *credo*, but simply said, 'Lord, remember me when thou comest into thy kingdom,' for which he was promised paradise.

"He believed. All believe who find salvation; yet all of these do not believe in *the* church or its creed, or yet in its long prayers and mummeries, such as 'Reverend Father in God.' 'And call no man your father upon the earth, for one is your Father which is in heaven.' (Matt. 23 : 9.)

"I cannot believe that I have found the city whose name is '*The Lord is Here.*'

ISRAEL KNIGHT."

## CHAPTER IV.

### ANOTHER OPINION.

BEFORE closing his present judgment upon this sect, Israel took the precaution to send the foregoing Notes to a friend whom, with his guardian, he was accustomed to consult. He received the following:—

"YOUNG SIR:—

"You have drawn your conclusions of the church in question, with more haste and heat than deliberation and wisdom. This, allow me to say, is characteristic of observers of your age.

"There are spots on the sun, but who would think of condemning that planet therefor as worthless! He who should make the attempt would prove himself another "dog, and bay the moon." It is not probable that the sun or the moon would take upon themselves to stand still in awe of such attacks.

"This people of God are too old, too venerable with precious associations of labor, suffering, and renown, too honored with names of the great and good, to cast about upon the fling of ordinary criticism. Like Jerusalem, she is the mother of us all; and who would think of looking too sharply upon the blemishes of that face to which we had turned for co encouragement and strength, from our earliest recollection!

"Her authors have contributed the most precious legacies of thought and research of those of any other church, and of all other churches together in Christendom. Her martyrs are most memorable upon the page of history. Her struggles for emancipation from oppression were the pioneer throes of the birth of Religious Freedom, the blessings of which all other religious bodies by the means have been enabled to share. It is true that this church has had her 'wandering stars,' who have shed their baleful influence over those who were so unfortunate as to come within the reach of their oppressive sphere; but in a system of such dimensions as this, this is by no means surprising.

"In particular respecting your notes, I do not like what you say about the ministers who appeared at the ordination service having been converts from other folds. Where will you find a set of clergymen on any one denominational platform who number not those who have been adopted there? Your own ideas of truth to profound conviction, and of charity for others in their movements, however seemingly inharmonious with yours, should repel the slightest acerbity of judgment of such matters.

"Neither do I like your observations respecting the love of this people for power. We should the rather admire them that, when possessed of such exhaustless resources through the centuries, they have abused their power so little. What other Christian people, endued with their gifts, would have deported themselves more wisely?

"Your remarks concerning their peculiarities in wearing clerical vestments, etc., are altogether unworthy. Why not head them with observations upon Revelations 1 : 13. 'And in the midst of the seven candlesticks, one like unto the Son of Man, clothed with a garment down to the foot, and girt about the paps with a golden girdle.'

"Let every people appear in their sacred courts as it seemeth them good, and be not presumptuous in speaking evil of dignities.

"Although I have no partiality for this communion, I desire to be as just and generous to them as to any other. To this end, I would recommend you to study them more faithfully and impartially, as you would a celebrated work of art, which, at the first, you may be inclined to undervalue. The longer you look, the more will you see to admire.
Truly yours,
J. ABELARD RIDLEY."

Somewhat troubled by this letter, Israel forwarded it with his Notes to his guardian, with an expressed wish for a judgment.

He received only this in return : —

"*Qui capit, ille facit,*" liberally rendered, "Whom the cap fits, let him wear it."
Yours in haste, but without heat,
EPHRAIM STEARNS."

# AMONG THE QUAKERS.

## CHAPTER I.

#### FRIENDS' MEETING.

ISRAEL began to be less hopeful of finding around him the city with the Lord's name and presence, and he went out one Sunday morning with no purpose whither to direct his steps. He was unhappy, almost miserable. There was not a church which he could call his home, not a people who seemed real and true friends.

Where was the fault? In the churches or in himself?

Presently he wandered away into a street apart from the great thoroughfares, with a design of going out till he should reach the open country, where he could worship in God's own temple, not made with hands.

A man walked before, scarcely noticed by him till he was joined by another who came out from an intersecting street. There was something in their manner of greeting each other which attracted his attention.

The unaffected friendliness of the words "Friend John, how does thee do?" and the reply, "I am able to go to the meeting, friend Isaac, and it is good to walk the old way once more," seemed to Israel a new note in the great concert of the world's society.

He looked more closely. The hat, the color of the

cloth they wore, determined the first impression. They were Friends or Quakers, evidently on their way to meeting. He resolved to follow them.

At length they stopped before a plain-looking building, which he should hardly have distinguished from a private dwelling. It stood within a small, neat enclosure, and had two doors of entrance, one on each side.

Israel now stepped forward and inquired.

"This is Friends' meeting-house," answered "Friend John;" "thee is welcome to come in." Somewhat in the look and tone which accompanied these words made Israel *feel* welcome to go in there. This friend showed Israel to a seat within.

Not a little was he at first interested to observe that "Friend John," as well as all other of the men who came in, did not remove their hats. Upon one side of the room sat the men, while the women together occupied the other, both facing one way, which was the wall behind the preachers' seats. Soon arrivals ceased, and all was still. Israel took the opportunity to cast several glances around him.

The walls were severely plain, as were also the seats. No sign nor sound of elegance intruded in that sanctuary.

The women were generally dressed with simplicity of color and shape, but the material was often costly. The plainest Friends wore the real Quaker bonnet, neckerchief and shawl; but these were only the few. Their faces were uncommonly smooth and placid in expression, as though the experience of daily life brought few distraining cares; or if they came, the alleviating simplicity of friendly hopes came with them. Some of the young women were very lovely.

The men had a comfortable, self-controlling look generally, though there were exceptional cases, where the expression admitted of a slight discount in favor of worldly wisdom. "Best wisdom" was prevalent, but did not universally reign.

After some time had elapsed, Israel began to be restless, and thought it was singular that no movement was made indicating a commencement of the services. He looked at the principal men who filled the more conspicuous seats, but they moved not, nor broke the solemn sound of silence. He now remembered reading that these people worshipped in the spirit, often coming together without public speaking, and composed himself "to do as the Romans did."

He began to look inwardly and listen to the silent teachings of the spirit. But no sooner was his gaze introverted than some indefinable impulse directed his thoughts before him toward a bonnet, not so plain as others, on the opposite side of the house. A slight turn of the head had revealed the fair and sweet face of a young Quakeress. Just as he looked, he thought the dark eyes under the bonnet looked also. The Quakeress turned quickly, and now the bonnet faced the side wall. Israel tried hard to think of subjects appropriate for that solemn occasion, but into his mind rushed unbidden the image of Cyprian Cutting. The sound of Methodist confusion filled his heart, and he was there in that Quaker meeting as though he were not.

The gentle swaying of the tall trees in a private yard behind this meeting-house was now heard through the open windows. It recalled Israel to himself and the scene of the hour.

"O, that I could reflect worthily!" he said to himself. Then he thought of the words which he had read that morning in Hosea 14: 5 : "I will be as the dew unto Israel; he shall grow as the lily, and cast forth his roots as Lebanon." "Here," reflected the youth, " is the Lord's presence, not as the thunder nor the trumpet. He hath not gone up with a shout, but he is as the silent, gentle, fructifying dew. Spiritual life grows in this soil like the lily, unheard, almost unseen, nevertheless sure, and with accretions of rarest beauty. As the roots of the great trees of the forest of Lebanon spread out underneath the surface into a web of strength and fortification against the passing blasts, so does the underlying principle of this people gather consistency and permanence from their most profitable silences, wherewith they are able to stand unmoved in the day of adversity."

Israel now thought of the god Heimdal, who was said to hear the wool grow on the lambs and the grass in the fields, and he wished that his spiritual hearing had been sufficiently acute that he might perceive the growth of the goodness which flowed from the united pause in the Friends' Meeting.

He ventured another look at the Quaker bonnet worn by the fair young girl, though this time it was not withdrawn so suddenly as before. Then he looked away at some of the demure men who occupied the preachers' seats, as though half-expecting one of them to rise. He now saw, with a sigh of relief, something new. The gravest looking of these men took off his broad-brimmed hat, and laid it down by his side.

Israel thought he was going to speak. The spirit had moved him at last. But no! he shook hands with his next Friend. This seemed a signal for a general stir. Friend after Friend shook hands, and it was plain that meeting was over. "Is this all?" thought Israel, somewhat disappointed. "Not by might, nor by power, but by my spirit, saith the Lord," he answered himself. All now gathered together very quietly for a friendly greeting and conversation. There seemed to be some Friends present who were strangers from England. These were welcomed by one and another with kind though measured words, which made Israel think that the lot of the stranger was indeed blessed among this people.

He had one more look at the bonnet which had more or less troubled the deep waters of his soul, through the meeting, and was rewarded by a full view of the face, radiant with calm delight, the remembrance of which lingered in his heart as something precious, and reluctantly went his way.

Like the traveller who visits the statue of Memnon, he had heard "a strange, sweet music from the cold and voiceless marble." When the Mahometans conclude their worship in the mosque, they smooth down their faces with their hands, take up their slippers, and go their way. Israel did not smooth down his face, for it was already smoothed by the viewless, noiseless tidal current of the Quaker worship; nor did he shake the dust from his feet. He felt, however, that his worldly shoes had been almost out of place on that holy ground.

## CHAPTER II.

### FURTHER OBSERVATIONS.

Some time later Israel was in a distant city, and remembering that this was the place of residence of one of his former classmates in an academy, who belonged to a Quaker family, he took occasion to call on this friend.

In his reception by this family there breathed the spirit of unaffected friendliness. His friend was absent; and though no one of these people had ever before seen him, nothing was wanting but the presence of the absent one to complete the spirit of their hospitality.

It was noticed by Israel that when all were gathered in their seats around the family board, instead of the blessing which he had often heard, each, with slightly bowed head, remained silent until the head of the family made the first movement to indicate that the silence was to give place to the courtesies of the hour. Israel had heard that in past time the men Quakers ate with head uncovered; he now concluded that this custom was obsolete.

It being Fourth day, Israel was asked by his friends to go with them to "meeting." He was told that that they met for worship on this day of the week as also on the first. He gladly went. The audience, for the most part, was composed of women. The Quaker men are generally busy in the marts of business on Fourth day. Of these women, a few were *plain* Friends, all elderly, who were real Quakers in appearance; the others illustrated Milton's words — " but Eve was Eve." Clothed in expensive fabrics of the mode somewhat modified, they would have scarcely been odd in the most fashionable congregation. Soon came on the silence of best wisdom, apparently in " calm and sinless peace." Israel looked at the grave elderly men who sat on the elevated seats, and wondered if the spirit would move any to speak. By-and-by his patience was rewarded by the rising of a woman, a very "plain Friend," who had a message of which her mind must be disburdened. Her position being in a remote part of the room from Israel, he was not able to hear her words sufficiently to obtain the full benefit of them. It seemed, however, to be an exhortation to the women to be less conformed to the vain show of the world, — a concern, which he thought not unwarranted in that audience. Not long after this, one of the men stood up, and in a pretty loud voice, addressed them.

He alluded to an esteemed friend who had lived in a past age of Quakerism, and quoted his example and words to incite them to lead a good and simple life. His speech occupied about five minutes, when he sat down. This concluded the ministry of Quaker service for that day. Afterwards it transpired that they were Hicksite Quakers, while another branch of Friends is called Orthodox Quakers.

The following is the substance of a conversation between Israel and these Friends: —

*I.* "May I ask why you are called Hicksites?"

*F.* "From Elias Hicks, who, about the year 1827, taught our people different views of doctrine from those before believed and taught by Friends."

*I.* "Wherein did this difference consist?"

*F.* "Elias Hicks denied the divinity and atonement of Jesus Christ, and affirmed that the Bible had no divine authority. George Fox, who founded the Society of Friends, having been educated in the Church of England, kept the principal articles of their doctrine, though he rejected some which they think important or essential. He was what is called orthodox upon the principal points of belief."

*I.* "What did he reject?"

*F.* "The sacraments of baptism and the Lord's Supper."

*I.* "On what grounds?"

*F.* "George Fox held that the Christian baptism taught in the New Testament is a spiritual one, which alone makes the true disciple a partaker of the mystical body of Christ, and that the baptism of John belonged to an inferior and decreasing dispensation. In like manner communion with the body and blood of Christ is only obtained by a union of the heart by faith, while all visible signs are promotive of dissension among Christians.

"Elias Hicks maintained that we need not go to the Scriptures for authority in this or other rule of life more than to any other book. The light that is within us, implanted by God, is sufficient to guide us into all needed wisdom, if we will hold our spirits in subjection to its teachings. He held that sacraments are unnecessary, but for other reasons. George Fox was a good man — a seeker after truth, as the Friends were first named — but he had not progressed into the best wisdom."

*I.* "Allow me to inquire why your sect was ever called *Quakers*, and not always Friends?"

*F.* "It is sometimes recorded that the name was given because Fox once told one of his judges in the time of his persecution for his opinions, to tremble at the word of the Lord; others say that it was because of their trembling manner of speaking. We call ourselves Friends."

*I.* "Was Fox a man of learning?"

*F.* "He was born at Drayton, England, 1624, and apprenticed to a grazier. His occupation of shepherd was good for solitary thought. While he watched his flocks he came upon many wise conclusions. One was that his days were evil and it was his duty to go out among the wicked world and seek to make them better. In 1647, he began to be a preacher of righteousness wherever he went. In a steeple-house at Nottingham, when the priest took for his text, 'We have a more sure word of prophecy, whereunto ye do well that ye take heed, as unto a light that shineth in a dark place, until the day dawn, and the day-star arise in your hearts,' and went on to teach the people that this light was the Bible, Fox spoke out by the strong moving of the Holy Spirit, 'O no; it is not the Scripture, but it is the Holy Spirit by which the holy men of God gave forth the Scriptures, whereby opinions, religions, and judgments are to be tried. That it was, which led unto all truth.' For thus saying he was put into prison. At other times in his life he suffered the pain of imprisonment. He died in London in 1690. William Penn said of him, 'He was a man that God endowed with a clear and wonderful depth; a discerner of others' spirits, and very much a master of his own; of an innocent life, meek, contented, modest, steady, tender.'"

*I.* "It would gratify me to know some other peculiarities of the doctrine and usage of the Society of Friends, common to the Orthodox and Hicksite divisions."

*F.* "We take no oaths. We affirm."

*I.* "On what grounds?"

*F.* "It was first our custom by reason of the words of Jesus, 'Swear not at all.' We go not to war with our fellow-beings, believing this to be a great sin in the sight of a God whose name is Love, and whose nature is Peace and Good-will to all. As a people we, and especially the Hicksites, were in favor of the abolition of the dark sin of slavery; but it was our view that this great and good work might be done by other means than shedding the blood of fellow-men.

"We do not believe in a hireling ministry or in a collegiate training for the making of ministers. The Holy Spirit is the only and sufficient guide in this matter. That can speak to us through women as well as men."

*I.* "If you accepted the letter of the Scripture as authority, I should quote to you the command of St.

Paul, 'I suffer not a woman to teach, nor to usurp authority over the man, but to be in silence.'"

*F.* "From the same Scripture, I will say to thee, it was prophesied by Joel and spoken by Peter, that in the last days, the daughters as well as the sons should prophesy, and on the hand-maidens God did pour out His spirit so that they should prophesy."

*I.* "Then any woman who feels the Spirit moving her to speak can do so in your meetings?"

*F.* "The meeting takes time for judgment before our ministers, men or women, are approved."

*I.* "You spoke of not favoring a ministry who had received a collegiate training. Do you not encourage your young men to obtain a liberal education?"

*F.* "We make it one of our rules to give our sons a good education to fit them for business; but we do not generally approve of their going to college."

*I.* "May I ask the reason?"

*F.* "It is upon our principle of use instead of vain show. We also think that they learn many things at college which will do them no good in after life, and may do them much hurt."

*F.'s wife.* "Our people do not approve of their sons and daughters reading unprofitable books, like many works of fiction."

*F.'s daughter.* "Yet thee knows that we do read some good novels."

*F.* "Thee need not call them novels, dear."

*I.* "I think I have heard that your marriage ceremony is peculiar."

*F.* "In monthly meeting, our people who intend to be joined in marriage appear with their parents or guardians, or in the absence of these, with certificates of their consent, and propose their intention. A committee is appointed to inquire if they are clear of other engagements respecting marriage. At a public meeting, if no such obstacle appears, the meeting consents to the marriage. The two persons then stand up and take each other for husband and wife. A certificate is read aloud, and these two persons sign, as do the relations and any others as witnesses."

*F.'s wife.* "A bride of our society is not allowed to wear a veil."

*I.* "A fortunate edict, since the Quakeresses are generally too pretty to require aid from any such outward adorning."

*F.* "George Fox taught that we were not to give compliments, as they belonged to the marks of a wicked world."

*I.* "But I am sure Elias Hicks is silent upon that subject. He lived under a newer light" (glancing at the Friend's daughters.)

*F.* (very gravely.) "We bury our dead also in a manner peculiar to ourselves. We did not believe in arraying a corpse in fine dress. The body, covered in a simple manner, was sometimes carried into meeting before being followed to the grave. At the grave a pause is made. Almost always some one of our ministers speaks a few words. This is the sum of our rite. But of late years we conform more to the world in the matter of the raiment for our dead."

*I.* "Do you believe in a resurrection of the natural body, or, in other words, a literal resurrection?"

*F.* "Some of us do and some do not."

*I.* "Probably the opinions of Quakers differ as much as do their dress."

*F.* "We support our own poor."

*I.* "Do you require any subscription to your articles of faith in order to membership?"

*F.* "We do not. We expect those who come into our society as members to be convinced of our belief; and after the usual inquiries and deliberation, they are formally admitted."

*I.* "Why do you say First day instead of Sunday, and Fourth day, as also the months by figures instead of their names?"

*F.* "The common names of months and days we hold to be relics of Paganism. They came from the heathen, who by these names intended compliments to their heroes or gods. We prefer the ordinal numbers."

*I.* "Why do you address each other and sometimes others not of your own body, by Thee and Thou, instead of the usual way?"

*F.* "The plural number used in address, comes from what one of our writers calls 'motives of adulation.' We believe in a sensible simplicity in all things."

*F.'s wife.* "It seems more friendly to say these words."

*F.* "We do not always use them to our friends who are not accustomed to us, lest they might feel that we wished to make them strangers. In all things we wish to be what our name teaches —*friends.*"

Israel thought that they could not readily wish a better or nobler object; but he remembered the injunction upon compliments, and was silent.

The next day Israel was in a public library. By chance his eye fell upon a book entitled "Quakerism, or the Story of My Life." He took it and read it with avidity. He paused not till he had concluded the last page.

This, with the account of the doctrines of Elias Hicks, decided him to go farther in search of The City.

Yet he ever accounted these "Friends" as some of the truest and most valuable of his life.

# AMONG THE SWEDENBORGIANS.

## CHAPTER I.

#### CONVERSATION WITH A SWEDENBORGIAN.

A YOUNG man, who boarded with Israel Knight, sickened and died under circumstances of trial. All the inmates of the house, save one, were gloomy; some were affrighted. Israel was both. From his earliest memory he had a morbid dread of contact with death and the cerements of the tomb. He absented himself from a funeral whenever he could in decent regard for the feelings of the living. In fearful words he ever spoke of the dying and the dead.

He thought this feeling arose from having lost his parents at a tender age; but persons in all favoring conditions often are not unlike him in this respect.

There was one of his fellow boarders who was never more serenely cheerful, more hopeful and happy than in this time of general gloom.

"How is it," asked Israel of this friend, "that you seem as tranquil as though this distressing event had not happened?"

"I can well remember when it was not so with me," he replied; "once I regarded such scenes as gloomily as any other person. Not until the true idea of death was taught me, did I come to a different mind."

"The true idea of death!" repeated Israel; "what have you of this which men of science and religion have not?"

"I have the substance of things hoped for, the evidence of things not seen. I have faith," answered his friend Stilwell.

Israel remembered that this man was a Swedenborgian, and knowing scarcely more of this belief than the name, he quickly rejoined —

"Faith! Yes, so had the followers of Mahomet when they credited the prophet's assertion that he rode to the third heaven on his white horse Alborak, in one night."

Stilwell calmly continued : —

"A beautiful alabaster results from the slow dripping of water in stalactitic caves; so does the quality of joyful faith form itself by temperate degrees, in the recesses of that soul which is blessed with the influences of a true doctrine."

"Whatever helps to rob death in the article, or in its associating idea, of its real terror, is worth considering," said Israel: "your fruits appear to be good, and I would know of your doctrine."

"Emanuel Swedenborg," said Stilwell, "is reckoned either an impostor or a madman by the majority of the Christian world. When I say Christian, I mean in distinction from Pagan or Mahometan. This is the result of crude reflection and the pitifulest superficial investigation. Many a theologian opens one of his books, and discovers at random some such words as these : —

(Stilwell took a book entitled "Heaven and Hell," and after carefully turning the leaves, read aloud a short passage, then continued,) "This reader soon closes the book in impatience, pronouncing summary judgment. But what does he really know of these sublime and beautiful truths?"

"Doubtless these works suffer from prejudice," said Israel, "like almost all others; but I am now chiefly interested to learn the Swedenborgian view of departed spirits."

"We of this faith believe that the spirits of the departed are about us. Those who loved goodness and good use in this life, perform corresponding work in the next. Death makes no change except in conditions. It disrobes us of the natural body, and clothes us with a spiritual one that is indescribably more capable of obeying the will. We do not mourn for the dead as do some others. We believe that they are near us as before, only in a much more favorable condition. Our friend who has just left our sight has only gone out of this state of existence, as it were, from one room into another, the separating door being what we call death. It was necessary that he should go at this time. He had fulfilled the appointed work of his mortal life. His spirit had completed its earthly conditions, and hence could not remain in the flesh another instant.

"I sometimes smile at the short-sightedness of those persons who speak of this or that contingent circumstance as controlling the death of a person. 'If the physician had done thus, or if another had omitted that, it might have been otherwise.' When we are ripe for death, we die, whether it be at one age or another, and no mortal power can speed or detain us. Death is always a blessing; hence an event never to be mourned. In the case of the good, who by a prepared life are capable of entering a glorious service there, all acknowledge that it is infinite gain. We believe it is gain to them, and in a certain sense, to us who are left. They are far more capable of doing us good than when here, subject to the flesh. They see more clearly and perform more perfectly.

"In the case of the wicked, it is also a cause of joy, for they are prevented from accruing evil and evil development of themselves. Sometimes this wickedness flows from ignorance and mistaken education. These are permitted to receive new and heavenly tuition: by degrees they become receptive of heavenly blessedness. Their understanding being opened, they, of their own free will, gradually turn to the light which is another name for truth.

"Those persons who have had the privilege of great light on earth, and yet set their faces as a flint against the truth, exalting their own wisdom above that which is divine, and refusing to love the Lord and the neighbor, by death are placed in more favorable conditions for the purification of their understanding and will. If they continue to resist this light, they become evil spirits, and consociate with the inhabitants of the hells.

"To these, also, death is a blessing, for longer life in this world would only have added to their capabilities of evil."

"Your theory of an intermediate state has plausibility, but, I apprehend, no Scriptural authority," remarked Israel; and added after a slight pause, "Do we not read in Ecclesiastes, eleventh chapter and second verse, 'In the place where the tree falleth, there it shall be," and also elsewhere, 'He that is unjust, let him be unjust still,' etc."

"Your quotation from Ecclesiastes," said his friend, "has no reference to a future state. Examine the context, which is an exhortation to benevolence, and teaches that we ought to give whenever needful, to all classes of persons, for we know not how soon we may fall into their power, when it will be in their hands to deal unto us. Vicissitudes of life are inevitable. Events must take place when the causes are matured, and no earthly power can change their course. If the calamity falls across our threshold, or our most remote project, to the north, or the south, it cannot be averted or escaped. Therefore we should be charitable unto all, that in the day of our suffering the bread which we cast upon the waters may return to us. This lesson of the inevitable course of events teaches us mutual love and charity.

"In regard to your other quotation, it is exactly accordant with the doctrine of Swedenborg as revealed to him by the Lord. I have just said that there are those who, from their own will and enlightened understanding are evil. These continue to be what they were at death.

"Let me read to you," continued Stilwell: "The first state of man after death is similar to his state in the world, because then in like manner he is in externals. * * This first state continues with some for days, with some for months, and with some for a year; and seldom with any one beyond a year. * * * The second state of man after death is called the state of the interiors, because he is then let into the interiors which are of his mind, or of the will and thought. * * * All men whatever are let into this state after death, because it is proper to their spirit. * * When the spirit is in this state of his interiors, it then manifestly appears of what quality the man was in himself during his life in the world, for he then acts from his own proprium. All who have lived in good in the world, and have acted from conscience, as is the case with all those who have acknowledged a Divine, and have loved divine truths, especially those who have applied them to the life, appear to themselves when let into the state of their interiors, like those who, being awakened out of sleep, come into the full use of sight, and like those who from shade enter into light; heaven also flows into their thoughts and affections with interior blessedness and delight, of which before they knew nothing; for they have communication with the angels of heaven: on this occasion also they acknowledge the Lord, and worship Him from their very life. But altogether contrary is the state of those who in the world have lived in evil, and who have had no conscience, and have hence denied a Divine. * *

"The third state of man after death, or of his spirit, is a state of instruction; this state appertains to those who come into heaven, and become angels, but not to those who come into hell, since these latter cannot be instructed; wherefore their second state is likewise their third, which closes in this circumstance, that they are altogether turned to their own love, thus to the infernal society which is in similar love. But the good are brought from the second state into the third, which is a state of their preparation for heaven by instruction. * *

"The good spirits who are to be instructed are conveyed thither by the Lord, when they have passed through their second state in the world of spirits, but still not all; for they who had been instructed in the world were there also prepared by the Lord for heaven, and are conveyed into heaven by another way; some immediately after death; some after a short stay with good spirits, where the grosser thoughts and affections, which they contracted from honors and riches of the world, are removed, and thus they are purified."

"He goes on to say," continued Stilwell, "that some of these suffer severely before being fitted for heaven, because they had confirmed themselves in falses, and still have led good lives.

"He next proceeds to describe in what way these different societies are instructed, and afterwards how they are admitted into the heavenly societies."

Israel continued: "I think you have alluded to the general belief of the resurrection of the natural body as somewhat distinctive from your own. May I ask if this is so?"

"The followers of Emanuel Swedenborg, accepting his instruction upon this point, do not believe in the resurrection of this body which we see, nor in any other resurrection than what takes place at death."

"Then you reject the doctrine of the Bible upon this point?"

"On the contrary we receive every word of Holy Writ which we deem the word of divine inspiration. You are aware that we as a church, accept as canonical only twenty-nine books of the Old Testament, and of the New Testament, the four gospels with the Revelations. But many Swedenborgians, myself included, reverently accept all Scripture as given by inspiration. Swedenborg affirmed that these were the books of the word, because only these had their internal sense opened to him. We who believe all, find no real difficulty in interpreting the words of St. Paul upon the resurrection, in consonance with the teachings of our faith. We have books written in explanation of his pneumatology, which are clear, convincing, and entirely faithful to our view. Of these, I would refer you to '*Foregleams of Immortality*' as one of the most valuable of this class. You will also find that many eminent thinkers of the various churches have received the Swedenborgian teaching upon this as well as some other themes, and engrafted it skilfully upon their own theologies, without the slightest acknowledgment."

"Will you state to me, concisely, your view of the resurrection?" continued Israel.

"When I explain our idea of the resurrection, I mean only our view of death. In the internal sense of the word death means a resurrection, or, as we most often call it, a *resuscitation*. When a person is said to die, we understand that he has been raised out of the material body. By this I mean that the spiritual body, or the man himself, has been set free from his earthly integument or covering.

"This is beautifully expressed in Ecclesiastes 12: 6, 7: 'Or ever the silver cord be loosed, or the golden bowl be broken, or the pitcher be broken at the fountain, or the wheel broken at the cistern.' The silver cord is the spinal marrow; the golden bowl is the head; the pitcher the heart, and the wheel the lungs. 'Then shall the dust return to the earth as it was: and the spirit shall return unto the God who gave it.' Observe, the words are, '*to the earth as it was,*' clearly teaching that no part of the Divine nature which was breathed into man when he became a living soul, is returned to the dust, or its former element of matter.

"The moment of this separation of body and spirit is when the motion of the lungs and of the heart ceases. Then takes place the opening of the spiritual sight, by the angels of the Lord. In some cases this commences before the cessation of the respiratory and systolic motions. Dying persons have been permitted to testify of what they saw and heard, to the living about them. In this connection I often think of the death-bed scenes of the spiritual-minded Payson, an unhappy theologian, but a devout Christian, who received remarkably clear views of certain things pertaining to the invisible life.

"Mrs. Payson observed to him, 'Your head feels hot, and appears to be distended.' He replied, 'It seems as if the soul disdained such a narrow prison, and was determined to break through with an angel's energy, and I trust with no small portion of an angel's feeling, until it mounts on high.' Again he said, 'It seems as if my soul had found a pair of new wings, and was so eager to try them, that in her fluttering she would rend the fine net-work of the body to pieces.' He also said, 'Hitherto I have viewed God as a fixed star, bright indeed, but often intercepted by clouds; but now he is coming nearer and nearer, and spreads into a sun, so vast and glorious that the sight is too dazzling for flesh and blood to sustain.'

"These, also, were his impressive words: 'And now God is in this room; I see him; and O how unspeakably lovely and glorious does he appear,— worthy of ten thousand, thousand hearts, if we had them. He is here and hears me pleading with the creatures that he has made, whom he preserves and loads with blessings, to love him. And O, how terrible does it appear to me to sin against this God; to set up our wills in opposition to his; and when we awake in the morning, instead of thinking "What shall I do to please my God to-day?" to inquire "What shall I do to please myself to-day?'"

"I remember," said Israel, "hearing an account of a little child, who, just before dying, raised her finger as if pointing to some one who appeared above her. In this manner she died, and her body appeared in the casket with the little finger pointing upward!"

"Yes," said Stilwell, "many are the cases which have shown that the spiritual vision is partially unclosed before the spirit is released. Persons often recognize their friends who are dead.

"Swedenborg teaches that the good angels are always present to resuscitate and introduce the spirit to the other world. But if the spirit is evil, he does not long remain with them, and separates himself of his own accord to be with those of a similar love to his own. The attractions and repulsions which we constantly see here, continue there with even greater force, since all motives to concealment are removed.

"Now the material body grows cold, and passes into

the conditions of decay like any other dead animal matter. We regard it of no more consequence, except out of a decent respect for its former use as the abode of the living tenant who has forever left it. The accidents of death, like the funeral paraphernalia and the place of interment, have no significance to us, save as signs established by custom. These signs, I wish you to remember, are always joyful emblems to a Swedenborgian. With our views how can they be otherwise? We feel that the departed one has gone beyond the sting of death, and has gotten the victory over the grave. Was there to be a necessity of another resurrection like that promulgated by the churches, the grave would retain its triumph, and death its sting.

"The injurious tendency of this unnatural doctrine of the body being recalled from the elements into which it has been scattered for uncounted ages, and accomplishing a reunion with the soul, is seen by the undefined and heathen notions of many Christian writers. These compare death and their resurrection, to winter and the awakening of nature in time of spring, leaving the inference of a period being passed by the spirit or real man in a state of unconsciousness. In one moment they will speak of the dead as in the other world and also as in the tomb; as having passed to a final state of rewards and punishments, and as waiting for the judgment of the last great day.

"From such instruction, it is natural that many became too confused to accept any clearer views than the sleep of the soul with the body in the grave. It is pitiful that they are thus robbed of some of the highest and purest consolations of our life. To them, it must indeed be 'a dread and awful thing to die,' or to have their beloved ones come under the shadow of such a grim conqueror who consigns his victims to the abode of darkness, silence, and final decay. The wailings, the gloom, and the despair which often accompany this event are seen to be consonant with this false and heathen doctrine."

Israel continued: "It must be a consolation to believe that our departed ones are still near us, and perfectly cognizant of what is passing in this life."

"How can we believe otherwise, when the history of the world, both inspired and profane, is replete with testimonies to this point. Could Moses and Elias have appeared unto the disciples had they not been in a state of existence, and knowing passing events in the world? You remember the words in the Apocalypse: 'And I, John, saw these things, and heard them. And when I had heard and seen, I fell down to worship before the feet of the angel which shewed me these things. Then saith he unto me, See thou do it not: for I am *thy fellow-servant, and of thy brethren the prophets*, and of them which keep the sayings of this book: worship God.'"

"This was called an angel and not a spirit," said Israel.

"Certainly, since all angels of whom we ever knew anything in this life, were once men," answered Stilwell.

"We are taught to believe by the Christian church that the orders of angel and spirit are entirely different, the first being superior to those who once lived in the flesh; and generally it is believed that angels only are permitted to minister to the world."

"You are so taught by Milton, whose theology contained more poetry than truth. There is no such teaching in the word of God. In Judges, thirteenth chapter, you will find that when the angel appeared unto the mother of Samson, he is called a man of God as well as the angel of God; again he is simply called 'the man.'

"In the book of Daniel, the angel Gabriel is called the man Gabriel.

"The angels who appeared unto Mary in the Holy Sepulchre were doubtless like men, as there is no record of her regarding them otherwise. They talked with her like men.

"In Revelations, twenty-first chapter and seventeenth verse, it reads: 'And he measured the wall thereof, a hundred and forty and four cubits, according to the measure of a man; that is, of the angel.'

"I recommend you, however, to read the words of Swedenborg upon this and other subjects to which I could not much more than allude."

"That will I do."

## CHAPTER II.

#### CONVERSATION CONTINUED.

ISRAEL continued: "I wish to hear your views of the character and mission of Jesus Christ on earth. Your words respecting the purification by an intermediate state of discipline and instruction, as also some of your observations upon the resurrection, have excited my interest. In short, let me first ask you if you believe in the doctrine of the Trinity?"

"Swedenborg teaches that there is but one God. This God was and is Jesus Christ. In Jesus Christ (as we are taught by writers of this faith) 'is a Trinity composed of the Essential Divinity, the Divine Humanity, and the Divine Proceeding, corresponding to the human trinity in every man, of body, soul, and operating energy. In eternity He was Creator, in time, Redeemer, and to eternity, Regenerator.' No other God will be seen in Heaven but Jesus Christ. His appearance there is as a sun high above the heavens. Hence, in the time of his transfiguration before the disciples, whose spiritual sight was partially opened, it is said, 'His face did shine as the sun.' (Matt. 17: 2.) Also in the apocalyptic vision to John, 'His eyes were as a flame of fire; and his feet like unto fine brass, as if they burned in a furnace.' The mission of the incarnate Deity was, in the language of another, 'to check the overgrown influence of wicked spirits over the minds of men, opening a nearer communication with the heavenly powers, and making salvation, which is regeneration, possible for all who believe in the incarnate God, and keep his commandments.'

"Let me read to you from the pages of a prominent disciple of this faith: 'It was not, then, any selfish regard to His own glory which led to this grand expedient; but in his *love* and his *pity* he redeemed us. There never was any *conflict* between his attributes. The justice of God is but his goodness in *restorative* action. He does *not* demand the punishment of an innocent substitute. (Gen. 18: 25; Ez. 18: 20.) He requires our repentance and reformation alone. (Jer. 18: 7, 8; Isa. 56: 7; Luke 24: 47-8; Acts 5: 30-1; 1 John 1, 9.) It is not enough barely to believe all this, though true; to repent in extremity; or to confess our sins in the gross.'"

"But how will you manage the case of the thief on the cross?" here interposed Israel.

"Christ only promised him paradise," said Stilwell, "and by what I have already told you, you can understand our view of the states after death. If the thief, on coming into paradise or the state of blessedness, found himself fitted for that society, he would remain; on the contrary, if he was evil in the ruling love, he would leave there of his own accord. None are banished from happiness or heaven by the Lord or His angels, more than are they excluded from goodness and its enjoyment on earth, save by their free will. It by no means followed that this person was a good angel after death, in his ultimate state, because he was to be with Christ in paradise that day."

Israel continued: "Since Paul uses the word 'paradise' as synonymous with the 'third heaven' in his account of his remarkable vision, into which he was caught up and heard unspeakable words, I think the condition of the repentant thief may be predicated as tolerably safe, especially as he was there to be with Christ."

"Place has no importance," said the Swedenborgian; "it is state or the condition of the soul and spirit. Here, what is heaven to one man is hell to another, and the converse. Precisely is it thus hereafter. Dives could speak to Lazarus, who was in Abraham's bosom, and yet between them was a great gulf fixed."

"That was a parable," said Israel.

"Certainly; but of what use is a parable save as a representation of truth? If it represents a nonentity, a falsehood, it is not a parable, but a myth. As such it could have had no introduction into the word of God.

"In this world," continued Stilwell, "there is also a great gulf between persons of different faith and life. For one of these to be admitted into the life of the other, would be, indeed, an indescribable torment. It is not the act of the good which banishes the evil from their presence or life; but they go away to their own place in the greatest freedom of choice.

"To proceed with my reading upon the manner in which regeneration is effected, and the death of Christ made efficacious unto men: —

"'Man must examine himself in detail; fight against his evils in the strength of the Lord; follow the great exemplar; (Matt. 10: 38; 16: 24; 19: 28; 1 Pet. 11: 21-2; John 12: 26; 1 Cor. 10: 13; 2 Cor. 3: 17, 18; 4: 16;) and thus, by an union of faith, charity, and good works, *without attaching any merit to either*, "work out his own salvation," or qualify himself for happiness. We know of no shorter road to heaven. A God of truth will not impute to us either the good or evil which was not and could not have been done by us. (Ez. 18: 20-21.) And though all are predestinated to heaven, yet none will be forced to accept it; nor will any be *elected*, but by that principle of spiritual affinity which leads those who are by reformation and regeneration made like Him, to choose Him freely and reciprocally. * * * As the ability to keep the commands is constantly afforded, voluntary *perseverance*, and constant vigilance are as little as could be expected in return.'

"Here follow words which I desire you to especially notice: 'Who then can estimate the importance of regeneration, when we reflect that man is by every thought, word, and act of his life drawing his own portrait and forming his own state for eternity? When we know that outward realities are but shadows compared with our own inward imaginations and desires, and that we are either good or bad, and, therefore, already in conjunction either with heaven or with hell, according as these and yet deeper principles are working within us.'

"Yes, my friend," continued Stilwell, closing the book, "we are already either in heaven or in hell. We may ourselves know whether we are children of God or of the Evil — for he that is born of God or regenerated into the truth, hath the witness in himself. The sign signifying the presence of the one is heavenly love — love to the Lord, which is also love to the neighbor, and leads us to do all the good unto others in our power. The sign signifying the other is hate — hate to all goodness and its source; hate to the neighbor, and a desire to accomplish evil to others in gratification of the ruling passion, which is love of self."

"Surely," commented Israel, "those ideas are more reasonable to the sense of right and wrong which seems innate, than those which make it possible to be in the church, and fully qualified for perfect happiness at death, with a life meantime replete with all manner of sin and corruption, or yet with a life while not especially flagrant in act, is yet disfigured with pride, envy, revenge, and a kind of refined, ecclesiastical hate. I have often wondered how prominent persons who were standard-bearers in the churches, could so far descend from their high privileges as children of God and heirs of ineffable love, as to bicker and strive one with another, and to manifest a will which evidently proceeded from self-love rather than the love of the Lord."

# CHAPTER III.

### WHO WAS EMANUEL SWEDENBORG?

ISRAEL made this note: "Swedenborg was either an impostor, a monomaniac, a superior clairvoyant, or what he claimed to be."

After reading extensively and carefully, he amplified his classification thus: "Was he an impostor? This man's father, a Lutheran bishop of Skara, West Gothland, and many years superintendent of the Swedish mission established in England and America, trained his child in his own severest doctrines. At seven years of age the boy fell into a trance while in prayer. After this, his devotions became more frequent and fervid, and the habitudes of his mind less natural to one of his years. Long periods were spent by him in abstruse meditation upon the profoundest questions in theology.

"His education was liberal. His life was ever open and free of all immoral taint. He wrote many books containing experiments and observations in mathematics and philosophy. In his twenty-eighth year, he was appointed by Charles XII assessor to the Metallic College. Afterwards, was ennobled by Queen Ulrica, upon which occasion his name was changed from Swedburg to Swedenborg. He was a fellow of the

Royal Academy of Sciences at Stockholm, and also of Upsal and Petersburg. These, with other similar honors, show the estimate in which the man was held by his contemporaries who knew him best. In his travels in Italy, France, and England, he was ever regarded with a respect commensurate with his claims as a profound scholar and a man of pure intentions. Plain in his habits and independent in his circumstances, he was removed from liabilities of the imputation of self-interest. Swedenborg could not have been an impostor.

"A monomaniac?

"Into the negative of this query, the foregoing statements may be projected as fair evidence. The Swedish prime minister, his friend of forty years' standing, exclaims in his eulogy — 'The amiable enthusiast'! What sort of specimen of that tame monster do they expect to find in this man of prodigious learning and science — whose unsullied honor, whose knowledge of mankind, and whose varied experience in life, had made him the companion of sages, of princes and nobles, of statesmen and heroes, and whose memory was honored with exalted eulogy, through the representative of the highest scientific body of his country?'

"On the other hand, it is to be noticed that he fell into trances in his youth. On one occasion he entered the presence of one of his most eminent friends, and announced himself as the Lord Jesus Christ. This circumstance was excused by his friends upon the plea of temporary aberration resulting from illness of body; by his enemies, it was cited as the legitimate result of his early impressions respecting his name Emanuel, and the forceful reaction of the normal condition of his mind.

"I find many things in his writings such as no sane spirit would conceive of heaven or earth. I know it is a convenient method of disposal for what we cannot or do not wish to understand, to say as Festus said of St. Paul.

"Besides, is not the man mad who teaches that truth has been revealed to him, after this manner, of which we, and especially the High Priests of our old faith know nothing? Is he not beside himself who says that a state of heavenly blessedness is secured, not through the door of any church or sacrament, but by conforming the hidden life to the love of the Lord and the love of the neighbor, casting out of the heart regard to the advancement of self by honors, wealth, and power?

(Afterthought.) "Every profound thinker is a kind of monomaniac, and every intense worker in any given direction is his fellow-sufferer.

"Was Swedenborg a superior clairvoyant?

"Those who deny this, call attention to the facts that his state was wholly independent of the agency of others; that he was in perfect possession of his consciousness during all his states of spiritual perception, and that he was also in the full enjoyment of his natural sight. They cite with confidence his own statement of the difference between his condition of mind and that of the subject of the state which has since been called mesmeric or spiritual. I copy this passage which, having been written in that early period of 'spiritual' phenomena, is reckoned somewhat remarkable; 'but they who believe this, (that spirits may talk with man), and are willing to believe it, *do not know that it is connected with danger to their souls.* * * But as soon as spirits begin to speak with man, they come out of their spiritual state into the natural state of man, and in this case they know that they are with man, and conjoin themselves with the thoughts of his affection, and from those thoughts speak with him; they cannot enter into anything else, for similar affection and consequent thought conjoins all, and dissimilar separates. It is owing to this circumstance, that the speaking spirit *is in the same principles with the man to whom he speaks, whether they be true or false,* and likewise that he excites them, and by his affection, conjoined to the man's affection, strongly confirms them: hence it is evident that none other than similar spirits speak with man, or manifestly operate upon him, for manifest operation coincides with speech.' * * *

"On the other hand, it is alleged that Swedenborg's revelations were on a similar plane with modern spiritual manifestations by clairvoyance, in proof of which, allusion is made to his announcement of the fire in Stockholm at the hour when it occurred, while he was in Gottenburg; of his telling the widow the place of discovery of her lost receipt; and his conversation with the merchant of Elberfield.

"Was this man what he claimed to be?

"In the forty-sixth year of his age, he affirms that his spiritual sight was opened by the Lord, so that he was enabled ever after to see and converse with the spirits of the other world. 'It was in London,' are his words, 'that a man appeared to me in the midst of a strong and shining light, and said, "I am God, the Lord, the Creator and Redeemer; I have chosen thee to explain to men the interior and spiritual sense of the sacred writings." He believed that he was chosen to establish a new dispensation of doctrinal truth, and 'that all those passages in Scripture which are generally supposed to refer to the destruction of the world by fire, and the final judgment, must be understood (according to the doctrine of correspondence) to mean the consummation of the present Christian Church, and that the new heavens are the New Church in its internal, and the new earth the Swedenborgian or New Jerusalem Church in its external form.'

"This church, he claimed, was spoken of in the Revelation of St. John. Upon the strength of this claim, he denies the authenticity of a large body of the Sacred Canon, since its internal sense was not disclosed to him.

"I cannot admit these claims.

ISRAEL KNIGHT."

## CHAPTER IV.

#### CONCLUDING CONVERSATION.

"I have now traversed the whole sea of Swedenborgian literature," said Israel to his friend Stilwell, "and my remarkable perseverance at least deserves honorable mention, if not a first-class medal." The other eagerly inquired his present opinion of the founder of the Church of the New Jerusalem.

"Shall I tell you just the few simple impressions I bring from those books?"

"Certainly; I want nothing less than candor."

"My opinion is," renewed Israel, "that Swedenborg would come under the category of men whom Mr. Locke describes in his 'Enthusiasm.' The subjective states of his mind passed unconsciously into the objective. He thought that he heard the voices of the other life while yet he was talking to himself, as do we ourselves, sometimes, on awaking from a confused dream. To be more special: Emanuel Swedenborg had been disappointed in love by death, as one of his biographers avers. It is bad for an intense man, independent in fortune, to be disappointed in love. If he had been poor, this incident would have made him great; as it was, it made him mentally dazed. Witness his work called 'Conjugial Love.'"

"Think now of the excellence of many of his writings which you may understand," rejoined Stilwell, very seriously.

"His style is immoderately diffuse. The story of 'The Locusts' illustrates it."

"Bear in mind that Swedenborg wrote in an age when men took time to think calmly, and to express those thoughts with equal deliberation."

"But contrast this style with that of the Bible! Verbosity is never the attendant of perspicuity. The strongest and grandest thinkers of all ages have been most concise, as flavors of the greatest power and rarest value are also most highly concentrated. The Inca Atahuallpa of Peru was more profoundly imimpressed by the name of God written upon the finger nail of the Spanish soldier, in proof of his power, than if he had displayed a volume. The Inca was ignorant. Likewise are we. Angels only can tolerate extension. God alone dwells in infinity. But one step bridges the sublime and the ridiculous."

"It is true," continued Israel more gravely, "that with all the discounting points in these works, they have a decided value as a contribution to the religious literature of the world. I admit what you said, that these views have tinged those of many a modern theologian of other churches."

"Why then refuse to admit that Swedenborg founded a new dispensation of Christian truth? He teaches that there are three senses in the Word—the celestial, the spiritual, and the natural. Before he wrote, the natural and the spiritual were only but faintly understood.

And these indeed were not really understood, only seen as in a deep, dark shadow."

"There lived before Emanuel Swedenborg's time, good men who died well," said Israel. "How much more might they have achieved and enjoyed, had they possessed the rational views of our faith!" continued Stilwell. "And what they did achieve and enjoy was on a similar principle or continent of belief, though as yet unconfessed and unknown. How many difficulties attending the explanation of the Christian religion are cleared away by our philosophy! In the language of another: 'This faith has nothing to fear from the progress of knowledge in any of its branches. The advance of science never can expel the Deity from his own universe, while we believe that preservation is continual creation. Discoveries in geology have no terrors for us. We do not believe that the world was made out of nothing or in six natural days; nor do we undertake to account for a literal flood which covered the highest mountains, or the ark which floated upon its waters, and the difficulties connected with it. Modern views of astronomy — with which all the eloquence of Chalmers cannot reconcile modern views of the atonement — are but part and parcel of our faith.'"

"Here appears a discrepancy of correspondence," said Israel. "I was deeply interested in Swedenborg's view of the most ancient church being designated under the name of Adam or Man; of the preservation of the doctrinals of faith of this church under the name of Cain, and this explanation of the words that a mark was put upon him, etc.; of the later compilation of doctrine under the name of Enoch, which being destined for posterity, was described as 'God took Enoch;' of the new or ancient church under the name of Noah, fragments of the word of this church being found in the books of Moses, allusions to which are in Numb. 21: 14, 27; but when I came down to the Divine manifestation in the person of the Lord upon earth, I was unreconciled according to his own laws of order and correspondence. In short, if Adam and Cain and Noah were not real personages, but representative names, why was not Christ? If the one had no real entity and historical personal verity, how could the other have had? I conceive a great difficulty in establishing a dividing line between the allegorical and the real. I have no doubt that much in the Bible is allegorical; and in that way I have explained those expressions which seem inharmonious with revealed truth; but when you strike under this head so much as does Swedenborg, an insurmountable difficulty arises to my view."

"You will bear in mind," said Stilwell, "that our view of the trinity as explained heretofore, is not like that of the churches who nominally accept this doctrine. We claim a far stronger correspondence here to the Invisible or Celestial sense in the natural letter of the Word than anywhere else."

"But will you say whether such a being as Jesus Christ, Man or God, or both, ever existed on the earth according to the version of the Gospels of Matthew, Mark, Luke, and John?" inquired Israel.

"Certainly; we believe the Gospels, though we explain them by divine correspondence rather than by

mere externals or the natural sense. The three senses
are requisite, and neither alone."

"If there were such a being as Christ, who once
lived on the earth, you know it by testimony and not
by external sight or any internal sense. Then by the
same reason, why may we not believe that there
really were such men as Adam, Enoch, and Noah?"

"Because there are accompanying difficulties in the
way of believing the letter of this history, which cannot be explained by any other doctrine than that of
correspondence according to the internal sense of the
Word."

"I do not entirely concede that," replied Israel.
"Your doctrine of correspondence has more worth as
a natural curiosity, than as a spiritual verity. I accept
it as a servant to truth, but not as its master. To me,
it is always deeply interesting to study the Holy Scriptures with reference to the inner and spiritual sense, as
also to study the uninspired scriptures of the earth,
and the nature and appearances of men with the aid
of the doctrine of correspondence; indeed, I have a
strong passion for the comparison of the visible with
the invisible, the exterior with the interior, and the
body with the immortal principle which animates it;
but this doctrine makes no laws for me which conflict
with my freedom of understanding and continued
scope of investigation. I will have no insuperable
barriers to thought. No despot, with drawn sword of
written dicta, shall stand at the gate of my investigation of truth. But mark you, my truth is complete in
itself. It is just as good at the beginning as at the end.
This is my dictator, master, and friend. I seek it,

often blindly, always, I trust, reverently. Do you ask its name? It is not divine correspondence nor spiritual influx; it is not progress nor emancipation. These all, I esteem and reckon good helps. But they shall keep their places by my side, and not in the van.

"It is God — revealed to me sufficient for all the designs of my existence here and hereafter, in His Word; and I accept these words: 'All Scripture is given by inspiration of God, and is profitable for doctrine, for reproof, for correction, for instruction in righteousness.'"

"So also do I," answered his friend; "but this does not prevent me from accepting Swedenborg's explanation of such portions of the Scripture as he has attempted to unfold. There is no doubt but that the apostles, who frequently refer to the Old Testament in their writings, regarded many portions as allegorical or written by divine correspondence," answered Stilwell.

"What proof have you of this?" continued Israel.

"If you turn to the Epistle to the Galatians, 4: 22, 23, 24, 25, you will find these words: 'For it is written that Abraham had two sons; the one by a bondmaid, the other by a freewoman. But he who was of the bondwoman was born after the flesh; but he of the freewoman was by promise. *Which things are an allegory:* for these are the two covenants; the one from Mount Sinai, which gendereth to bondage, which is Agar. For this Agar is Mount Sinai in Arabia, and answereth to Jerusalem which now is, and is in bondage with her children. But Jerusalem which is above is free, which is the mother of us all.'"

"Are those the words in our version?" now asked Israel in surprise.

"Certainly; you see that I have your Bible in my hand. Read for yourself."

Israel took the book and read.

"I never noticed that passage before in this light," he said.

At this moment they were interrupted by the appearance of a gentleman, a friend to both parties, who said in a loud voice: —

"Allegories! I have been listening to some of your conversation, and I think the finest allegory for the present point, is found in Virgil: '*Claudite jam rivos, pueri; sat prata biberunt.*' Although you are both learned 'veal,' I must give a translation, lest you escape the force thereof. Hear! 'Dam the rivers, boys; the meadows have drank enough.'"

"Of what use is so much talk about Abraham and his women-folk and all the rest of it, in the New Jerusalem light? I went to that church, once, and I came away swimming like a mote in the beams of the sun. I could think of nothing but heat and light, light and heat, love and wisdom, wisdom and love, the Lord and the sun, the sun and the Lord, all of which was of inconceivable good to me!"

"Nevertheless," said Israel, laughing quietly, "this doctrine as explained to me by my friend Stilwell, has done me more good than I can suitably acknowledge. Never again shall I regard death as before. A new light has been shed upon that else dark and appalling scene. The friend, whose body we have lately followed to the tomb, is not dead, but ushered into a life a thousand times more real than ours,—while yet he is cognizant of what we say and do!"

"I could have told you that without the aid of Emanuel Swedenborg," rejoined the other; "only last evening I talked with him for a couple of hours. By the way, he desired to be remembered to you."

Both young men regarded the speaker for a moment, as though they questioned his sanity.

"Nothing remarkable in that, is there," he continued, "when there is a 'medium' in the next street. You have heard of the celebrated Mrs. Kennett?"

"What!" exclaimed Israel, "is she in town?"

"Yes; and I was at one of her sittings, last night."

"I should like to see her," said Israel.

"Certainly, that is reasonable. She has forgotten more than Swedenborg ever knew. She says she has spoken with him several times, and he always tells her that he was wrong in some respects when he wrote his books on earth. In short, Emanuel Swedenborg is played out."

Stilwell looked disgusted, but was silent; Israel was thoroughly curious.

"You shall go with me to listen to Mrs. Kennett, and you will soon be a Spiritualist," concluded the gentleman.

# AMONG THE SPIRITUALISTS.

## CHAPTER I.

#### A SITTING WITH A SPIRITUAL MEDIUM.

Israel, with his friend Thomaston sitting a little apart, was placed in a position just before the medium. She rubbed her eyes, dropped her head, on which she made passes, and giving one or two long breaths, all was ready. The chasm between earth and the invisible world was bridged.

"I see," she began in a low, disjointed, but yet confident voice, "some one standing just behind you who is out of the form, I think. Yes, she is out of the form. By that, I mean, she is what we call dead. She is of medium height, is slight in figure, and graceful in her movements. I think she must have died of consumption. Her face is thin, and wears a hectic flush. Her eyes are sunken, but very bright; they are of a dark hazel color. Her hair is also dark, and is put back from her brow in two or three long curls. She must have been beautiful when in health. She has a small scar upon her right temple. She wears a black dress, and appears to be in mourning. They come to us as they looked in life, that we may identify them. Do you know who this person can be?"

"No," answered Israel, with a slightly unsteady tone. The assertion that one who was dead stood just behind them, with a hand on his head, made him rather uncomfortable.

"I should think," said the medium, "that she was about twenty-seven or thirty years old when she died."

She paused now, her eyes remaining closed; and after a few minutes, resumed by saying, "she tells me you are her son. She must be your mother. Is your mother out of the form?"

"My mother is dead," answered Israel, with increasing awe.

"She says, 'My dear boy, how glad I am that you have come to talk with me. For this privilege I have waited long and prayerfully. I am almost always near you, though you do not know it.'

"Another person out of the form appears now at her side. It is a man who was considerably older than your mother when he died. He was rather full in figure. He breathes with difficulty, and he often lays his hand on his heart. This is to show that some disease connected with his heart was the occasion of his death. He has very light hair, a blue eye, but penetrating and dark in its expression, and a Roman nose. His mouth is wide, firm, but pleasant, and his whole appearance is of a man of superior culture. I think he was highly educated. By the books and papers which I see about him, I should judge he belonged to one of the professions — the Law, I think. Can you tell who this person is?"

"If my mother is here, ask her," said Israel.

After a brief silence, she said: "Your mother tells me it is your father. Are your parents both dead?"

Israel admitted the fact rather reluctantly. "But my father was not a lawyer," he added.

"Perhaps he was a physician, though I see no special signs of that profession. No, I think now he was a clergyman. He appears to be reading a book which I think is in some foreign language, and I see something there which looks like a written sermon. But if he was a clergyman, he did not preach as much as he — he did something else — I cannot quite make it out. Let me examine further. He wrote books, I think. Was it so?"

"If he preached," said Israel evasively, "he would write manuscripts."

"But I think they were more than sermons," she persisted; "they look larger; and then — I see — them afterwards like books. Will you please to tell me if I am all wrong?"

"Go on," said Israel smiling.

"But it is better to be frank with me," said the medium, appearing troubled.

"All right, Mrs. Kennett," now interrupted Thomaston. "Pray go on, and not mind his scepticism."

"Your father now speaks," said the medium, "and his voice is a little peculiar. There is a slight impediment, I should think. He says this was the reason why he wrote more and spoke less in public. But I think he had a great influence over others while he lived — and — through his books, his influence continues."

"What is his message to me?" asked Israel.

"He says — 'my dear son, you have been searching a long time. You are in a state of — indecision about

— what is it? I cannot yet understand — a church — religion — some such thing as that, I believe.'"

"Does he say that?" asked Israel, in a surprise which he could not conceal.

"Yes. And he says that you are very dear to his heart. Your mother says that, too. She looks very happy. I think she was a very sweet person when in the form."

"But about what I am searching for," said Israel; "can he assist me? I should be intensely glad to have him tell me what is right for me to do?"

"He says he can and does assist you. He has always helped you."

"Will he tell me where I am to go for peace?"

"He answers, 'God is a spirit, and they that worship Him must worship Him in spirit and in truth.'"

"But how does that apply to me?"

"He says, by the spirit operating upon your spirit. Every effect has its cause — many causes sometimes. You have to go through what you are now going through, in order to arrive at the result."

*Israel.* "What will be the result?"

*Medium.* "You will come to a more settled and peaceful state of mind. You will be happier than ever before. You will see things in a truer light, and your soul will expand under the influence of an enlarged sphere of truths."

*I.* "Will he please to be more definite. What church had I better join?"

*M.* "He says it is not permitted him to tell you. Whatever is for your good, he will freely impart; but there are things which they must not divulge to those who are in the form, however much they are desired to do so by their beloved ones. He adds, 'I am no bigot, nor never was when in the form.' Other spirits now appear. I see a child about you — a little girl with fair hair like your father's, but eyes like your mother's. Had you a sister?"

*I.* "No."

*M.* "Perhaps it is one who is yet to come into the form. Or, it may be one of the children of some of your friends. I think you are very fond of children."

Another pause.

*M.* "Your mother says the child was one you knew where you boarded, when you was at school. You made a great pet of her, and she loved you very dearly. She died suddenly of croup or some difficulty of the throat."

*I.* "There was such a child. Ask her name."

*M.* "I hear, Kitty, Katie, and Caddie."

*I.* (Much moved.) "Yes, I called her Kitty. Others called her the other names. What does she do now?"

*M.* "She says, 'I play now, but it is all more beautiful.' She says, 'I also learn heavenly things. I am with my aunt, who died the year before I did. I am very happy. I have so much that is lovely! I visit my dear mamma and papa very often.'"

*I.* "Truly there must be something in this. You have given me so many tests, I begin to believe that my parents are here."

*M.* "Your mother says, 'Believe, my dear son.' She lays her hand again on your head, and she weeps — weeps tears of joy."

*I.* (In tears.) "Mother! dearest mother! if you are really here, give me some strong test."

Another pause.

*M.* "Sometime ago you went to a place where all the people sat very still. No one spoke a word. It was on a Sunday. I think it was a meeting of some kind. You saw a young girl over across from where you sat."

*I.* (Starting.) "Possible! that she tells you this? Some one must have informed you."

*M.* "You forget, sir, that I never saw nor heard of you, before this evening."

*I.* "What of this young girl? Go on. I am eager to hear."

*M.* "She wore a very plain bonnet and shawl. She was pretty and intelligent looking. I think she is your kindred spirit."

*I.* "My kindred spirit! Ask my mother what she means?"

*M.* "She says you will marry sometime—rather soon, I think."

*I.* "Indeed! how soon?"

*M.* "Time is nothing in the other life. I cannot tell you. Sometimes they mean quite soon, as we understand it; again they do not. Their ideas of time are different from ours."

*I.* "Am I to marry that girl?"

*M.* "She replies that all are free. There is no rigid and immutable law of control. Yet there is a way which one cannot escape. It is not to be explained."

*I.* "But will she answer me, directly, the question?"

*M.* "I will see, and tell you all I am permitted to. Perhaps she will tell me, and perhaps not. They tell only what is for our good to know. (After a pause.) She says, 'I think that you will take her for your wife. I think she is the complement of your being.'"

*I.* "Does she advise me to do this? Is the lady one whom she would have loved if she had lived?"

*M.* "She says 'No one is perfect. You must not look for perfection, my son.' These are her words. But be thankful that your lot is as good as it is."

*I.* "Will she tell me her name?"

*M.* "I hear the name of Mary, also Charlotte. But Mary I hear most. Perhaps it is Mary Charlotte."

*I.* "Ask if she is interested in me."

*M.* "She says that she is. She thinks of you much of the time, and has even taken pains to find you out."

*I.* "How shall I proceed to make her acquaintance?"

*M.* "She says 'I cannot tell you now. There will be a way.' We see results without understanding all the connection. But another spirit has now come. He seems anxious to speak to you."

*I.* "What is he like?"

*M.* "He is tall, very grave-looking, and is black on one side of his face, as if he had been bruised severely."

Both Thomaston and Israel started. They recalled their friend who had died under the same roof, some time before, and with whom Thomaston said he had conversed a few evenings since.

*I.* "Ask his name, if you please."

*M.* "He says you know who he is. He calls himself an old friend who sat around the same board some time before he passed out of the body. He is very glad to have a chance to talk with you."

*I.* "Ask him if he is happy."

*M.* "He says, 'I am happier than I was on earth, but not so happy as I shall be when I have progressed to a higher group.'"

*I.* Does he believe, on religious subjects, as he did when on earth?"

*M.* "Not altogether. He was much deceived here about some things."

*I.* "May I ask what are those things to which he refers?"

*M.* "He says you will remember that he had a great reverence for the Bible; the same as you, yourself, now have."

*I.* (Much startled.) "Well; has he not a reverence for the Bible *now* ?"

*M.* "He has now a reverence for all good books. Not one is free from erroneous views. Not one is absolute and infallible as a standard of perfect thought."

*I.* "What! not the Word of God, the Holy Scripture, written by inspiration!"

*M.* "That, he says, is by no means perfect. It was written by men no more inspired than Confucius, or Seneca, or Thomas Paine. Your blind adoration for the Bible — these are his words — leads you into many false ideas and devious paths. It makes you unhappy when you ought to rejoice in the God who has made the beautiful world and all things therein. I should think by his manner that he was very positive in his opinions when in the form. He gesticulates peculiarly, extending his forefinger, and then striking the other hand, ending with a motion like this." (She imitates him, and Thomaston and Israel both smile as they identify the peculiarity of their old friend.)

*I.* "I am much surprised at this. Will he speak to me further respecting his views of religious truth? I am anxious to know what is the true doctrine."

*M.* "Yes, he says you are; he says, look into your own heart and the great, beautiful book of Nature. Talk, also, with those who have progressed in a knowledge of true Spiritual philosophy. Frequent Spiritual circles. Deliver your mind from the iron shackles — of — of old prejudices. You will then see clearer, know more perfectly, and enjoy much."

Not long after this, the medium announced, — "The state is passing off me. You must hasten, if you have more to say this evening. The spirits are going to leave me."

*I.* "My dear father and mother! What shall I do to please you most?"

*M.* "They both place their hands upon your head, and they engage in prayer. Now they both stoop over you, and imprint a kiss on your brow. They say, 'Dear son! come often and talk with us. Live up to the higher life. Be hopeful. Be happy. We are ever near you. We often elevate your spirit when you are depressed. We smooth your pillow by night, and waken you in the morning. Never feel that you are alone. Good night.' They move away. I am going to come out of it."

The medium now rubbed her eyes, gave a few deep

sighs, and a slight start, then slowly opened her eyes as if waking up from sleep, and looking vaguely at Israel, asked: "Have you had a pleasant sitting?"

"I have, madam, thanks to your skill," answered Israel, while he threw down twice the customary fee upon her table.

"I hope to see you again — thank you," she said, in a very low voice.

"We shall be sure to come," said Thomaston.

## CHAPTER II.

### MORE ADVICE.

"It is very strange," said Israel to his friend Thomaston, on their departure from the medium, "very strange indeed. All she told of my father and mother, so far as I know, was perfectly true. I have often looked at the small scar on my mother's forehead in her picture; and as she buried her father a few months before her death, undoubtedly she dressed in mourning."

"It was also true about our friend who has lately died," said Thomaston. "They do tell many remarkable things. How can you help believing?"

"I do not know," answered Israel, thoughtfully.

"If you require further investigation," said Thomaston, "I have books and papers which I will lend you."

"I shall be glad to read them," Israel replied.

The following day, Thomaston brought Israel several copies of a noted Spiritual newspaper, which Israel examined with great interest and with much care. He came to the following conclusions, viz:

"That the aim of Spiritualism is to destroy all respect for the Bible, or, that no more should be held for it than would be for any other book of its age, and less than should be for the writings of 'Apostles of Liberty.'

"To annihilate the divine mission of Jesus Christ, and rank him below any other prominent man who has influenced the minds of men for good.

"To pull down all the religious faith of evangelical Christendom, and on its ruins erect a temple of Spiritualism which shall reach the heavens, and by which men may constantly unveil mysteries of far more value to mankind than the most sacred annunciations of God's revealed Word."

The arguments were nothing more nor less than what he had read in the books of all the celebrated infidel writers. They were old acquaintances in new dress. They neither astonished nor angered him; for his astonishment and anger had both spent themselves long ago over the pages which he had read. Meantime he constantly prayed to God for wisdom and right discernment. He was greatly strengthened when he read such words as these, found in 2 Thess. Chap. 2:
"That ye be not soon shaken in mind, or be troubled, neither by spirit nor by word, nor by letter as from us, as that the day of Christ is at hand. Let no man deceive you by any means: for that day shall not come, except there come a falling away first, and that man of sin be revealed, the son of perdition; who opposeth and exalteth himself above all that is called God, or that is worshipped; so that he, as God sitteth in the temple of God, shewing himself that he is God. * * * For the mystery of iniquity doth already work: only he who now letteth will let, until he be taken out of the way. And then shall that wicked be

revealed, whom the Lord shall consume with the spirit of his mouth, and shall destroy with the brightness of his coming. Even him, whose coming is after the working of Satan, with all power, and signs, and lying wonders, etc. * * And for this cause God shall send them strong delusion, that they should believe a lie."

As was his habit, he wrote to him who had been his guardian, (for Israel had now more than attained his majority,) and received this reply: —

"MY DEAR OLD FELLOW:

"Be assured that Spiritualism, so called, is nothing new. It had not its date with the Fox girls of Rochester. It astonishes the ignorant who have not read the history of the world, but disturbs not one jot nor one tittle the equanimity of those who are in any wise posted in the affairs of Satan's kingdom. The same old adversary who told our grandparents in Eden, 'Ye shall *not* surely die. What! will you make fools of yourselves in minding the law of God, when by breaking it ye can become as gods, knowing good and evil, without any help from your Creator!' is, and has ever been, busy at his tricks in beguiling unstable souls.

"In all ages of the world there is a record of the devil's mission. He succeeds often, but his work does not stand through the years and cycles. His track is sin, which covers remorse, desolation, and broken idols. These ruins are 'ivied o'er' with the attractive rhetoric of flowers, purling streams, diamonds, and whispering leaves."

(Israel here remembered having read in one of the spiritual newspapers this sentence: "Therefore it [the Bible] is to us no authority and no absolute guide in matters of faith or practice. Reason is the soul's guiding star, and nature the soul's commentary. O, nature, accept us as thy disciple! We love thy inspiration, thy freedom, thy flowers, thy fruits, those voiceless orbs that look down so calmly in the night time; those rich, roseate sunsets, suggesting visions of magic lands and spirit-homes floating in space, all radiant with crimson and purple and gold, and those still summer nights, too, when the heavens kiss the oceans, and dancing fire-flies illume woods and fields, enzoning the earth, as it were, in a mantle of stars. O, nature, we are thine; thou art ours forever!")

"Beautiful nature! Glorious nature! is the harp, on which he causes his votaries to play tunes of adoration to himself. Beautiful human nature is the organ-swell of the great diatessaron of infernal harmonies! Anything, everything to break down Christian faith and pull up the old land-marks of Christianity. According to prophecy, many, even choice Christians, will be deceived and led away into the mazes of error and sin. There will be just so much done in the world. But remember, Israel, you are free — free to choose or refuse. Remember that he that endureth to the *end* has the promise of salvation. 'To him that overcometh will I give a white stone, and in that stone a new name which no man knoweth save him that receiveth it.'

"The magicians of Egypt imitated Moses very cleverly in his miracles, but there were some things which they could not do. The magic Spiritualists imitate Christ and the Apostles, but there are things which they cannot do. Of these, they cannot raise the dead body, nor lay the devil that is in a man, both by nature and practice. Man, being made out of the breath of God, has a great many good things in him, both by heirdom and education; but all these goods require evoking by a spirit as far above these cabalistic jugglers as the heavens are above the earth. Satan being a rebel angel, knows how to put on the garments of light, and act almost to perfection. He does it in all manner of ways. It would take more books than all living men could write to describe the half of his works. No sentient being is free from his influence, through his myriad emissaries. But we are also free to choose the influence of our good angel. Resist the devil and he will flee from you. Avoid these 'teachers with itching ears,' of whom Paul wrote — 'And they shall turn away their ears from the truth, and shall be turned unto fables.'

"However, I do not censure your spirit of investigation. It is natural that you should have a curiosity to open Pandora's box. Be not alarmed. This thing will waste and wear itself out in due time. The more it is opposed, the better will it thrive. People who go to them for bread and get a stone of falsehood, will amuse themselves a little while by making a 'stone-broth;' but the dish will not digest. The stone does not become bread. The lie does not prove true. The shadows of future events vanish in the dust. The false gods do not save in sickness, calamity, and death.

"Finally, my young brother, be steadfast, immovable, always abounding in the work of the Lord, forasmuch as your labor is not in vain in the Lord.
         Yours, faithfully,
                    EPHRAIM STEARNS."

## CHAPTER III.

### TALK WITH A SPIRITUALIST.

Israel showed the letter of his former guardian to Thomaston, who read it with a look which signified half compassion, half contempt.

"The old gentleman," said he, indifferently, "has not kept pace with the progress of the enlightened world. The sense he has is not ventilated in God's free air. His ideas of the devil are worthy of the Salem witchcraft. They make me think of the girl in France whose case is detailed by Dr. Picknell. She, by an old woman's advice, drank water saturated with the earth of two priests' graves, believing thereby to insure to herself a great spiritual reward. She got only the larvæ of beetles, and twelve days after, a green insect flew out of her mouth."

"You talk like a man of charity, a many-sided mind, delivered from the self-hood or the *Ichheit*, as the Germans call it," said Israel.

"But I cannot help commiserating such ignorance," responded Thomaston, "whether it appears in an old man or a young girl."

"This man whom you despise," said Israel, "has the works of all the German and French rationalists, the English infidels, and the American transcenden-

talists in his library. He is as familiar with them as
with — I was about to say his Bible. He reads easily
and speaks fluently the ancient and modern languages.
With several eminent Germans he has sat under their
vine and fig-tree, and held long discourse upon the
subjects on which they have treated in their books. I
think that we, who have hardly shaken the dews of
college walls from our sapling branches, can ill afford
to rattle defiance at the ignorance of the sturdy old oak
with an experience gathered from the centuries."

"I beg pardon of the venerable shade, but I hope
he will remember that the world revolves on its axis,
even though he survives all change and chance in
unparalleled dignity," retorted Thomaston ; "I believe
what our American philosopher says: 'Wherever a
man comes there comes revolution. The old is for
slaves.'"

"Truth is eternal," answered Israel ; "hence as good
at the beginning as at the end. Truth is God. He
is the same yesterday, to-day, and forever. The old
*ex cathedra* uttered to the first family-child : 'If thou
doest well, shalt thou not be accepted? and if thou
doest not well, sin lieth at the door,' is just as plain
and true to-day as it was then. Cain was one of your
men. He thought for himself, independent of God.
He was jealous of Abel, whose sacrifice found more
favor than his own. He did not see any use in atoning
blood, when the earth was full of inexhaustible resources for 'self-adjustment,' which he could secure by
his own hand. Then came a revolution. He struck
Abel out of sight. This man thought his brother's
work meet for slaves, not for himself. He made a

mistake. The revolution was in himself; not in the earth, nor in the Everlasting God. The blood of his brother cried from the very ground beneath him. As well might he have made a shield and carried it between him and the morning star, announcing afterwards that such star was no more. How petty is such a design! how infinitely small its attempt at execution! As though a man could strike out Christ and his revealed word!"

"Such talk is but fustian — mere rant," said Thomaston.

"Perhaps it is," answered Israel calmly; "but my theme is worthy of a better advocate, and yet it has no need of any human voice to be uplifted in its behalf. Perfect in itself, it requires no imperfection to consummate its mission. But setting aside all abstract argument, let us look at the practical bearings of the two schemes — the Gospel plan and the self-hood; the Christ and the Man. What countries have been civilized, what neighborhoods elevated, blessed and truly enriched, or what poor, down-trodden heart permanently refreshed and comforted by such words as have been left on record by Bahrdt, Loeffler, Lessing, Reimarus, Paulus, Strauss, Renan, Herbert, Collins, Tindal, Blount, Shaftesbury, Voltaire, and Paine? Souls have been made giddy with a presentiment of emancipation from the old. They have been stultified with their own divine. They have dreamed of drinking the nectar of Olympus from the muddy ponds of their own hearts. They have grasped diamonds in fire-flies, and seen angels in rotten wood. They have lived charmed lives. But which of them all has died a charmed death? Which of them all, in the face of the inevitable event which was about to carry them into the visible presence of the great God, could rapturously say, with the apostle, 'For I am now ready to be offered, and the time of my departure is at hand. I have fought a good fight, I have finished my course, I have kept the faith. Henceforth there is laid up for me a crown of righteousness, which the Lord, the righteous Judge, shall give me at that day; and not to me only, but unto all them also that love his appearing'?"

"But what has all this to do with modern Spiritualism?" asked Thomaston, after an embarrassing pause.

"Very much," answered Israel; "from what I gather out of the papers and books which I have had from you, upon this subject, I understand that this thing, Spiritualism, is only a new phase or demonstration of an infidelity which has run through all the ages since the beginning; nature and the self-hood against the law and God — against revelation and the Christ. These new supernatural sights and sounds are only a recasting of the old characters, and a revamping of the old stage-machinery. Every quarter of an age must have its spiritual sensation."

"That is to say, you think it all trick and humbug — of a piece with the Salem witchcraft?" pursued Thomaston.

"By no means. The trick and humbug are not with the machinery, (that works fairly in most cases; no doubt there are some counterfeits,) but they belong to the underlying principle from which this operation springs — the invisible law. Neither was the Salem demonstration a pure humbug, nor yet have been the sorcery and magic, and the thousand pronounced demonstrations which work under this system of causes that encloses the scheme whose name is a lie! These are the principalities and powers, the rulers of the darkness of this world. And we need the whole armor of God to withstand them,—the most valuable piece of which is faith."

"Yes," said Thomaston, ironically, "I think it is. But why not have more faith in Spiritualism? You admitted that you knew what Mrs Kennet said to you was true."

"Only in regard to certain alleged appearances. There was just enough light borrowed to make the darkness more visible."

"How can you prove that?"

"I have not told you my experience about the 'kindred spirit' revealed to me by the medium greatly to my surprise and satisfaction?"

"No! How was it?"

"On a Sunday after that, I obtained the company of one of my friends who knows the people where the girl appears at meeting,—'the girl with the plain bonnet and shawl,' whom I recognized as soon as the medium described her, as one I had once seen about a year since,—and together we went to that place, I for the second time. I wished, if possible, to get my friend to identify her and inform me who she was, for I did not even know her name. What was my delight to find that the lady was the happy wife of a man, who, with herself, was well known to my friend! Thus ended the 'spiritualistic' shadow of my kindred spirit, designated by the care of my sainted mother! The fault was not in the saint. It was in the sin and its author!"

"But they certainly tell many wonderful truths," persisted Thomaston.

"And as certainly tell many falsehoods, as every one who has ever dealt largely with this thing knows full well. The poor mediums, who are often innocent and well-meaning, make good cat's-paws for the arch enemy."

"You think he has horns and cloven feet, I suppose! No wonder you believe so much!" laughed Thomaston.

"When I speak of a person or one being under the designation of the arch enemy, I refer to evil and its angels, who were once men like us. These are the opposites of God and the good angels, who also were men."

"Why may not these good angels talk to us through mediums."

"It is not for me to say that they cannot. But I would as soon listen for them on my own pillow in the night hours, as at the speech of a medium. Sooner far would I watch for them in the province of my common life. For the food of my soul, my daily bread is all I need ask of the good Father, and not miraculous quails."

"Well; every one to his taste; *chacun a son gout*," responded Thomaston.

"Be careful that you do not taste the meat which will not keep and stand the test of time."

"Ah! it is not us, free-thinkers, who have to do with the ages. The now is all in all, to us. What a man is, abides with us forever," exclaimed Thomaston triumphantly; "the present of the human soul is the acorn in which are folded the gloriously infinite possibilities of the Divine Eternal."

"Thus saith the Lord: 'I am the Lord, and there is none else, there is no God beside me: *I girded thee, though thou hast not known me.*' He girds you with all the strength you have, whether you know him or not. Who can contemplate a more sublime spectacle than that of the Lord girding His creatures with the strength which they use in their attempts to rebel against His law? Truly He is good, and His mercy endureth forever-!" exclaimed Israel.

"We know and acknowledge God sooner than we do his 'professed' children, — the elect of his love. We believe that all are his children, and may hold communication with Him. Not ever are we talking about Him, but our life is surrounded and lost in Him.. I have a young brother — the delight of all our hearts. Our love is repaid in love. He lives in us, but he is unconscious of it to any pronounced standard," said Thomaston.

"That beloved brother," continued Israel, "furnishes me a test question in point. If you knew that he must be left alone in the world, would you not place him in the care of a truly Christian man, instead of one who may be called an infidel Spiritualist — a disbeliever of the Bible?"

"It would depend on the man," answered Thomaston; "not on his external opinions."

"But the man and his opinions are identical, in a free land like ours," said Israel.

"Some of our most remarkable free-thinkers have been gracious to all young people, kind and benevolent to the neighbor, and as true souled in all points of honor and right as man ever was," said Thomaston. "And I need not remind you of the difference in this respect between them and what are called ministers of the Gospel," he continued. "I know of orthodox pastors who scarcely nod at the young people of respectable families in their parish, from year to year. They seem to think that all attention to such members of their flock will subtract from their elect, priestly superiority. Such young people go out into the world for themselves, and finding that those whom they have been taught to class with the 'son of perdition' are kind, tender-hearted, sympathetic, the springs of their love out-flowing, they naturally turn to them and finally become their disciples. No wonder that these priestly autocrats find comfort and refreshment in the doctrine of sovereign decrees, election, and reprobation!"

"I know also," he continued, "men first and foremost in these orthodox churches, who are more dangerous in business than common burglars, because, forsooth, their work is not one for which we can obtain redress in case of detection. Their strength is to cheat; their play to make long prayers, which are as tasteless 'as the white of an egg.' The sins of these men go beforehand unto judgment, for they are in the mouths of everybody but their fellows in the church. Think you I should prefer to place a young and innocent child in such an earth-sphere as that?"

"In all ages," replied Israel, "there have been

hypocrites. Our Saviour denounced them in the strongest terms. Were there no genuine disciples, there would be no counterfeit. But surely you will not deny that there are good pastors and good people in the Christian churches. These are the salt of the earth."

"Said I not, it depended on the man and not his opinions? But that was not all of the matter. I mean that a good man will have a good rule of action underlying all his motives, whether among one people or another; and the same of the bad. But such opinions as are taught by these churches are most dangerous and destructive of good. Were not men who are not sacrificed to the spirit of their doctrines very good by nature, and were it not for the restraints of society, they would be ruined by them."

"Let us remember," said Israel, "that the greatest of all virtues is charity."

"It says also, 'they that fear the Lord hate evil,' and a curse is pronounced upon 'him that justifieth the ungodly,'" Thomaston quickly interposed.

"But we must forgive those who trespass against us, if we wish to be forgiven. We must be more quick to see the good than the evil. We must be mindful that not one of us is without sin. It makes a man unhappy and unhealthy to harbor censorious thoughts of others," said Israel.

"True; and allow me to remind you of all these good words of yours, when you sit in judgment on the Spiritualist-infidel or the Neo-Spiritualist. They are not without their good points as well as those which you may think are evil. I quite consent to the proposition that the greatest of all spiritual gifts is love. And with it in the ascendant in your mind, you will oblige me by stating your idea of the origin and nature of what are called Spiritual manifestations — that is, more definitely than you have yet done. For when you set them down to the score of the devil, you talk as intelligently as do the Turks, who say that their most exalted pachas are the pachas with three tails."

"I think that His Darkness works often in this thing by means of animal magnetism and electrodynamics. By eliminating common sense, the experiment is a success," said Israel.

"But the devil would not require to call in such aid," said the Spiritualist.

"I do not give him the credit of omniscience. He is not greater than God, who works by means," answered Israel.

"There is no use in reasoning with one who has no reasonable basis," said Thomaston, impatiently.

"I trust I am not so prejudiced as to be unwilling to listen to what is really reasonable," returned Israel.

"Then," said Thomaston, "consent to accompany me to-morrow evening, to hear the noted Spiritualist speaker, Denatra, who speaks in Granby Hall."

Israel assented.

## CHAPTER IV.

### A SPIRITUAL TRAJECTORY.

THOMASTON was prevented from attending the meeting designated, and Israel went without him. The next day they met, and thus discoursed:—

*Thomaston.* "So you had the rare privilege of listening to our great apostle, last evening?"

*Israel.* "I heard him."

*T.* "Distil some of the dew of his lips upon me, if you please."

*I.* "Rather some of the poison from under his serpent-tongue."

*T.* "Thou unbeliever in all that is high and beautiful!"

*I.* "He said what I could not have believed possible for a man in any reputable place of this land to dare utter."

*T.* "Dare! Indeed, a great, true soul will dare even death for truth's sake."

*I.* "I would dare death, I think, sooner than the responsibility of his words."

*T.* "Why did you not cry out and shout '*Amen*,' thou inhabitant of Zion?"

*I.* "It would have been Jonah's cry."

*T.* "When he entered the golden gate of heaven?"

*I.* "No; when in the recesses of the hell he pictures. Like the expatriated prophet, I was stifled, suffocated; and had I not soon escaped, would have cut my throat with a file."

*T.* "What heard you so disturbing?"

*I.* "After aiming the usual shafts against Christ, the Bible, and God himself, he was particularly eloquent in irony of prayer, — that divinest privilege of the soul, — against remorse or consciousness of sin, and finally against law. In this latter division of his theme, the man with his unhallowed lips dared to talk of woman and her rights."

*T.* "Good; that is what people of your set do every day with impunity, — and not only men, but women. I hope you are sufficiently gallant to be willing to accord to the sex those rights which many now claim?"

*I.* "Yes, when they claim to be women."

*T.* "You could not but like our true spiritual idea of woman's sphere, if you only understood it."

Israel now arose and began to walk the room in silence. At last, striking his forehead with his hand, he exclaimed, "Thou God of my mother! thou knowest I should fall dead under the axe of self-torture, were I to mistakenly link myself to one of these women who accepted this 'doctrine of devils!'"

*T.* "Would you not tolerate the right of ballot in your wife — that privilege now clamorously claimed?"

*I.* "I believe that a man in all ways should shield the companion of his life, with a sacred consciousness of his heaven-delegated right so to do, unutterably tender, yet with a fidelity to judicious purpose, which should be a quality of the 'sterner stuff' of his make. Whoso professes this, and through wilful negligence comes short, let him be anathema (I speak *ex cathedra*.) Grave yet sweet should be his recognition of her parallel existence. The picture to him will be the haloed Christ knocking at the door of his heart. The fact, a divine gift approaching his approach of providential circumstance. His compassion for this woman's faults will be unqualified with the hauteur of self-poise; his faithfulness to her needs bounded by a manly scope.

"But to marry a woman," continued Israel, "who asserts her right to go to the ballot; to think for me; to lead battles like Semiramis on an elephant, though of words; to allow herself and her good works, whatever they are, to be trumpeted about the world; and to go up and down seeking what conquests she can acquire, — would be, in short, like the attempt to make a bosom friend of the statue of Minerva in a public square."

*T.* "But what remains to do! The women are rushing that way. Much learning doth make them mad."

*I.* "I cannot accept your universal sweep. If it was so, I, for one, would put forth my utmost exertion to form a new society called the Young Men's Independent Union. The principal article of its constitution shall read — *We, the undersigned, do solemnly pledge ourselves not to knowingly marry a woman who is a modern Spiritualist, or who claims the right of elective franchise, or who believes in exhibiting herself to the public as a speaker or writer.*"

*T.* "Ha! Now you are forever lost in the regards of great souls! All the blue-stockings and their doughty esquires will be pelting your devoted head with their brickbat arguments, till you will not know your right hand from your left. It is woman's privilege to scold with tongue and pen, and at present she seems fully disposed to live up to it."

*I.* "Very well; there is one staff yet in our hands; nay, two staves. They cannot make us love nor wed them."

*T.* "As though they desired to! It is amusing to contemplate the amount of conceit which a man like you can carry about him! A lady Spiritualist would scorn your ghost; a voting lady would scarcely deign to extinguish you with the power of her ballot; and an authoress or speakeress would draw away her royal robe from the slightest contact with your ignoble presence."

*I.* "Remember, however, that I make a sharply defined distinction between the classes indicated. Not all lady writers or speakers are Spiritualists or would-be voters."

*T.* "You would not mind breaking your staff or staves in defence of the one class upon an emergency, I conclude, when the Spiritualists would have to suffer drowning because you declined an introduction for their rescue."

*I.* "I borrow the name of my staves from Holy Writ — Beauty and Bands. The Spiritualists do not recognize the Bible, consequently they would not me nor my staves."

*T.* "The classification of those ladies and you

should be rather Beauty and the Beast. I pity the woman whom you shall vouchsafe to endow with yourself."

*I.* "Possibly your emotion would be wasted." (Smiling).

*T.* "I am proud and happy to say that my wife shall be free — free as a butterfly among the flowers of a garden — free to think, to speak, to act. She shall vote, if she likes. She shall live and die without being fretted with my petty chains.

*I.* "Provided you find her. But it is one thing to talk of freedom — another to live in that state."

"Who talks here of freedom?" now interrupted a loud, hearty voice; "and what is the burden of this valley of vision?"

Israel recognized a man who, a few days before, had been announced to him as Captain Brewster. He had once followed the seas, but was now a retired gentleman, living upon his fortune.

"Pray, sir," said Thomaston, rising, hat in hand, "whose dog are you?"

"I wear no collar around my neck. I belong to the great universal family of man. God is my father. No man is my master. All men are my brothers for time and eternity. We shall all make one port at last."

"We have been talking upon religion in its various moral and social relations pertaining to our fellow men and women," said Thomaston; "will you join us and classify yourself?"

"I glory in my name — a Bible Universalist," said the captain.

"In some things we agree; in others, not. But both of us, I am sure, deny the existence of that imputed relative, Old Nick, who came from the northern sea-god Nicken; and we affirm, by paronomasia, that men are not fiends but friends, and that God is but another name for Good; hence his attributes must be all summed up in Love!" continued Thomaston.

"It is a pity that our young friend, Mr. Knight, (turning towards Israel.) is not more perfectly instructed in the way of God. He seems well-disposed, but —"

"Dreadfully be-knight-ed," added Thomaston; "suppose, captain, that you take him under your tuition awhile. I have been too clumsy, I think, to hammer his mind into the shape of a good horseshoe that will effectually keep off the devil."

"Most willingly, if by his own free act and deed," answered the captain.

"I have no objection to investigation," said Israel.

"Then hold yourself in readiness to go to my meeting next Sunday," said the captain.

"Certain I am," said Israel, "that I have not yet found the City."

"What city?" asked the captain.

"That with the precious name of which mention is made in the Bible as 'The Lord is there.'"

"We know that we have that name, for truly God is with us," said the Universalist.

# AMONG THE UNIVERSALISTS.

## CHAPTER I.

#### THE UNIVERSALIST SERMON.

The following Sunday, Israel was on his way with Capt. Brewster to attend the Universalist meeting. Another gentleman, who, though not of this faith, sometimes went to this church, accompanied them. His name was Ackerman.

This man said: "I can tell what 'our text' will prove this morning; at least, I should not be afraid to lay a heavy wager that it will be one of twelve verses, which twelve are headed off with, 'For as in Adam all die, even so in Christ shall all be made alive.' Then comes, 'That in the dispensation of the fulness of times, he might gather together in one all things in Christ;' next 'Who will have all men to be saved, and to come under the knowledge of the truth;' 'God shall wipe away all tears from off their faces,' and—"

"You forget," here interrupted Capt. Brewster, "that we now have a new minister. He is peculiar in treating old truths in a new way."

"Out of the Bible?" asked Ackerman.

"Yes," answered the captain, "our preacher is a Bible Christian, I am proud to say. He does not belong to the left wing of Universalism."

"Then you acknowledge two wings to your denomination?" said Israel.

"Certainly; our people, like all others in Christendom, have their Cagots," he said, good-humoredly.

"What is that?" asked Israel; "I do not comprehend."

"When I was in the south of France, I found a race of people who wore an egg-shell on their clothes, by way of distinction. I asked what it meant, and was told that it was a sign by which to know who were Cagots. In former ages they had been shunned as lepers; then it had got down to only an egg-shell."

"I have heard of its all lying in a nut-shell," said Ackerman.

"The difference," said the captain, "is as small as that, to appearance; but after all, they have the taint in the blood. There are those who cannot think as we do, in all points. It isn't in them."

"What is the difference at last?" asked Israel.

"Finally, none at all. He will reign till He has subdued all things. There are first and second fruits," answered the captain.

"You were not brought up a Universalist," here remarked Israel.

"How do you think that?" asked the captain.

"Because I know it must be so. You have the language of the mixed nation. Your parents, or guardians, or tutors, whoever they were that had your first years in training, were either Congregationalists or Baptists. By nature, you are what you are, which is not what you were by education."

"Guessed right, messmate. My father and mother

were Baptists — real hard-shells. They doubted the salvation which is not got out of the water. I expect that was one reason why I took to the sea."

They were now at the church. Israel noticed that the comers were in excellent spirits, to appearance. Every man greeted his neighbor, and all knew each other, from the least to the greatest. The ladies wore many bright colors, which generally were arranged with more reference to show than elegance. They greeted each other with voices which indicated a substantial breakfast, and he missed the subdued mouse of superior refinement running along their tones. Nothing was constrained, measured, fastened. On everything seemed written: "All things are yours, and ye are Christ's, and Christ is God's.'

They found their seats, as they would at a lecture on secular occasions; and one or two elderly men took out a political newspaper and read till the minister ascended the pulpit steps.

The minister was an intellectual looking man. Evidently he spent more hours in his library than in visiting or fishing. He had the cast of him who fashions his own mallet with which to beat the oil for the sanctuary. His commentator was not Hosea Ballou, nor Walter Balfour, nor Paige, but rather his own reflection.

His prayer was moderate in length and devout in spirit, offering all in the name of "the Great Mediator and the Adorable Saviour of all mankind." His text was *not* one of Ackerman's twelve standards. It was, "I press toward the mark for the prize of the high calling of God in Christ Jesus." (Phil. 3: 14.) Also this: "And he said, of a truth I say unto you, that this poor widow hath cast in more than they all." (Luke 21: 3.) From these words he derived his theme of PRIZES; the prize of the high calling and the prize of the low calling.

Israel made notes, which ran like this:—

"When men, like the ancient Greeks, went to the great national festivals with a spike of hyacinth blossoms at their ears, it was fitting that those festivals should award prizes. The old Alcibiades' shoes looked well stamping applause at the announcement of a favorite winner. The Grecian youth who delighted in his dancing dog, and the leading choragi in a robe of gold-colored silk, were at home in the work of struggling for prizes.

"The Christian teacher whose God was a wrathful Jupiter, dispensing smiles and frowns upon a system of debt and credit, rewards and punishments, found the scheme of visible prizes, both in this world and the next, serviceable to illustrate his heathen idea. It was a grand goad whereby people were driven to build up enormous denominational pyramids,— or monuments in which was the dead body of their king, an old defunct Idea. It was the part of a truly enlightened Christian to teach people another interpretation of the words of the text.

"That ambition was natural to the human soul, no observer, philosophical or common, could deny. You could not eradicate it — root it out. If you succeeded in crushing it down beyond the plane of activity, the man was no more a man. He was demented, robbed of his mind, of himself. There was no use in calling ambition a sin. The sin was in its development, its aims. Every sane man works for an end in view, a prize. The tendency of the age is to rapid extremes; hence great strife for what is called great prizes.

"The ambition of the people should be directed toward the prizes of the high calling. These were of the spirit, and not the matter; the substance, and not the shadow. Goodness should be loved for itself, and not for its name and sound, however profitable. The prize it holds out is for the degree of this love, the manner whereof it is followed, the spirit in which it is taken up and appropriated to the faith and life. Hence Christ awarded the glory to the poor widow who had cast into the treasury her all, rather than to the rich who had given of their substance.

"At present, the state of the public mind was unhealthy upon this subject; it was not normal. False stimulants of all kinds were doing their pernicious work in all grades of society and every scope of effort. The prize-fever upon the low calling gains ground with every year; and this not only in the lower stories of life, among half-cultured races, whose blood and bone are made from the pabulum of sensations, but in the star-chambers of religion and learning.

"Churches which claim perfection of creed and practice, churches which command all others to stand aside as less holy than themselves, which reckon themselves born under a covenant of Partial Grace while all outsiders are Pariahs to be stigmatized, prayed over and ground over, are now busiest of all in this unchristian and debasing work. So long as the business was confined to wrestling, rope-walking, foot-racing, and the like, in which those who strove for the mastery anointed with anserine oil before entering the lists, it had much less importance than now, when men with the odor of sanctity offer prizes for attainments in the curriculum, and also for the writing of tracts, pious tales in newspapers and in book form.

"These children of the light are borrowing wisdom from those whom they are accustomed to call the evil generation. The tricks of the evil generation pay. They are like the Hospitallers of Jerusalem, who bound themselves to refrain from touching the filthy lucre of the infidels, but were afterwards found owning castles and towns, and governing territory after the fashion of the most earthy of princes. While these good knights in their long gowns were ever burning a light at night that they might be prepared for the enemy, a subtler foe stole in among them, and ere they were aware, their hearts' citadel was captured by that power which they had solemnly abjured.

"In a catalogue of a New England college for this year, — a college wherein an avowed Universalist has no chance of the least degree of justice being given him, — you find, out of an attendance of less than two hundred and fifty students, thirty-six prizes are awarded.

"It is said, for a single institution of learning to offer a few prizes, or for a student in his curriculum of four years to compete now and then for a prize, is an insignificant matter. Besides good accrues in various directions.

"Nothing is insignificant which goes to make up

one man. That one man will help make other men; the men make community; and then come results. Those results react upon the man, and act upon him who comes after.

"A single polyp, building his little castle of calcareous matter in the ocean, seems but a trifling affair. But other polyps build around him, until a tribe of zoophytes are at work on a structure which becomes a giant tree blooming with a thousand flower-architects. The unwarned ship comes that way, strikes what is now the coral reef, sinks, and is lost. The specimen prize often cited as a good, is but a part of a formidable system, against which principle must be damaged, if not wholly lost.

"The tendency of this system of getting young men forward on the scale of the low calling, of which gambling is one of the series, is a development of the meanest class of moral qualities. The fiery brain of undisciplined youth is a good soil for these seeds of pride and envy to fructify therein and bear crops which shall curse themselves and others with a deadly poison.

"An intense selfism is the result of a system which secures the advancement of one individual to the deterioration of his fellows.

"What is less like God than the proud consciousness of the acknowledged possession of that which gives the individual priority! How does it violate the spirit of the divine command to love the Lord with all our heart and our neighbor as ourself! also, that he that is greatest should be as a servant! And yet it is entirely worthy of the doctrine which teaches that

God is a partial being, who punishes men to all eternity for — what? Not for ill-desert; for if so, then would their choicest members take an eternal prize of damnation for their deeds of injustice and wrong; but it is because the innocent child of Adam *does not believe as they do*, — he does not look through their microscope at the infinitely glorious God and His plan of salvation!

"It is worthy of the doctrine which teaches men to pray for the children of 'believers,' and forgets or condemns the sons of those whom they think are in bonds of iniquity; yet everybody has heard of the hopelessness of the ordinary run of orthodox ministers' sons and deacons' daughters.

"Not only does this system of low prizes react unfavorably upon the spiritual and moral character, but upon the intellectual as well. The student who aims at the premium cannot afford to indulge in thorough and, comparatively speaking, exhaustive investigation. The rules of this race-course do not tolerate originality. There can be no independent thought nor deviating experiments — no divine silence of the mind, in which descend the inspirations of invisible teachers and the restful music of interminable spheres. Original demonstrations which do not belong to the common proscribed track are counted an unsightly freak, to be cast aside, as the unlearned eye sees the growth of seeds on the back of certain leaves, when they are the perfect result of a perfect law — the epiphyllospermous.

"The student may really know twice as much as another, of the spirit of a passage in the classics, or of the philosophy of a mathematical problem, and yet report himself so poorly as to take the lowest figure of the scale, while the other student seizes the words and the formula by the means of a parrot memory, and victoriously wins the prize. Hence, it so often occurs that prizes are unjustly awarded, and that these prize-students, in after life, make so poor a figure as practical and useful men.

"Again, it often appears that one of these zealously affected toilers falls by the way before reaching the goal. His clergyman then says 'his bounds were set,' but his physician pronounces it a case of excessive excitement of the brain. For years before, his fond parents had been setting before him all sorts of false stimuli. He had been prize boy at the preparatory schools, and earlier, in the infant classes, a winner of numberless 'rewards of merit.' One of the signal triumphs of his early career was a prize in the Sunday school for repeating the greatest number of verses from the Bible and pious hymns.

"The system of prizes on the low scale is aptly illustrated in various ways connected with popular life, but in none more forcibly than the regattas of the boating clubs of colleges. Men who condemn horse-racing and betting will frequent this spectacle and show an interest worthy of a nobler race. Censors of the religious press who deftly peck away at the follies of the times, and particularly at those of other religious denominations, get complaisant over these fashionable water gambling arenas, and are profoundly silent about the 'little peccadilloes' which transpire as a sequel to the exciting dissipation."

(Here the speaker expatiated largely, but as I was one of them at college, I don't transcribe.)

"We test the working of this system of prizes in the diffusion of moral influence and religious knowledge. Where prizes are offered, fewer books are issued, and these at a more expensive rate for the buyer. Often it appears that the book which most pleased the awarding committee was really not so good as several of the competing works. This is true, also, of the prize newspaper story. But the sensations which attend the issue of the superior work, as they would make it appear, are expected to indemnify the publisher for his extra expense in proclaiming them.

"It is like the early times of the art of gunnery, when the size of the ball was the main object to which engineers addressed themselves. Marble bullets of from one hundred and fifty to two hundred pounds weight were fired in these big guns but once in each day, and if they hit the mark (which they rarely did) their work was signally devastating. The consolation for a miss of the mark was a tremendous noise!

"The quality of the book must be, according to order, commonplace enough. You must not spin glass, but yarn, for glass is 'highfalutin' and yarn is useful and sensible. A touch of erudition is fatal as, according to the ancients, was that of a kingfisher to a bush. What the 'committee' do not know must be instantly extinguished. The story must be truth, and yet representing real life about as much as does the 'roc's egg' interpret Wesleyan '*lay representation.*'

"The moral must be good, albeit carefully noncommittal on all subjects which touch the committee's taste or habits.

"The true dignity of the Christian church forbids resort to such enginery as prizes of this stamp. These bounty moneys for books and tractates carry us back to the days of the sale of indulgences, and the barter of the feathers of a certain bird as a safeguard against thunder and family quarrels. Although the tendency of the times is for prizes of all sorts, the church should be clean from this corruption. The leading conservators of her morals should not enter the indecorous lists. The youth who are trained to think themselves better than others because nurtured in peculiar forms and ceremonies, from such examples and tuition derive encouragement to pursue gaming and a career of the most debasing character. What is learned under the green tree will be practised on a more liberal scale under the dry.

"Jupiter was wise to save the horn of the goat which he nursed; afterwards it became to him 'a horn of plenty.' The child that is nursed on church grab-bags, fish-ponds, guess-cakes, and wheels of fortune, with all the other nameless appliances of these fairs for pious purposes, will save that in his soul which will mature into a greed nothing can satisfy. His hand, ever outstretched for the horn of plenty, will grasp only the little end, while the other will empty its fabulous treasures into the unsightly abysm of his false ambition. Unhappiness, born of unrest and disappointment, is his sure portion."

(Much more in this strain did the preacher say, when he announced the final portion of his text: "Of a truth I say unto you, that this poor widow hath cast in more than they all.")

"The poor widow found a prize in a sense of having received the divine approval. She had done what she could in a spirit of simplicity, truth, and unbounded faith. For it is certain that she must have had this faith, else she would not have cast in her all. A sense of the infinite goodness filled the vacuum in her soul created by poverty. She knew that He who careth for the sparrows would not forget one who was destined to be an heir of immortality. This woman was truly happy. My hearers, had she not found a prize even in this world — one which the man with his millions knows not of?

"The prize of riches is not to be despised, if accompanied by a spirit like that which this woman had — simplicity, truth, faith. Said Confucius: 'The man to whom God hath given riches, and blessed with a mind to employ them aright, is peculiarly favored and highly distinguished.'

"It should be always our care to both learn and teach that lesson in the work of creation. 'And God saw everything that He had made, and behold it was very good.' The commonest things may be exalted into prizes, when the heart sees in them what certain men of old time found written on every leaf and flower — the name of God!

"Every heart may prove a nest of singing birds if swung in the branches of infinite love.

"Angels are ever our guests — the highest and purest in those hearts which love most.

"Existence itself is a prize, though we, who love not, but hate much, are blind.

"The consciousness that we were born with a destiny which is to be evolved in the presence of heavenly hosts, should ever wrap our spirits in a delicious content, so that it will signify not much whether our earthly feet are shod with golden sandals, and walk the streets of towns, or thrid the green lanes of quiet hamlets with shoes so worn and clumsy we cannot but feel the prick of thorns.

"The scale on which God distributes prizes, equalizes fortune in reality. A man should remember that his lot, whether full or scant, like the city which was measured by the golden reed, has 'length as large as the breadth, and the height of it is also equal,' here or there, in this life or the next."

Yet other words in this strain did the preacher utter that morning; but these were all which were entered in the note-book, except the very last, which were these: "Friends, like the apostle, press forward towards the mark for the prize of the high calling. Like the poor widow, cast in your all, which is love. This alone is substance and life. Whatever is done in any other spirit is worthless. Whatever is done to be seen of men, and to obtain their poor, ephemeral rewards, impoverishes the soul, and retards your preparation for eternal felicity. With the prize of your high calling in view, all work shall be glorified, all aims shall be sanctified. Every man will be your neighbor, your brother, whom you would no more injure designedly than you would injure yourself. Nay, you will strive in all ways to help him to press forward toward the mark for the prize of the high calling of God in Christ Jesus."

After the service, conversation began in the vestibule. Israel heard such fragments as these: "Our minister is a fearless man, and I am glad of it."

"Yes, he said things to-day which no one in this city will dare say in the public desk."

"I don't agree with him in all the particulars, but I honor a man for stating his honest convictions in an honorable manner," spoke the gruff voice of a man whom Israel recognized as one of the city government.

"We must look out for our fairs," was the soft whisper of a young lady to her friend, who replied, "I don't care; I think there is real fun in a guess-cake. I got the ring once, and I don't think I am any the worse for it."

"Nor I," here interposed one with a mustache, who had been listening unperceived, "for I got a colored lady out of a grab-bag, myself; and I have been popularly in love with those ladies ever since."

"Well, young man," said Captain Brewster, as they reached the clear sidewalk, "what d'ye think of the sermon?"

"Is it a specimen of what you hear in your pulpit regularly?" asked Israel in reply.

"I told you he was a little peculiar, you will remember; but we get much the same from him always."

"I wish to take time for my answer to your question," said Israel; "he crossed many of my 'established opinions' most slashingly."

"I thought as much. Queer, that he preached about prizes to-day, when you happened to be there. Better go again this afternoon, and see what you will get."

"I think I will," responded Israel.

## CHAPTER II.

#### CONVERSATION WITH A UNIVERSALIST.

THAT day Israel dined with Captain Brewster. The conversation naturally turned upon Universalism. Israel inquired if the denomination acknowledged any particular creed. The captain replied, "We have what is called the Winchester Confession. In 1803, a committee composed of four leading Universalists prepared for the annual convention which met at Winchester, New Hampshire, certain articles of belief, which to this day are reckoned the standard ground of our church theology. The reason of giving out a formula of doctrine at that time, I must not omit to tell you, as it furnishes an interesting item in our history. The Supreme Court of New Hampshire decreed that Universalists and Congregationalists were one, in law, in order to get a tax out of the Universalists for the support of Congregational parishes. So they announced themselves in a fashion which they intended should either make a breach, or clear away all but the breach. This was the 'Profession of Belief,'" he continued, on opening a book which he took down from his library : —

"'1. We believe that the Holy Scriptures of the Old and New Testaments contain a revelation of the character of God, and of the duty, interest, and *final* destination of mankind.

"'2. We believe there is one God, whose nature is love, revealed in one Lord Jesus Christ, by one Holy Spirit of Grace; who will finally restore the whole family of mankind to holiness and happiness.

"'3. We believe that holiness and true happiness are inseparably connected; and that believers ought to maintain order and practise good works; for these things are good and profitable unto men.'"

"There was no danger of the Universalists being identified with the Congregationalists, after that," said Israel.

"I should think not. What think you of such a creed?" asked the captain.

"It is not clear to me what value is attached to the mission of the Lord Jesus Christ."

"The words are plain —"

"If so, why then are Universalists divided in their opinions upon this point? Some of them with whom I have conversed speak of him as a man who lived a very good life, but not more a mediator or atoning sacrifice for the sins of mankind than was Seneca, Confucius, or Peter. Others of whom I have read are quite orthodox in their idea of the atonement. In the library which was left me by my father I found a collection of hymn books used by the different denominations. Among these is one which was 'selected and designed for the use of the Independent Christian Church, of Gloucester'— the church of the earliest American Universalists. It was printed in 1808. Nearly every hymn of this collection has some reference to Christ as the Son of God, who was the Mediator and is the Saviour of mankind. They are hymns which, for pure doctrine upon the character and mission of Christ, the straitest member of the strictest sect would not censure. Many of those whom the Universalists claim as their particular lights have been orthodox on the doctrine of the Atonement."

"Mr. Ballou has written a work on the Atonement, which I wish you to read," said the captain, taking down another book.

"May I ask the nature of his views?" said Israel.

"It is hardly doing justice to any work on theology, to select only specimen pages," he replied; "yet I will read a little on 'Atonement in its Nature,'—a small portion of Ballou's Treatise upon the Atonement:—

"'I have already observed, that atonement and reconciliation are the same. Reconciliation is a renewal of love, and love is the law of the spirit of life in Christ Jesus, of which St. Paul speaks in Romans 7: 2, by which he was made free from the law of sin. The soul, when governed by the law of sin which is in the members, of which St. Paul speaks in Romans 7: 23, is in a state of unreconciliation to the law of the spirit. And it is by the force and power of the law of love in Christ, that the soul is delivered from the government of the law of sin; the process of this deliverance is the work of atonement or reconciliation.

"'The reader will now see, with ease, that that power which causes us to hate sin, and love holiness, is the power of Christ, whereby atonement is made. All the law and the prophets rested on this spirit of love, by which alone they can be fulfilled. This eternal spirit of love is the *word* or *logos*, which was, in the beginning, with God, and was God, which was hidden behind the letter of the law, and in the cabalistic allegories of the prophets, until it brake forth in the official character of Jesus, and rent the vail of the temple from top to bottom. Our Saviour, in his official character, is always called by the name or names, which is, or are, applicable to God, manifest in the *flesh*, which figuratively means the *letter* of the law; this circumstance will fully account for all the Scriptures which my opponent would urge in support of Jesus being essentially God.

"'Christ came not to destroy the law and the prophets, but to fulfil them; the law is as far fulfilled in the soul, as it is brought to love God, in his adorable image, Jesus; and a complete fulfilment of the law and the prophets will effect love in every soul, on whom the law, in a moral sense, is binding.

"'Let it be asked, by what means are we brought to love God? Answer: "We love him, because he first loved us." God's love to us is antecedent to our love to him, which refutes the notion of God's receiving the atonement; but the idea, that the manifestation of God's love to us, causes us to love him, and brings us to a renewal of love, (in which spirit we all stood, in our spiritual head, Jesus, before formation; and from which we in a certain sense elapsed, after being made subject to vanity) is perfectly consonant to the necessity of atonement; it shows us what atonement is, and the power which the Mediator must have and exercise, in order to reconcile all things to God.' \* \* \*

"Again he says: 'Christians have for a long time believed that the temporal death of Christ made an atonement for sin, and that the literal blood of the man who was crucified has efficacy to cleanse from guilt; but surely this is carnality, and carnal mindedness, if I have any knowledge of the apostle's meaning, where he says, "To be carnally minded is death." The letter killeth, but the spirit giveth life. The apostles were made able ministers of the New Testament, not of the letter, but of the spirit. Christ saith, "except ye eat my flesh, and drink my blood, ye have no life in you." Must we understand this in a literal sense? If we do, how shall we understand what he further says of this matter? "The flesh profiteth nothing; the words which I speak, they are spirit and they are life."

"'The apostasy of the Jews happened in consequence of the lips of the priests not preserving knowledge; they fell from the spirit of the law, were lost in the wilderness of the letter, and therefore were blinded indeed. This was a figure of the more dreadful apostasy of Christians, as were various circumstances recorded in the Old Testament. The Christian apostasy happened in the same way; and the church has been led into the wilderness of the letter by an hireling priesthood, who knew nothing of the spirit of the law; who have preached, in the name of the Lord, the *letter* which *killeth*, in room of the *spirit* which giveth *life*.

"'The literal death of the man Christ Jesus is figurative; and all the life we obtain by it, is by learning what it represented. The literal body of Jesus represented the whole letter of the law, with all the allegories contained in the word of prophecy. The death of the body of Jesus represented the death and destruction of the letter, when the spirit comes forth, bursting the veil thereof, which is represented by the resurrection of Jesus from the dead. Agreeably to this, the reader will understand all the sacrifices, under the law, by which the high priests entered within the veil.

"'Being thus enabled to pass from the letter to the spirit, we see what death it is which is the proper sacrifice for sin, and what blood it is that cleanses from guilt. The blood is said to be the life; it is therefore the spirit or life of the law which does away sin, and gives life to the soul.

"'I am sensible there are thousands who profess Christianity, who are blind enough to object and say, "Then the Gospel has nothing to do in the salvation of mankind." But suffer me to say, the Gospel is nothing but the spirit of the law, which is the word, or *logos*, spoken in the law, brought forth from the shadows of the first dispensation. To believe in any other atonement than the putting off the old man, with his deeds, and the putting on of the new man, which, after God, is created in righteousness and true holiness, is carnal mindedness and death.'"

"I see now," commented Israel, "the view of the atonement as held by at least one Universalist. It strikes me that the spirit of the great atoning sacrifice for sin, as apparent from the plainest reading of the New Testament, is pretty well killed out of this explanation of the letter."

"His theory makes me think of the griffin of the ancients," he continued, "which was part eagle and part lion. The wings and beak indicate capacity for a flight into celestial regions, but it is held down by the lion. The creature must work himself out of the wilderness of sin by means of his carnality alone; the eagle part of the atonement serves only as an ornament or mere impetus in the work. In other words, the Christ of Ballou's atonement does not rescue the sinful man, or work in any more efficacious way than as a present adornment of the scheme and an animating principle in its execution. After all, the lion does the work. It is the man who moves."

"Is that not rational?" said the captain, "if you leave all the work of redemption to either the eagle or lion alone and singly, it is inconsistent with reason and revelation. I like your figure. Without the eagle, the creature would be but a beast which could never fly heavenward. With that royal bird, it finally is enabled to plume itself for an immortal flight. The scheme which leaves all the work to the eagle is most dangerous, in my view."

"Did Mr. Ballou believe in any punishment after death?" now asked Israel.

"Upon this I will quote his words from another of his books, entitled 'Notes on the Parables.'

"'St. Paul says, "As in Adam all die, even so in Christ shall all be made alive." And he is particular in stating the constitution which all men will receive in the resurrection of which he speaks. * * * He makes no distinction. He says nothing of the good works of some and the evil works of others. His testimony is, in fact, directly against any distinction or difference in that immortal state; *all* are made alive in Christ, and as this life is spiritual, incorruptible and immortal, this testimony agrees with the testimony of Jesus to the Sadducees on the same subject of the resurrection, in which he says that in the resurrection they are the children of God, equal unto the angels, and can die no more. In this debate with the Sadduces, Jesus gave no intimation that any would rise from the dead to a state of condemnation, but was particular in saying that *all* live unto him.'"

"But do all the standard Universalists agree with Mr. Ballou upon this point?" continued Israel.

"No, they do not. Some believe in a limited punishment after death. Some reject the word 'punishment,' and interpret the same idea by such words as 'the necessary consequences of sin.' In 1827, our people were considerably agitated upon this question, and for a time there was an apparent division into Impartialists and Restorationists. Of these latter, the Reverend Paul Dean wrote thus: 'The Restorationists maintain that a just retribution does not take place in time; that the conscience of the sinner becomes callous, and does not increase in the severity of its reprovings with the increase of guilt; that men are invited to act with reference to a future life; that if all are made perfectly happy at the commencement of the next state of existence, they are nor rewarded according to their deeds; that if death introduces them into heaven, they are saved by death, and not by Christ; and if they are made happy by being raised from the dead, they are saved by physical, and not by moral means, and made happy without their agency or consent; that such a sentiment weakens the motives to virtue, and gives force to the temptations of vice; that it is unreasonable in itself, and opposed to many passages of Scripture."

"James Kelly of England," continued the captain, "whose disciple was Mr. Murray, the first Universalist preacher in America, believed that there would be 'a resurrection to life, and a resurrection to condemnation — that believers only will be among the former who, as first fruits, and kings and priests, will have part in the first resurrection, and shall reign with Christ in his kingdom of the Millennium; that unbelievers who are raised after, must wait the manifestation of the Saviour of the world — under that condemnation of conscience which a mind in darkness and wrath must necessarily feel; that ultimately every knee shall bow — and every tongue confess,' etc. etc."

"As there seems to be a diversity of opinion upon essential points of doctrine, I should think it would be difficult to know who should truly be called a Universalist, or who they may cast out as heretical from among themselves," remarked Israel.

"Of this, let me read you from Whittemore's 'Plain Guide,'" said the captain.

"'There has been some discussion within a few years past, on the appellation *Universalist*. The question seems to have been, whether this word ought to be applied to all who believe in the eventual restoration of all mankind, or only to a particular class of them. On this subject we have never had but one opinion, and that opinion we have frequently expressed, namely: *that all persons, who truly believe in the eventual salvation of all mankind by the grace of the Lord Jesus Christ, are Universalists.* This is the rule laid down in the modern history of Universalism. For instance, Richard Coppin and Jeremy White, who both flourished in the time of Cromwell, are put down in that work as Universalists, although they differed much in opinion on minor points; the latter being a Trinitarian, and a believer in future punishment, the former discarding that doctrine.'"

"I like that definition of Whittemore's," said Israel; "all persons who truly believe in the eventual salvation of all mankind, *by the grace of the Lord Jesus Christ*, are Universalists. The more you strike out 'the grace of the Lord Jesus Christ,' as found in the Revealed Word, the more you lose your glory and your power."

"So think I," responded the captain; "as a denomination, or as individuals, we have a transient pretence of a power, if we look only to ourselves. I rejoice in every effort which is put forth by our faithful watchmen on the forecastle of the good ship of our Zion, to keep the doctrines pure. I will be one to contend earnestly for the faith once delivered to the saints. If there are any who sail under our colors, who believe not in this Gospel, let them go out from us and enter the service after their own heart. The sea is broad and free to all."

"Do you believe in any punishment subsequent to death?" asked Israel.

"I do; but my idea is that no punishment inflicted by God is vindictive, but corrective. It is intended only for the good of the erring, and not to appease His wrath. I confess that those words, 'the wrath of God,' smite one with shame that an intelligent being of this enlightened age can ever consent to use them. How unworthy the divine character!"

"But we must not be wise above that which is written," said Israel; "you remember that there is much in the Bible, the New Testament as well as the Old, which shows the possibility of the literal sense of such words."

"Not when we compare Scripture with Scripture, and rightly understand the context. Many such an expression is a Hebraism or Grecism."

"This last interpretation of yours is a convenient subterfuge for a multitude of troublesome passages," said Israel, with a smile.

"You should read our standard authors, and learn from them an explanation of the apparently difficult places."

"To whom do you refer the origin of Universalism — to Niel Douglass of Glasgow, who prayed to God for the devil, as 'his ancient servant,' or to Kelly?" continued Israel.

"Now you are far astray of the mark," answered the captain; "the first Universalists after Christ and his apostles, of whom we have any distinct account, were Clemens Alexandrinus, president of the Catechetical School of Theology and Philosophy at Alexandria, Egypt, and Origen, who is called the greatest scholar of the early church. It is said that he wrote six thousand volumes."

"I now remember," here interposed Israel, "that Origen left on record these words respecting the doctrine of the final salvation of all men: '*The sentiment ought to be kept secret among such as may be fit to receive it, and not publicly exposed.*' You will find this in 'Marsh's Ecclesiastical History.'"

"Is that so?" said the captain.

"It is; and I think Origen was a man of good sense and keen perception. If I were a believer in the doctrine, I would not let my left hand know of it. It can do no good, and may do infinite evil, if untrue. Yet I have no doubt that many benevolent, large-hearted apostles of the orthodox churches secretly believe it, or at least devoutly hope it may be true. It is, however, a faith hidden at the bottom of the well of their hearts. There are more Universalists, according to Mr. Whittemore's definition, than the world will ever dream of."

"I do not consent to your statement that the promulgation of the truth can do no good. In the first place, it does a man's own soul good to be perfectly honest and open. Candor is the fructifying dew of heaven, which enriches the soil of the heart; while the opposite contracts and exhausts its powers and graces. The law of giving is increase. The exercise which brings expansion multiplies capacity and resource. Not only does it benefit one's self, but it blesses others, to preach this truth which brings a glorious immortality to light, through our Lord and Saviour. It lifts the natural veil of darkness which surrounds man, and affords him cheering glimpses of his coming, immortal destiny — cheering indeed are they, amidst the trials and privations of this sin-stricken state of existence. With this view men are saved from religious despondency, blighting infidelity, and atheism."

"Perhaps you are right," said Israel; "yet I think there is danger of crying peace at a fearful risk."

"Not when you believe that every man shall be judged after death, according to his works," said the captain. "In addition to these names," he went on, "I must not omit to mention among the fathers of Universalism, Titus, Bishop of Bostra, Gregory Nyssen, Evagrius Ponticus, Didymus the Blind, president of the Alexandrian School, Theodorus, Bishop of Mopsuestia, and others of the fathers. Universalism was condemned at celebrated councils, which proves that it continued to flourish. In 1660, appeared Jeremy White, chaplain of Cromwell, who published his 'Restitution of All Things.' Archbishop Tillotson, Dr. Burnet, and William Whiston were Universalists. So was the German philosopher, Kant."

"A German philosopher never stops at Christian Universalism," said Israel.

"Petitpierre's 'Treatise on the Divine Goodness,' was first published at Amsterdam, Holland," he continued.

"There is the bell for church," exclaimed Israel.

"Yes; so for the present, our conversation must be suspended," the captain concluded.

# CHAPTER III.

#### SECOND SERMON.

The minister arose and announced his text to be "*He hath no hands.*" Is. 45: 9. These words are found in this connective reading — "Woe unto him that striveth with his Maker! Let the potsherd strive with the potsherds of the earth. Shall the clay say to him that fashioneth it, What makest thou! or thy work, He hath no hands?"

Israel made a few notes, which ran in this wise: —

"The ministry of Universalism is specially the ministry of reconciliation — reconciliation of man to his Maker, and not of the Maker to his creature, man. The first idea was worthy of the most exalted character of God, — as the Creator and Sovereign; the other idea fitted those whom the inspired writer had likened to a potsherd of the earth, or a fragment of a broken earthen vessel.

"Addison mentions in his travels in Italy, the republic of Lucca, which has the word *Libertas* in letters of gold over the only gate of the city. The whole administration of government at that period passed into different hands every two months. This was like those people who, in their views and corresponding actions, give out that God rules one day and they the next; changing about the administration of the affairs of the world with every other moon. In some things they allow a divine oversight which virtually amounts to government; in others, they and their fellows are all and in all. This is Liberty in golden letters over the gateway of their souls!

"God either rules or He does not. Man likewise is a sovereign, or he is not. He cannot be God unless he does rule, and is the alpha and omega of power. Any other idea at once sinks his nature and attributes to a level beneath even that occupied by man. If God rules as a sovereign, all things pertaining to his plan of government are absolutely right, perfect, infinitely good. Whatever appears to the contrary, is the fault of him that striveth with his Maker. For God to rule and yet man be free, is wholly inconsistent.

\* \* \* \* \* \*

"There are many in the Christian world who believe that God created all men for salvation; that He is willing that they should be saved, and has provided a way whereby they may be saved. But his creature, man, is able to refuse this salvation, go utterly out of this way, and be finally lost. In support of this theory they adduce the testimony of all ages, which they claim cannot be broken, viz: the lives of bad men, reprobates, those who create only evil, and that continually. Of any one of these men they use language which may be figuratively translated into the simple sentence, '*He hath no hands.*' That is, there is no developed power in him to do anything fitting and right. The word *hands*, as used here, I take to proceed from a root (this preacher, though furnished from all the schools, never used a Greek or Latin word in his pulpit) signifying to be strong, straight, right; which would give the sense of fitness and beauty. This is one of the definitions of a standard lexicographer. He hath no power to do that which is straight, right, and beautiful; or if, having the power, it is dead, and hence the same as no power. He hath no hands.

"These, say they, are the bad men who, like their arch prototype, go to and fro on the earth, seeking whom they may devour, breaking into the houses of innocent citizens, despoiling men of their goods, leading astray the unwary, thirsting for blood, and performing all those numerous deeds which, if exposed and adjudged, send the performers to the gallows or the place of confinement. These are also the bad men who believe and teach false doctrines.

"These are, also, they affirm, the men who do not join 'our church,' nor walk on our plank, and refuse openly and boldly to acknowledge fraternity with those who walk on any other. These all are they who have no hands; the one class as well as the other; they do nothing straight, right, and beautiful; or if they do accomplish that which seems to have some right to be so called, it is all filthy rags. All of them deserve the vengeance of eternal damnation; and all of them are sure to get this just reward of their works.

"Certainly, we may here pause to consider that the orthodox hell is a curious place, inhabited by such a variety of elements. It almost matches for curiosity the orthodox heaven, which is composed of all sorts of persons who, in this life, were illustrations of profound convictions of the utility of selfishness, crime, and unbelief.

"'How can these men who have no hands,' cries the Calvinist, 'be finally saved, after a life of such unqualified depravity, superadded to which is the most heinous unbelief in the only true way of salvation! They have neither works nor faith.' And every one of these exclaimers has some example to thrust before your eyes as an incontrovertible evidence of their proposition — some terrible image of depravity in human shape — some dragon of iniquity, the rehearsal of whose career is enough to make the blood curdle in your veins.

"Here, my hearers, I invite you to let the anthem of divinest praise go up from your hearts, that God, the Maker of heaven and earth, seeth not as man seeth! Praise God! let all the people praise His great and holy name!

(A deep, serious voice in the congregation responded *Amen*.)

"Cain is more to be pitied than Abel, because he had a distorted getting-up — a deformed spiritual, mental, and moral organization. We say not this to complain or strive with his Maker — shall the clay say to him that fashioneth it, What makest thou? or thy work, He hath no hands? This also was for the glory of God. Cain was not made for any other purpose. To believe that God made him for endless woe, is the most daring impiety. 'Who hath declared this from ancient time? who hath told it from that time I have not I the Lord? and there is no God else besides me, a *just God and a Saviour!*'

"The venomous snake of the recesses of the northern rocks, the slimy reptiles of the dank ravines of the tropical lands, the grim alligators basking in the waters under the tree trunks which can scarcely be distinguished from the gigantic boa constrictor that winds around them — these all are His works. These all are creatures of that creation which God called very good, alike with the bird of most beauteous plumage or of the sweetest voice, — alike with the white-robed, peaceful lamb, or the patient and useful beast of burden. A divine purpose is answered by the fierce lion of Bilidulgerid, the leopard from Hindostan, the unicorn from Thibet, the rhinoceros and river-horse from Senegal, the antelope from the Zaara, the reindeer from polar latitudes, the elephant from Ceylon or Siam, the ibex of Angora, the bison, buffalo, the camelopard, the quagga, the zebra, and chamois. These, too, with others, may be said to be representative of various tribes and peoples of the earth, of whom it is written: 'Look unto me and be ye saved all ye ends of the earth!' In that glorious day, 'The wolf also shall dwell with the lamb, and the leopard shall lie down with the kid; and the calf and the young lion and the fatling together; and a little child shall lead them. And the cow and the bear shall feed; their young ones shall lie down together: and the lion shall eat straw like the ox. * * They shall not hurt nor destroy in all my holy mountain: for the earth shall be full of the knowledge of the Lord, as the waters cover the sea.'

"In wisdom hast thou made them all, O my God! Do you wonder that the saint Chrysostom was called in all history, '*the golden-mouthed!*' For it was he who was accustomed to say, 'Praise God for all things!' He saw nothing which had no hands!

"My hearers, I tested this glorious view of mankind, fallen man, in my boyhood. Suffer the word of narration for an interlude. I used to recite some of my preparatory lessons in the classics to a clergyman, who, I believe was the most Christ-like in his thinking and doing of any man I ever knew. I was with him in his study, and he had been pausing to recite a passage in the life of Christ, one peaceful day of the decline of summer, when our attention was arrested by rude noises in the street below, accompanied by a volley of oaths which made one shudder. We looked from the window. There stood a man, his grey hairs falling down upon his threadbare coat, his eyes flashing an almost unearthly fire, while his hands clenched a bottle. Several boys were endeavoring to get it from him. My teacher opened the shutter, and called out. One of the boys said, 'It is only that old brute (calling the name of a notorious man of that town). He wants his bottle so as to beat his wife, and starve his children again.' The wretched man looked at them, then looked up to our window. He saw the well-known face of the clergyman, and raising his clenched fist, shook it towards him while he screeched out '*Go to hell!*'

"My friend went quickly down. I next saw him in the street with his hand upon the arm of the wretched man. Then he led him within, where I found them in the grandest room of the house, the drunkard in a luxuriant chair near the centre of the floor, my friend walking up and down, without speaking. The drunk-

and trembled like a leaf, as he sat there, muttering and moaning by turns. At length the good man went up to the wretched wanderer, and said in his own low and compassionate voice, 'Brother!' 'Going after an officer, I suppose,' was the response, as he ventured to cast up a stealthy, fiery glance. 'No, I cannot accuse my brother, however much he may deserve it. Thou art a broken vessel, but what am I, that it is not as well with you as with me! God made you. God is our Father. His name is also Love.'

"'No, it is not,' said the poor man, with an oath, 'else he would not have let me come to *this!*' Then he went on to tell how he was once the son of respectable parents, how he grew up, by dint of much striving, a temperate and honest youth. The strife was often terrible, for his mother had thirsted for liquor before he was born. But it did not get the mastery till, during a severe sickness, his physician held the draught to his feverish lips. He took it, day after day, according to direction, till he was lost.

"'Since then,' said he 'twice have I been in the house of correction; once, a term of three years, in the penitentiary of Columbus, Ohio, and once in a lunatic asylum of Massachusetts. What have I not suffered and what have not others suffered on my account!'

"The good man listened; there were tears in his eyes; he only said, 'Poor man! thanks be to God that he has provided a place of purification.' The other thought he alluded to the house of correction, and said as much with an oath of defiance.

"'No,' said my friend, 'I was thinking of heaven, your own home!

"'Heaven! what have I to do with that place! I have been damned to hell more than a million times. I have bought up stock in that company, years ago!' The poor fellow actually laughed.

"'He shall let go my captives, not for price nor reward, saith the Lord of hosts,' repeated the clergyman, as to himself.

"The poor man stayed in that house for days, during which time he was used like a brother indeed. Words of love, of an almost maternal tenderness, were spoken to him. Prayer was offered without ceasing in his behalf, and yet he was not worried with prayer, nor with advice. When he went out again from that door, he was clothed anew and partially sane. Money was furnished him with which to go to a distant city. He went, provided with a letter of introduction to an estimable and truly benevolent man, written by the clergyman's own hand.

"For some time, nothing was heard from him. At the expiration of about four years, a gentleman called to see my friend, the clergyman. He was unrecognized; but it was the once wretched drunkard. He had come to tell his benefactor how much he owed to his instrumentality. 'That day when you took me in, poor wretch that I was — was the day of my new birth!' he said, 'but I never broke down till you *spoke of its being possible for me to go to heaven.* When you called it my home, my own home, I began to think out of another heart. I seemed to be somebody else beside the outcast I had been. All at once, I said to myself, "If I am going to heaven, I must fix up myself or I shall be ashamed when I get *there.*

But I tell you as long as I believed that I was going to hell, I didn't care to behave any other way than the worst, for that was good enough for such a home as I was going to. Then, after a day or two, God did not look to me as He used to. I did not hate His name as I had done. It appeared to me if He had made such a man as yourself, sir, who could *pity me*, that His own Son certainly would not turn me off. Then I loved the Lord Jesus Christ, and he seemed to lay His hand on my head just when you did as I sat there in your room, one night. After that, I felt willing to go to heaven, though I knew I wasn't fit at all!'

"My hearers! that man afterwards became a citizen of usefulness and honor. I knew when he died. Good people mourned for him, and the poor bewailed his loss — for he had learned to pity them. His love was great, for he had been forgiven much. Think you that clergyman who saw in the poor outcast, a brother who should one day heir a glorious immortality — a child of God of whom it could not, it should not be said, 'He hath no hands! but rather '*He hath hands*'— hands which are capable of a work, straight, right, and beautiful, hands which shall one day write the blessed name of Immanuel upon hearts of his stricken fellow-man, — think you he could not say ' In the Lord have I righteousness and strength. In His word do I hope, for his promises are Yea and Amen in Christ Jesus!'

"Yes friends, even to Him shall men come, and all that are incensed against him shall be ashamed. All that say of any of His creatures, however sin-stricken. 'He hath no hands,' shall be ashamed. All that despise the lowest, the meanest, the most apparently worthless of God's creatures, shall be ashamed. They shall call on the rocks to cover their confusion in that day of power when every knee shall bow, and every tongue shall confess to the glory of God!

"Do you ask me, 'What will become of those wretched souls who do not repent in this life, who multiply their transgressions to their latest breath?' You will observe in a few verses preceding my text, that it reads, 'That they may know from the rising of the sun, and from the west, that there is none besides me. I am the Lord and there is none else!' This I take to be a beautiful illustration of the truth of the boundless provision for man's redemption from ignorance and idolatry of false gods, or evil passions. Some will be led to acknowledge Him in the land where the sun rises, or in the early portion of their existence — in this life; while others will not confess him till they reach the west — that is the world beyond which the sun of this life goes down — the continuation of the endless existence.

"There Christ preaches unto the spirits who are in prisons of ignorance, misconception, and sin. He opens the door of their souls, and sets his captives free, without price or reward. I remember being greatly impressed, in my youth, by reading of the return of a celebrated conqueror, to one of the continental cities, where the inhabitants exhibited their joy by holding up birds in cages, and giving them their liberty as he passed in triumphal procession! But what is this to that release of the captive children of men from their cages of sin and blindness of mind, in honor of the victorious march of Him who is described in the vision of the apocalypse: 'And I saw, and behold a white horse: and he that sat on him had a bow; and a crown was given unto him: and he went forth conquering and to conquer!

> 'Hosanna to our conquering King,
>   All hail, incarnate love!
> Ten thousand songs and glories wait
>   To crown thy head above!
>
> 'Thy vict'ries and thy deathless fame
>   Through the wide world shall run,'
> And everlasting ages sing
>   The triumphs thou hast won!'

"When you contemplate this glorious event of the setting free of the captives, can you not newly understand why the angels veil their faces before the brightness of His ineffable glory, and in honor of the triune name, cry, 'Holy, holy, holy, art Thou, Lord God Almighty, which art and which wast and which is to come. Holy, holy, holy is the Lord of Hosts; the whole earth is full of Thy glory. Thou art worthy, O Lord, to receive glory, and honor, and power: for Thou hast created all things, and for Thy pleasure they are and were created!'

"Dare any of you, then, look on your fellow-man and refuse to recognize the divine image which he wears — that photograph of infinite possibilities of joy! Durst any one of you go forth from this house of our God to-day, and see a single fellow being, no matter who or what he is and has been, and say 'He hath no hands!' all capacity for making strong, straight, right, and beautiful paths for his feet is gone! Dare you cast eyes of scorn and hate on degraded and fallen woman? Dare you say of her, that mournfulest knell of the soul — 'No more! No more in the image of God!'

"Dare you pass by, beyond the side of reconciliation with him who has injured you; who has deeply, lastingly, irrecoverably wronged you? Dare you say of your bitterest foe, 'He hath no hands?' Never again can he make straight, right, and beautiful paths for my feet! Perhaps he never will in this life; but what, after all, is this first chapter of existence — but a span long! You cannot evade the truth that an eternity is before you, where God is the visible presence which draws all men to Himself. The sooner you are in a state that can be assimilated to the divine, the more glorious your hereafter — for one star differeth from another star in glory. You cannot be in this state unless love reigns — a perfect reconciliation to your Maker possesses your heart and life, so that all His work shall appear harmonious, beautiful, infinitely right. 'Where we can't unriddle, we must learn to trust.' There is 'seeming evil' here, but from it we must only 'educe the good.' A heart full of the love of God will not pause in the unhallowed indulgence of reasoning strife with the dear Father concerning His incomprehensible work.

"As the river Clitumnus was fabled to turn all things white which drank of its waters, so let your souls drink of the river of God, whose fountain is exhaustless love, till they become purified and meet for the saints' inheritance in light."

## CHAPTER IV.

#### THREE MONTHS LATER.

"Since you insist upon my opinions of what I have heard from Universalist pulpits, and read in their books of standard theology," said Israel, "I must say, with your leave, that it seems to me I find, at least, one decided blemish."

"What is that?" quickly rejoined Captain Brewster.

"They too freely deal in hard words against those who differ from themselves, and especially against what are called Orthodox Christians."

"Yes," said Ackerman, "I have noticed that, as Tillotson says, 'The scoffers twit the Christians.' It is inelegant as rhetoricians, insignificant as philosophers, unworthy as Christians. Great men, conscious of bearing the precious archives of truth, can afford to be more magnanimous."

"I have sometimes thought," continued Israel, "that they believed in what amounted to a hell for their opponents."

"Their pious imprecations, as well as those which are impious, are often very amusing," Ackerman went on.

"I listen to you, sirs," said the captain, "as the angels must have heard the buccaneers who used to pray before going upon their piratical excursions. You rave at my people with a commendable zeal for godliness."

His genial smile disarmed the severity of his words.

"He thinks us far gone in the sin of prejudice," said Ackerman.

"No; I confess the justice of your criticism in part. But it is easily accounted for. Many of our preachers, and nearly all whose words have become our standards, were men converted to Universalism from the orthodox denominations. They had been Baptists or Congregationalists. It was impossible that they should entirely lose the marks of their early habits, associations, and education. No man is so bitter to the Universalist as the real Baptist; and several of our leading lights were Baptist preachers. Our young ministers read their works and catch their spirit. It is a pity, but a fault, considering its origin, which cannot at once be rectified. As our denomination is more thoroughly developed, and hence becomes more self-contained, we shall show better manners."

Ackerman laughed heartily as he said, "You have extricated yourself, I confess."

"There is truth as well as wit in what he says," added Israel.

"Certainly," said Ackerman; "if you would get models of bad temper and its exhibition, consult what artists would call evangelical studies."

"The sea-serpent envy is master of the situation," said the captain; "but let us pass on to number two — for I dare say the objections stand along the coast of your mind like a forest of masts."

"Wherever we see Universalism in the ascendant

in any community," said Israel, " is there not apparent an absence of good order, such as observance of the Sabbath, and all those evidences of a God-fearing people that mark a really desirable home?"

"Where Universalism goes to seed," said Ackerman, "the place is unsightly and barren of good things."

"That atheism," replied Captain Brewster, "brings forth some such results, I, myself, have noticed. But Universalism, — true, Christian Universalism is eminently productive of good fruits. What people of modern times have done more for temperance than have Universalists. Some of the noblest advocates of that holy cause, you will remember, are from our ranks. Besides, who giveth more liberally to the poor and distressed than the Christian Universalist? His heart overflows with the cream of human kindness, and his purse equals his heart so far as it is endowed. If I were in trouble, without name or credentials, without an inkhorn and pen whereby my benefactor could be reported, think you, sirs, I would apply to the Calvinists? As soon would I ask for a hug from a bear, or a kiss from a gorilla. Sooner would I expect to double Cape Horn in a wash-tub, as to successfully circumnavigate their hearts."

"The quality of your mercy is not strained," said Ackerman.

"Nor skimmed," said Israel; "but his figure of the tub reminds me that Hercules, when he went to unbind Prometheus, sailed the length of the ocean in an earthen pot. Mr. Locke, the metaphysician, says that this represents human nature, and describes Christian resolution that saileth in the frail bark of the flesh, through the waves of the world. Now the captain's

Christian resolution in his earthen wash-tub should accomplish wonders with these Calvinists, who, indeed, have often shown the disciples, as did the barbarians to St. Paul, 'much kindness.'"

"Yes," said Ackerman; "the examples of the true liberality of the straitest sects are not to be forgotten."

"They cannot be forgotten," said the captain, "since they are paraded beyond all chance of escape from the world's recognition."

"They are known also for many acts of private benevolence among them," said Israel.

"We do not boast, like other denominations," continued the captain, but we raise moneys for denominational and charitable purposes, equal in amount, to say the least, with those who blow their own horns the loudest."

"My next objection," said Israel, "is that a large proportion of those who are numbered among your people do not believe the authority of the Bible, and hence reject the most precious Christian doctrine of the divine mission of Christ."

"When all the other Christian denominations have cut off their left wing, or changed it to match the right one, and so make a perfect flight in an imperfect world, to heaven, we will accept your criticism in self-abasement. He that is without sin, let him begin to stone us. Let that religious sect which has no offending members, cut off ours," answered the captain, curtly; "what next?"

"Nothing more at present," concluded Israel, "except that your doctrine has much that the Bible can be adduced in disproof."

"What doctrine has not?" concluded the other.

# AMONG THE UNITARIANS.

## CHAPTER I.

#### PRELIMINARY OBSERVATIONS.

WHEN Israel Knight had progressed as far as the foregoing in his investigations of the existing forms of the embodiment of religious truth, his inclinations took him to the pale of the Unitarian belief. He was not yet satisfied that he had found the "City" for which he sought.

Some one told him that there was really no difference between the Unitarians and Universalists, only "on the social plane;" but, as he saw considerable apparent distinction in their operations, he wished to learn for himself. This wish was, in part, stimulated by circumstances. About this time, it was his fortune to reside in the family of an eminent Unitarian clergyman. He thought that a better opportunity for his purpose could not have been presented.

His first observations were practical. In this family he soon noticed a young girl who acted the part of an assistant domestic. He thought her the ugliest child he had ever seen. This impression of her face was not a little assisted by frequent exhibitions of an irrascible temper. Conversations which were held in the study and parlor of the clergyman were interrupted or broken up by her furious outbursts of passion on occasion of the slightest crossing of her will. In her unreason she seemed insane. In her vicious propensities there was "method in her madness." She was strangely ingenious to accomplish wrong against her benefactors, who were the younger ladies of the family.

Israel could not but wonder what had induced these refined, intellectual, and amiable persons to undertake such a disagreeable charge — and concluded, at first, that this greatness of torment had been thrust upon them by unavoidable circumstances. Certainly nothing less could have brought such a blight upon that else well-ordered and elegant home.

The history of her introduction to that household transpired in this account by one of the daughters: " Some time after leaving school, we found a considerable portion of our time unoccupied by any sufficiently *absorbing* object of interest. We attended to our music, we read, visited, and so forth, but we required something more stimulating. Our lives were getting too same to suit us. An idea struck one of us, which all welcomed. We immediately applied to father for permission to execute it. This was to go abroad and perfect our knowledge of the French language in a celebrated *pensionnat* of Paris, where were already some of our friends and correspondents. He asked for a day's reflection upon our project, though we hardly believed he would give it many thoughts, as he was writing all that day. He only took time to dignify his assent, as we thought. That evening he called us to his study, and said he had concluded to recommend an object of pursuit, which in point of interest and real use to us, he thought far outweighed the other plan. Had we sufficient confidence in his affection for us to allow his judgment to prevail? he asked. We replied unqualifiedly our affirmative.

"The French boarding-school, then, would be given up for the time, and he would bring home, on the morrow, the new object of interest and action. He declined to tell us what it was. That night, before we separated, he read to us the beatitudes in Matthew's Gospel. Upon the words, 'Blessed are the merciful, for they shall obtain mercy,' he dwelt with a peculiar tenderness of spirit; and I thought I had never heard him explain so clearly the nature of that beautiful sentiment. The next day we were all expectation. He went away accompanied by our mother, and it seemed to us they were gone a long while. But at last we heard the sound of the carriage-wheels in our yard, and we ran down to meet them, expecting to hear about an order for a new piano, a sewing-machine, or a complete set of artist's materials, when we discovered that they were accompanied by a strange child.

"Father introduced her to us as the new object of interest and action. They had found her in an asylum whose authorities had come to consider her 'hopeless,' 'incorrigible,' and 'irreclaimable,' and were about to cast her upon a reform school. Her name was Maggie, though they said it should have been Magdalene, for she had as many evil spirits as that personage. 'Then,' said father, 'there is hope for her; her prototype became a follower of Jesus; let me have her for a trial.' She has been with us but a few weeks."

"Are you not disheartened in the pursuit of such an object of interest and action?" asked Israel.

"Not yet," she answered; "she has not sinned against us the seventy and seven times."

"Not more than fifty," said one of the sisters.

"Your system? Allow me to inquire, if you please," continued Israel.

"Love, forbearance, long-suffering."

"Let patience have her perfect work."

"Believeth all things, endureth all things, hopeth all things."

"And when we get faint in the pursuit," said the eldest, "we apply to papa, who reads to us the beatitudes anew. Then he points us to Jesus, and tells us where we may get new strength."

"Can you make the sacrifice, both of Paris and your own ease, without one pang of regret?"

"Father has brought our work to appear to us so magnificent in comparison to any selfish enjoyment, that we are ashamed to ever speak of what we might enjoy abroad now. Even when one of us received a 'black eye' from the blow of her hand, the other day, as she was learning to read, we all agreed — that is, after a few moments of confusion succeeded by some of calmer reflection — that it was a good thing to do alms without wishing to be seen of men."

Here a pleasant ripple of merriment ran through the group, and the conversation ended. Afterwards, the clergyman, when alone with Israel, said, "Perhaps we give less for denominational purposes than almost all other sects; but we encourage all forms of unostentatious benevolence. We believe in striving to be Christ-like — to build up character, less by societies and groups of laudatory selfism which centre around a creed, than by deeds of simple justice to our fellow-beings."

Israel had occasion to notice repeatedly that this clergyman proved himself "the highest style of man," in his gracious attention to all who applied to him for any office of kindness in his power; and this, without reference to name or caste. Letters were frequently received by him from entire strangers, upon items of business, which had little claim upon his notice; but these were invariably answered in the utmost courtesy. In this, he truly resembled his divine Master and Exemplar — nothing was too small, no one too obscure, to escape his gentlest consideration. *The measure in which he meted out to his fellow-beings, returned to him again a hundred fold.*

When Israel had watched the working of this system of life, he exclaimed to himself: "How different is this man from others whom I have known — who reckon him a heretic to be set beyond the pale of their slightest recognition, as a true Christian? I shall listen to his teachings from my heart as well as my head."

On the following Sabbath this clergyman preached one of his characteristic, elaborate, and great sermons. His text was: "For what man knoweth the things of a man, save the spirit of man which is in him? even so the things of God knoweth no man, but the Spirit of God." (1 Cor. 2: 11.)

The spirit of man and the spirit of God were discussed with a metaphysical acuteness and logical profundity worthy of any of the authors quoted, as Kant, Sir William Hamilton, Berkely, Hartley, Horne,

Tooke, Descartes, Feder, Garve, Fichte, Krug, Schulze, Malebranche, Helvetius, and the like. This brought Israel to a state of mental lucidity, as though he had been contemplating the "ephod and teraphim," made by the man Micah. The world around him seemed toned down to a *reductio ad absurdum*, while the Hartleian "vibrations and vibratiuncles in the medullary substance of the brain," with the "nihilism," "empiricism," and the kindred "isms" wound him up to exploding fragments of transcendental synthetics.

He was in a state of vapor like Bonnot de Condillac's theory of *la faculté de sentir*. This is no uncommon condition of minds in churches. He saw men as trees walking through the majestical illustrations of the preacher. The stronger his efforts to hold upon the argument the more weary he became; and all thoughts of notes were out of the question, as indeed, were all thoughts of anything rational or connected. He fell asleep.

The minister beheld him, and the words of Whately darted through his mind: "I cannot but think that the generality of sermons seem to presuppose a degree of religious knowledge in the hearers greater than many of them would be found on examination to possess. "I have made a mistake," he reflected.

Israel knew not whether he was in or out of the body, till he began to be recalled by the sight and sound of the exchange of civilities on all sides of him. Of these civilities one thing impressed him — the ladies of the clergyman's family were very cordial to all whom they met — not only to those who appeared "congenial" and upon a similar "social plane," but to those less favored by fortune. He mentioned this afterward to a friend, who said to him: "Those ladies, descendants of colonial governors, state representatives, judges, and other eminent men, and at present connected with some of the leading families of the land, know no other way than to be gracious to all the members of their father's parish. They are not of that degenerate and insignificant order of *new* people, who affect airs and make petty distinctions. Besides, their religion teaches them to follow the example of their Master as well as to profess faith in Him."

## CHAPTER II.

#### CONVERSATION.

When Israel had listened to the teachings of the Unitarian clergyman until deeply interested, the following conversation occurred between them: —

*Israel.* "Your views of Regeneration, which, I suppose are similar to, or the same as, those of the Universalists, are not quite clear to my recognition."

*Clergyman.* "Not accepting the dogma of the total depravity of mankind, we believe (and I draw from our standard authorities,) that man has, by nature, a divine principle within him, which, coming from God, will return to Him. This divinity in man can never be totally extinguished; no power in heaven or earth can annul the holy relationship existing between the Creator and Creature. We believe that the creature requires a transformation of heart, a regeneration from the natural into the higher spiritual life, and that this will eventually take place, here or hereafter, before the consummating event of union with the Creator. The divine union which is effected between the reconciled heart and God, in this life, constitutes the most excellent Christian character. He who truly lives in God, is truly regenerated.

"There are, however, degrees in the regeneration.

We do not attempt to estimate how many of these degrees it shall take to complete the standard of excellence. Here let me read to you a sentence from one of our standard writers,\* which expresses my idea: 'Unitarians do not feel at liberty to define or restrict the mode of the divine operation in this spiritual, any more than in the natural birth. Recognizing as of indispensable necessity the hand of God in both, they know and acknowledge that "the wind bloweth where it listeth," and, consequently, that now a child of God may be raised and trained under the gentle care of a Christian mother's hourly love, and now may be brought forth amid the throes and pangs of the terror and distress of a conscience smitten by sudden calamity, or by the truthful words of a mighty "man of God." \* \* Regeneration, in their opinion, is not coercion, nor supercession, but a stage in moral growth, a process of spiritual development, a revival of dormant energies, a renewal of suspended life. Regeneration has its perfect work in salvation. \* \* Salvation is not only freedom from sin, but it is the perfection of virtue: in other words, it is humanity instructed, enriched, refined, and elevated to its highest pitch, in virtue of the power, and after the model of Christ.'"

*I.* "Your views comport more nearly with the work of God in Nature."

*C.* "We do not encourage belief in that regenerating process which is said to take place in one point of time, and in an equally defined point, lapses into a

---

\*Rev. Dr. Beard.

state which is no better but worse than the first. Conversions which are the work of a freak of the mind, make unsightly characters; whereas those which are the result of a steady purpose of the enlightened will, gradually develope characters of symmetrical structure upon good foundations."

*I.* "In the allusion to the power of Christ in this work, how much am I to understand is referred to this power?"

*C.* "It will be necessary to consider the Atonement, in order to reply to your question. We believe (and again I draw from our standard authorities) in one God and in his Son, our Lord Jesus Christ. We believe in the Holy Spirit as the impersonal power of God which works in the heart of man. Christ was the first-born of every creature, consequently he cannot be equal to God the Father. The precise nature of his relationship to God and man, we regard as unwarrantable presumption to define. That there is a three-fold office in the work of regeneration we acknowledge. In the work of reconciling man to God, the Father, Christ the Son acts the part of Exemplar, Teacher, elder Brother, and Saviour. God so loved the world that He gave His only-begotten Son, that whosoever believes in Him may be saved from his sins in this life and the next. It was not the anger of God towards man which gave the inestimable gift of His Son, as is erroneously taught by some forms of belief. The Holy Spirit is the power of God in the heart which draws it to discipleship to Christ, and moulds it, in favoring circumstances, into His likeness. These circumstances are a part of man's destiny in this life or the next. The complete work, as also the work on all its parts, is one of Infinite Love. The creature, man, cannot love the Lord Jesus too much, nor, as second only to the Father, can he exalt him too high. His work in the regeneration of man, is that of ineffable tenderness. As such, it is passing all speech in the realm of the beautiful and the good. 'Behold, I stand at the door, and knock: If any man hear my voice, and open the door, I will come in to him, and will sup with him, and he with me.' 'It is the voice of my beloved that knocketh, saying, open to me * * for my head is filled with dew, and my locks with the drops of the night.' What words could more truly portray the mission of the Christ to man than these?"

*I.* "But what use do you assign to those passages in the Bible which clearly show that Christ was also a sacrifice for sin — thus pointing to a work of propitiation with the Father?"

*C.* "Those words which indicate a sacrifice were used in accommodation to the existing ideas of sacrificial offerings for sin, which had been transmitted from the earliest periods. But I prefer to read to you, concerning this, from the author already quoted: 'It is not denied that sacrificial language is applied in the New Testament to the passion of the Saviour. But that language, it is maintained, had parted with its primary import, while the strictly vicarious sufferings and literal atonements of heathenism were unknown in the Hebrew church.' The general idea of atonement, it is thought, passed, in the religious history of man, through several stages. In the rudest

religious conceptions, sacrifices were vicarious means
of appeasing the Divinity, and so averting the consequences of His displeasure and wrath. Here we have
the offender, man; the being offended, God; and the
atoning medium, the most precious of man's possessions — his substance, his captive, his child. By the
Mosaic law, God was set forth as essentially good, and
surpassingly merciful; willing, therefore, to accept
man's offerings, not so much as means of appeasement
on his part, as tokens of a submissive, grateful, and
obedient heart on the part of the repentant sinner;
consequently, atonement, in the Hebrew Church, was
a system of covering, and as of covering, so of oblit-
eration for sin; a system by which God threw a vail
over human transgressions, and, receiving marks of
man's homage, graciously remitted the sin, and fore-
went the penalty. Another stage in the conception is
found in the prophetic view of atonement, which,
based on the internal nature of religion, the necessity
of internal obedience, and the abuses to which the
externalities of sacrificial observances had been found
to lead, disallowed, and even severely reprobated
all outward oblations and propitiatory tokens whatever, declaring that God could accept only a pure
heart and a benevolent life. (Is. 1:11; Amos 5:21;
Micah 6:7; Jer. 6, 20; 7:22.) The final step in this
process of revelation and of spiritual refinement was
set by the Lord Jesus Christ, when teaching men to
regard God as the Father of all, especially of those
who believed (1 Tim. 4:10) he taught them also to
consider his own sufferings as an expression and
exemplification of love — of everlasting, unpurchased,

and unprompted love — on the part of the Father; and of pity, and the widest and most generous philanthropy on his own part. Coming, however, as he did, to put away sin by the voluntary sacrifice of himself, (Heb. 9: 26,) he became the great sacrifice — the ideal atonement — the completion and the fulfilment of all divinely-recognized sacrificial ideas, types, and observances, — so that, while all the phraseology connected therewith was applicable, and in its highest import applicable, only to him, that import was not physical, not material, but divested of all merely human and earthly elements of wrath, equivalence, and propitiation; had risen into pure spirituality, and represented as its essential ideas, sin and suffering on man's part, love on the part of God and Christ, and such a remedy emanating from the latter as would inevitably cover, obliterate, and remove the former. Thus eliminating all the gross conceptions which had their reason, if not their origin in low states of moral culture and early periods of civilization, the Gospel presents in its atonement, "a new and better way" — a way in which mercy triumphs over justice; love has "free course and is glorified;" and, while sin is subdued and extirpated, the sinner is redeemed, restored, renovated, and made everlastingly happy, by becoming essentially holy.'"

*I.* "The view is a philosophical one upon the basis of human reason; but as a religious view, upon the basis of the word of God, there are many difficulties accompanying it to my mind."

*C.* "It is plain to understand, provided you admit the same process takes place in the human mind of different ages as in the operations of Nature, namely — *change."*

*I.* "You believe, then, in the progress of ideas of Christian truth?"

*C.* "Most certainly. We glory (if the term is ever permissible) in our scope of liberty of thought and enlightenment in the domain of truth. This, though sometimes abused by our people, we hail as our precious, inalienable right. Were I bound to a creed made by any man, I should feel as if chained to Ixion's wheel. In any human prison of thought, I should stifle into inanity. There is no bondage like that of the soul in chains of religion. Man's spiritual nature having come from God himself, is allied to the infinite. Hence, all attempts at its prescription and limitation are nothing short of positive tyranny, as cruel in its sensations as it is fatal in its capacities for growth. I often think of what that excellent man, John Robinson, wrote to the Congregational Church, which he had founded, after their departure for Plymouth, New England. Here it is. (Reads): 'For my part I cannot sufficiently bewail the condition of the reformed churches, who are come to a period in religion, and will go at present no further than the instruments of their reformation. The Lutherans cannot be drawn to go beyond what Luther saw. Whatever part of his will our good God has revealed to Calvin, they will rather die than embrace it. And the Calvinists, you see, stick fast where they were left by that great man of God, who yet saw not all things.

"'This is a misery much to be lamented; for though they were burning and shining lights in their times, yet they penetrated not into the whole counsel of God; but were they now living, would be as willing to embrace further light, as that which they first received. I beseech you, remember it is an article of your church covenant, "That you be ready to receive whatever truth shall be made known to you from the written word of God." But I must herewithal exhort you to take heed what you receive as truth. Examine it, consider it, and compare it with other Scriptures of truth, before you receive it; for it is not possible that the Christian world should come so lately out of such thick antichristian darkness, and that perfection of knowledge should break forth at once.'"

*J.* "I remember hearing a Congregational clergyman read extracts from this letter, but he omitted this which you have read."

*C.* "Yes; I should suppose he would."

*J.* "And yet it is evident that Calvin saw not all things, especially when he failed to discern the right of his opponent Servetus, to whose death he consented."

*C.* "Servetus, a good man, as all admit, could not accept the Calvinistic idea of the Trinity. He was burned in conformity to the Calvinistic idea of God's punishment of his enemies. How true is it that we act towards our fellow-man as we think that God deals with them. In other words, our characters take on the semblance of our idea of God. If we think He is a being full of wrath, hate, and vengeance, the tendency is hate to all others but those who are like ourselves."

*J.* "However, Robinson's caution to his people

respecting the obligation to examine an alleged truth with the Scriptural canon, is not to be disregarded."

*C.* "We accept the Scriptures of the Old and New Testament as a compendium of faith and duty; but we do not admit plenary inspiration."

*I.* "It seems to me that the dividing line between reason and revelation is hard to draw. Dr. Priestley's idea, that the words of the writers of the Bible should be received just as we receive that of other credible historians, but without ascribing infallibility to them, is attended with great difficulty to me. If I reject their infallibility, I am compelled to resort to my own fallible judgment — a subterfuge altogether unworthy of such a subject."

*C.* "But, if you accept them to the fullest import of inspiration, you are yet compelled to do the same thing, in order to arrive at an intelligent understanding of their annunciations."

*I.* "This intelligent understanding, as I believe, can only be gained by the assistance of the Spirit of God. Our hearts do not burn within us while we read, till Christ talks to us by the way, and opens to us the Scriptures. This takes place, when, as you have intimated in that beautiful passage quoted in another connection, we open the door of our hearts to Him. We get from the Scriptures the measure of truth or error, which is the result of what we bring to them. If we carry hearts of unrest and hate to the Written Word, we bring away the same in kind, but more in degree; and if we carry love, we bring away the effluence of love. Since prophecy came not by the will of man, but holy men of God spake as they were moved by the Holy Ghost, I cannot see that it is to be understood by the will of man, but rather by the spirit of God within us."

*C.* "We differ, if at all, more in terms than in reality. Like yourself, I believe that the Scriptures are to be interpreted *by the spirit of God within us.* This spirit exists in the heart of every sentient being. It does not work by any private interpretation vouchsafed to a Calvin or a Wesley; but it is free to all as the air we breathe. What you believe is truth to you, but it may not be so to me, for the reason that the mediums through which it operates upon the understanding are unlike. If I see yonder landscape through a red glass, all things are red; if you look at the same scene through a green one, all the scene is green. Yet vision is perfect in both cases; so is the landscape the same, and unchangeable. This comports with your idea of our bringing out of the Bible what we carry to it. Theologians form systems of divinity from the same texts, as unlike in their nature and tendencies as light from darkness, because the theologians themselves are unlike in the conditions of mind. Consequently I attach little value to all theologies. *He that doeth His will* shall know sufficient doctrine for all purposes essential to a good life and a good death. And that will is found in the Bible."

*I.* "While I am explicit in avowing my belief in the full inspiration of the Holy Scriptures, I confess to unqualified admiration of the stress laid by you and your co-believers upon works, or moralities. The little attention paid to these, by the expounders of orthodox creeds, so called, has often been a great stumbling-block in my way. To me, it is nothing short of absolute impiety or heathen mythology to claim a surety of the highest happiness, immediately after death — the result of a life spent in the service of deception and the other devious ways of sin — under cover of a mere expression of faith."

*C.* "Here you will understand why we do not make the atonement cover so much as do those men. We regard the idea of those who are self-styled evangelical, as most dangerous and often fatal to thorough foundations of virtue and good faith in dealings among men. You will observe the character of those communities which hold such doctrines. They strain at a gnat in a profession, but swallow camels in their practice. It would seem that nothing but the laws of the land restrain them."

*I.* "I admit what you say. And yet I must add that it is my faith, if I am ever saved, it will be by the atonement of my Saviour Jesus Christ, and not by any works which I have done."

*C.* "At the same time you believe that we shall all be judged according to our works?"

*I.* "I do. And I also believe that the death of Christ avails nothing where these works do not exist."

*C.* "We differ, as before, more in terms than otherwise."

*I.* "It is surprising to me that your sect does not gain followers more rapidly and more extensively over all the classes of society, when you inculcate such pure practice."

*C.* "Our teaching of the necessity of a moral life

in order to please God, is the offence of the cross which fails to suit the popular ear; whereas a doctrine that teaches a faith without any works but those of your own will, is most agreeable to the general heart. They do indeed teach good works, but rather as an outgrowth and adornment than the elements of the structure of which the Christian character is composed. Our foundation, alike with theirs, is Christ; but we believe that the building will not stand the test of time unless rightly composed."

*I.* "Allow me to add an opinion respecting this. It seems to me if your preachers brought their sermons more on a level with the great heart of the people — those active, impulsive, and yet mostly unlearned and unread people — that they would be more attractive, and hence more operative upon popular thought. With some few exceptions they are not sufficiently in earnest. The laws of rhetoric, you know, sir, inculcate earnestness in the speaker, in order to kindle a corresponding emotion in the hearers. They do not bring enough of the vital interest at stake. They indulge in theories, while their hearers, for the most part, are wholly unprepared for such food. They sacrifice their true power in an attempt to sustain the dignity of a life of profound study interspersed with elegant leisure and the most refined social exchange."

*C.* "I admit that there is justice in your criticism. But we do not wish to evoke an earnestness which will soon consume itself and its possessor. You remember that in the time of Godfrey of Boulogne, certain people of Nivers were burned with invisible fire, and Krautzius says that some of them cut off a hand or a foot where the burning started, in order to arrest the calamity. It is indeed a calamity to have a fire kindled within you, which consumes. The true warmth of the soul is created by the rays from the sun of righteousness; but every soul has the capability of this divine fire, which is a blessing and not a curse."

*I.* "I remember that De Castro said of Doctor Alexandrinus Megeteus, that fire came out of his backbone which scorched the eyes of beholders. Now, those beholders could not help looking at the Doctor; they would go far to see him. He drew crowds. I would have ministers with such backbone. The few have it, whom all men draw after."

*C.* "Such sensational men have no real permanence in the confidence of the people. You never know who they are or what they really believe. They know not themselves. Neither are the sensations begotten in the people of more account, save as a havoc and damage every way. Witness the aspect of the people on their return from a camp-meeting. As a brother once said to me on one of these occasions, 'I've got religion enough to last me a whole year, till the next one.' They look as though they had to continually assure themselves of this, in order not to lapse into a state of profound misery."

*I.* "This is the extreme. The golden mean — the *juste milieu* in all things, is certainly best. We must take people as we find them; for if we stop to make them over quite to our liking, they are gone, and so likewise are we. In our short lives we have not time to do what we would. The people demand excitements. If they cannot get them here, they will seek for them there. If your sect can get along without the people, you may well afford to hold the even tenor of your refined and elevated way. But if you want them, you must provide things meet and suitable for them. While you, Unitarians, are discoursing from the sublime heights of philosophy and refined experience to the few who know whereof you speak, the other populous sects are coursing thoroughly the defiles and gorges of sin, scouring the plains of every-day life, and making their difficult way through apparently unexplored regions of unbelief and ignorance, and so gathering numberless raw recruits of way-farers, plodders, fools, villains, and all the heterogeneous mass which swell their formidable array of denominational statistics. Their mission is like His who came not to call the righteous, but sinners to repentance. Hence they prosper."

*C.* "Not every one that saith 'Lord! Lord!' and doeth many wonderful works in his name, will be found all glorious within, on the day of the revelation of the true life. We live not for to-day. We look not to time for the trial of our work. Statistics made by partial men are of no account to us. The homely adage is not forgotten, 'Easy come, easy go.' There are, however, transition periods in all denominations. And were I to indulge myself in prophecy, I should say that ours was approaching one of these."

*I.* "May I inquire to what you refer?"

*C.* "The thinkers of our people seem awaking to the consciousness of a necessity for a more active spirituality. Their hearts are getting more sympathetic with the popular heart. Research and speculative reflection are becoming tiresome. (Israel thought of the metaphysical sermon.) A need is springing up in the soul. Christ's knocking is heard and heeded. The deflection of certain portions of our people into what is called pure Rationalism, has been the occasion of this awakening of the other portion, called Christian Unitarians or Unitarian Christians."

*I.* "You, like other sects, have to bear one another's burdens of 'heresy.'"

*C.* "Yes, without admitting the word heresy. We do not consider those who differ from our own views, whether within our own pale or beyond it, as heretics. That word belongs to a dark age. The children of a common Father, whose name and essence is love, can ill descend so low as to deal in stigmas. Who art thou that judgest thy brother? Judgment belongs to God."

*I.* "I think if some of you Christian Unitarians were to come out with a more apostolical zeal, so that the common people of the highways and by-ways would hear you gladly, your power would prevail over that of your brethren who deal in refined speculations."

*C.* "And the exercise of our powers would be promotive of their development into higher and nobler channels of thought and action."

*I.* "I trust that you will pardon my presumption in venturing these criticisms. Your unvarying freedom of communication has caused me to forget all else but your goodness in listening to one who has no claims upon your attention."

*C.* "I honor your draft upon my courtesy. The

expression of one's honest convictions is never to be undervalued. I am certain that this you say of us is truth. We must feel more the necessity of speaking directly to the people of the great vital truths of Christianity. We must urge them to seek a new heart and a right spirit. Thought and feeling must go hand in hand in the onward march of progress; then will there be kindled a noble, God-like fervor, not only in our hearers, but in ourselves. We preachers need to bring new fire from off the altar in order to be true Christian Unitarians."

*I.* "I infer that you, in common with all other Christian sects, date your first period to the time of Christ."

*C.* "We do, as Christian Unitarians; but as Unitarians, we go back to the times of the patriarchs who believed in only one God. In the earliest Christian churches we find that the believers of our doctrine were opposed under the name of monarchists, because they held to the sovereignty of one God, the Father."

*I.* "In connection with your denomination, I have always associated a few eminent leading names as the personal embodiment of its teachings. Of the first of these, is Arius. I remember of my early reading of this man, and his contest with Alexander, bishop of Alexandria."

*C.* "This was in the begining of the fourth century. He owned Christ to be God, but in a sense that angels are styled gods in the Scripture; that he was not co-eternal with the Father, consequently not co-equal. Arius is represented to have been venerable in appearance, and irreproachable in his habits."

*I.* "I used to be much impressed when I read of his restoration to favor by Constantine, notwithstanding the opposition of Alexander — how he, with his followers, on being recalled, walked the streets of Constantinople in triumph, and when, according to the language of the historian, 'he was suddenly seized with an anguish in his bowels, and soon after expired.' I thought that it was a visitation of the judgment of God, for his errors. But since, I have found in more truthful sources of history, that the evidence was conclusive; that his opponents cut short his career by poisoning him."

*C.* "We have suffered our share of persecution."

*I.* "Next, I recall the names of Martin Cellarius, of Stuttgart, the friend of Luther and Melancthon, and Michael Servetus. Lælius Socinus adopted a similar system of antitrinitarianism, which was introduced into Poland by his nephew, Faustus Socinus."

*C.* "The doctrine of Socinus differed from that of Arius, in that he taught that Christ had no existence until born of the Virgin Mary."

*I.* "I think that Socinus must have held a higher view of Christ than did some of his followers, as it is stated in history, that he persecuted Francis David on account of rejecting the worship of Christ, and cast him into prison, where he died."

*C.* "There were different parties of antitrinitarians in those days as in the present time. Some believed Jesus Christ to be a God of an inferior nature to the Father; others held to his peculiar sonship like Arius; yet others believed only in his humanity endowed with superior wisdom for a special mission which he sealed with his blood. The latter view has prevailed more extensively in Germany, in recent periods. In our land, they of this faith are now quietly passing into the ranks of the Rationalists or Transcendentalists."

*I.* "Next the names of Priestley and Belsham, in England, come up to recognition in this connection."

*C.* "But the first public advocate of Unitarianism in England was John Biddle. He, with others, published a series of Socinian tracts which aroused controversy, and established conviction in many hearts. The progress of our views during the latter part of the last century, in England and America, is chiefly ascribed to Dr. Priestley."

*I.* "Dr. Samuel Clarke might also be styled a Unitarian, I suppose, since he maintained a difference of rank between the Father, Son, and Holy Ghost."

*C.* "Yes; and also John Milton and Sir Isaac Newton. There are other eminent names belonging to evangelical bodies, who have not been considered 'sound' on the doctrine of the Trinity."

*I.* "In this country, the name of Channing is precious to every sincere and liberal lover of truth. I have read his works with the deepest interest. Some of his words I have transcribed into my memory, and so have them always present at my call."

*C.* "What are these?"

*I.* "One of the beautiful mosaics is this: 'Books find their way into every house, however mean; and especially that book which contains more nutriment for the intellect, imagination, and heart, than all others; I mean, of course, the Bible. And I am confident that among the poor are those who find in that one book more enjoyment, more awakening truth, more lofty and beautiful imagery, more culture to the whole soul, than thousands of the educated find in their general studies, and vastly more than millions among the rich find in that superficial, transitory literature which consumes all their reading hours.' "

*C.* "We do well who imitate Channing in reverence and love for the Bible."

*I.* "Then of all his writings I most like this passage: —

" 'I call that mind free, which jealously guards its intellectual rights and powers, which calls no man master, which does not content itself with a passive or hereditary faith, which opens itself to light whencesoever it may come, which receives new truth as an angel from heaven, which, while consulting others, inquires still more of the oracle within itself, and uses instruction from abroad, not to supersede, but to quicken and exalt its own energies.

" 'I call that mind free which sets no bounds to its love, which is not imprisoned in itself or in a sect, which recognizes in all human beings the image of God, and the rights of his children, which delights in virtue, and sympathizes with suffering wherever they are seen, which conquers pride, anger, and sloth, and offers itself up a victim to the cause of mankind.

" 'I call that mind free which is not passively framed by outward circumstances, which is not swept away by the torrents of events, which is not the creature of accidental impulse, but which bends events to its own improvement, and acts from an inward spring, from immutable principles which it has deliberately espoused.

"'I call that mind free which protects itself against the usurpations of society, which does not cower to human opinion, which feels itself accountable to a higher tribunal than man's, which respects a higher law than fashion, which respects itself too much to be the slave or tool of the many or the few.

"'I call that mind free which, through confidence in God, and in the power of virtue, has cast off all fear but that of wrong doing, which no menace or peril can enthral, which is calm in the midst of tumults, and possesses itself though all else be lost.

"'I call that mind free which resists the bondage of habit, which does not mechanically repeat itself, and copy the past, which does not live on its old virtues, which does not enslave itself to precise rules, but which forgets what is behind, listens for new and higher monitions of conscience, and rejoices to pour itself forth in fresh and higher exertions.

"'I call that mind free which is jealous of its own freedom, which guards itself from being merged in others, which guards its empire over itself as nobler than the empire of the world.

"'In fine, I call that mind free which, conscious of its affinity with God, and confiding in his promises by Jesus Christ, devotes itself faithfully to the unfolding of all its powers, which passes the bounds of time and death, which hopes to advance forever, and which finds inexhaustible power, both for action and suffering, in the prospect of immortality.

"'Such is the spiritual freedom which Christ came to give. It consists in moral force, in self-control, in the enlargement of thought and affection, and in the unrestrained action of our best powers. This is the great good of Christianity; nor can we conceive a greater within the gift of God.'"

## CHAPTER III.

### THE PRACTICAL SERMON.

A FEW Sabbaths after the foregoing conversation, the Unitarian clergyman preached a sermon upon these words: "And the Lord said unto Joshua, Get thee up; wherefore liest thou thus upon thy face?" (Joshua 7: 10.)

Of this discourse, Israel made the following memoranda: —

"Joshua was faint-hearted. He had found difficulties. He, with his people, had recently come into a strange land, among an unfriendly people. Regretting that the Lord had brought them over Jordan, Joshua with his elders rent their clothes, fell to the earth, and put dust upon their heads. Then the Lord said, 'Get thee up; wherefore liest thou thus upon thy face?'

"There are many like Joshua in our day and generation. Indeed this state of mind is, doubtless, that of every one at some period of life. But some do not hear the words of the Lord as did Joshua; or, if hearing, they do not heed them. They continue to lie on their faces and grovel in the dust and ashes of tribulation. They go mourning all their days.

"There are two or three points which I shall consider in connection with the text: —

"*First.* Who are these that lie on the ground upon their faces?

"*Second.* How can they obey the command 'Get thee up,' involved with which is the question, What are they to do after they get up?

"Under the first head, I would point out, among the representatives of this class who lie on their faces, that young man who has no defined purpose of life, no object above the existence of the present hour, no aim more exalted than his own present gratification. Do you say, 'let me alone — I have no means, no opportunities whereby to do more. There is no greatness in me. I never could do much when at school. My endowments do not qualify me for any higher sphere than that I now occupy. Besides, whenever I have tried to get up, I have surely fallen. I see no way for me to do better or greater. It does not pay for me to make any such extra efforts.'

"Another representative of the class is the man of business who shuts his soul to all the higher impulses of his being; who, seeing that it fares better with others than himself because of his inferior conditions for culture, remains prone upon his face, with no thought of recognizing a higher life and a nobler scope of vision.

"The third representative man is he who has passed middle life, and is now looking towards the decline of his years. He says, 'If I had my life to live over again, I should do very differently; I should know what to do in order to get great things for myself. But it is too late now. I am getting to be an old man. My remaining business is to keep pretty still where I am till I feel the cold touch of the grim messenger, Death.'

"Suffer me to say to all these classes of persons, and to all others who are in the condition in which was Joshua, ' *Get thee up;* wherefore liest thou thus upon thy face?' Every effort you make in this life adds something to the development of the immortal man within you. Nothing of strife for the better, the nobler, the holier, is ever lost. If you had but one day more to live, it would avail more than I can describe to make all the advances possible before that day was over. Just so far as you get in time, so far ahead you begin in eternity. Therefore, lose no time in getting up, looking about you, and discovering what the Lord would have you to do. * * * *

"Under the second head, I shall notice some of the means whereby you may obey the command, 'Get thee up.' Men are prone to forget who and what they are; they forget their kinship; they forget their destiny. You are not only sons of men, but sons of God. You are made in the likeness of God. You are dowered with a freedom of will, the exercise of which, if in accordance with the laws of your being, is pleasing to God. You are not mere machines. You are not doomed men. You are not made under a curse for the sins of Adam. No dark, impenetrable cloud of divine wrath hangs over your devoted head, shrouding your way in mystery and gloom.

"Think, my friends, you are the children of God! If earthly parents know how to give good things to their children, how much more shall your Father which is in heaven give good things to them that ask

Him. If you take this home to your hearts, can you not see how easy it is to get up from your posture on the ground?

"Nothing is more disastrous, more utterly to be deprecated in the course of the events of your life, than to believe in your fate, to talk of luck, to cry over your evil stars. Fate! Luck! Stars! What are they all before the power of God! And has not God vouchsafed to promise the exercise of this power according to the measure of your faith and corresponding effort? 'Help yourself, and heaven will help you.'

"'How shall I help myself? How can I get up?' do you reply?

"Believe what I have just told you. Begin with believing, and according to the adage, 'The beginning is the half of the whole.'

"You, young man! to whom I have already spoken, be true to the divinity within you, in order to work yourself up into the recognition of men. Wherever you are, do *all* your present duty,— no matter who sees you, or who sees you not, — no matter what it may cost you of self-sacrifice. Live up to yourself. Cut off your evil habits, if you have any, if it takes your right-hand sin. Divinity does not grow in an atmosphere of impurity. It stifles. Sin brings you flat on your face. You cannot walk upright so long as vice clings to you. As St. Gaull, the apostle of Germany, ordered the bear who served him with bringing wood to kindle his fire, to retire to the farthest fastnesses of the forest, and nevermore to show himself again to the injury of man, so do you command the sin which serves you with fuel for the fire of your life, to depart hence, and disturb you no more. The legend states that the bear obeyed the Saint until his dying day. So, will the sin obey you, if it discovers that you are in earnest — that you are really determined to get up, and prove yourself an upright-going man. Resist the devil, and he will flee from you. Put away the accursed thing from among you, even as Joshua was commanded to do by the Lord. This is one help to your getting up.

"Another is, to throw yourself upon the undeveloped capabilities within you. Who knows what he can do, until he tries! The career of all the great men in all departments of laudable effort illustrates this. And the Lord said unto Joshua — (this was the next thing after the putting away of the hidden sin which was among them) — Fear not, neither be thou dismayed; take all the people of war with thee, and arise, go up to Ai; see, I have given into thine hand the king of Ai, and his people, and his city, and his land.

"How many of you, young men, want to go up to Ai?

"This has seemed to be a favorite text among certain preachers of late — *And he pitched his tent towards Sodom.* One of these said in the pulpit, a short time since, that it was pitching the tents towards Sodom when young men left their homes to seek their fortunes in the West. As though God were not the God of the West, as well as of the East, in our own little speck of continent on the earth!

"These men who delight in holding up Sodom for contemplation, seem afraid of the outgrowing enterprise of our people. They wish to crop it off with the dull blade of religious bigotry and self-conceit. I would sooner look for Sodom where John Randolph directed the woman who was soliciting missionary funds — at our own doors. The ministers who would check off laudable ambition in young men, have the Sodom in their own hearts. For where would they have been, if they had not pitched their tent beyond the horizon of their own paternal doors! If you pitch your tent in this world, you will find more or less of Sodom.

"Therefore, I say unto you, young men, who of you desire to go up to Ai? Where is Ai? Ai is wherever there is work to be done — hard work of which you are capable. Wherever there are souls to be conquered to the dominion of truth, is Ai. Wherever there is a city to be built in the name of the Lord, is Ai. Wherever there is a king like Slavery, Intemperance, Avarice, and Unbelief, to be overcome and destroyed, is Ai. Get thee up; wherefore liest thou thus upon thy face, when there is such glorious work to do — first to conquer the foes to your own peace, then to vanquish the foes of the peace of others. Are you all ready to get up, and go out on your feet, new men, with new life within you?

"No; I see that you are not. You lack entire preparation. The Christ within you has not been invoked. In the name of the Lord, can you only do this great thing. It was God who gave to Joshua the might to go forth and conquer. It was He who gave unto them Ai and his people, and his city, and his land. Will you take Jesus for your guide, and make the effort, or do you prefer to lie where you are, and let the swift coursing tide of opposing events roll over you. When Alexander and his army marched to Mount Hæmus, he found that the enemy occupied the summit of the mountain, which was covered with a line of wagons which were to be rolled down precipitously upon the ascending phalanx. He then ordered his soldiers to open their ranks, so that these wagons could pass through the intervening spaces. But soon the wagons came down so fast and hot upon them, they threw themselves on the ground, and locked their shields together, so that the wagons went over them with a bound. The sensations of those Macedonian soldiers could not have been very pleasant while lying there under that advancing foe of clattering wagons. You, who lie flat on your alleged destiny while the artillery of the enemy rolls over your backs, defended only by the shield of your philosophical resignation, know somewhat the sensations.

"'But,' do you say, 'I have tried more than once to advance and take the enemy. Their wagons are always too thick for me. I have to lie on my face in order to escape with my life.' Joshua felt just this, or he would not have torn his clothes and powdered his head with dust, in the anguish of his spirit. There is no disgrace in failure if unlinked with sin. To try a thousand times and fail only shows that you are a man with a spirit worthy of the gods. It shows that you are determined to succeed some time, and success crowns the brave soon or late. 'Men want industry more than time or abilities,' says Sallust. *Work*, WORK, WORK, is the secret of getting up and getting on. If you fail here, apply there; if you fail there, return

here; only keep on working. No matter if your
schemes come to nought; try others. The dream goes
by, but the man is here. Don Quixote returned home
from one of his great expeditions, stretched upon a
truss of hay on the bottom of a cage, in a wagon
drawn by oxen, instead of coming in the great glory
which he had foreseen. But he was none the less the
indefatigable flower of chivalry, than if drawn in state
in a gilded chariot, harnessed with royal lions, like the
gods, with angels for outriders.

"Before the commencement of earthquakes, the
clouds are fixed and motionless. So when your lot
seems to have come to a dead and forlorn standstill,
look out for the revolution which shall turn up great
things in your path.

"I said another representative of this class was the
man of business, who is content with keeping his face
to the earth, because, forsooth, he has not had the
benefit of advantages for superior culture." This is
looking backward to no good, after the style of Lot's
wife. Of what avail are useless regrets? Of what
use is it to pound in your weak points? Rather bring
them out and accustom them by use to sustain burdens
by degrees.

"But do you worry how you are going to sustain
them, when you were not trained for the work? 'O
Lord, what shall I say?' cried cowardly Joshua, there
on his face, 'when Israel turneth their backs before
their enemies?' Not content with lying on the ground,
he goes to borrowing trouble about the future. That
is the style of your cowardly souls.

"'For the Canaanites, and all the inhabitants of the

land shall hear of it, and shall environ us around, and cut off our name from the earth; and what wilt thou do unto thy great name?' continues Joshua. As though the Lord could not take care of His great name without any of Joshua's help!! As though, too, it made any real difference with Joshua and his people, what the Canaanites should say when they heard of his weakness, or what they should attempt to do!

"But how much this is like the men of to-day, who fear to get up and go on, lest they will not know what to say! Say what you honestly think, or keep still till it is time to say it. That is better in all straits than any quotations from the Greek or Latin poets; it it is better than the Sanscrit; it excels the 'dark sayings' which were uttered upon the harp of David. (It excels quotations from the old schoolmen, thought Israel.) There is no need of taking thought what you shall say when your backs are turned to your enemies. The best way is to right about face, and say nothing.

"Next, you trouble yourself over what the Canaanites will say about your defeat. This is the greatest folly of all. Who are the Canaanites? Only men like yourself; they do not even eat angels' food. They, too, have their defeats. The Canaanites are unworthy your notice, or they would not comment upon your troubles. Hence, take no notice of those Canaanites. Or if you do notice them, let it be after the fashion of the Mahometans who, at the place where they say Abraham offered up Isaac, throw seven stones at a pillar, crying, 'Stone the devil, and them that please him.' I do not counsel you to stone your enemies. Far from that; but I do advise you to stone their words with your sublimest indifference. There are invisible, noiseless shots, far more powerful than the roar of a cannon.

"The best way for you, who are struggling in discouragement, with an ever-painful consciousness of your deficiencies, is to transmute your dross into gold by the powerful alchemy of the name — '*Make the best of it.*' Mythology ascribes the invention of wreaths to Prometheus, who imitated with flowers the fetters which he had borne for his love to mankind. So, likewise, can you who have been forced to wear fetters of any kind in the days that are past, or even up to the present, call your chains wreaths, — laurel wreaths worn for your love of others! Beautiful crowning of a lot of self-sacrifice and pain! Every one of your trials should be reckoned a flower of fairest hue and sweetest fragrance. God so reckons them if they have been sanctified.

"Therefore I say unto you, as was said to Joshua, 'Up, sanctify yourselves against to-morrow!' Sanctify all your sufferings and hardships. Sanctify your hearts in the name and for the love of Jesus. Get ready for to-morrow's work!

* * * * * *

"To the third representative man — he who, being past middle life, despairs of ever doing more or better than he has already achieved, — suffer me to say that you have but just begun your existence. It is high time for you to attend to the monition, 'Get thee up; wherefore liest thou thus upon thy face!' Do you imagine that God has taken all this pains to bring you over Jordan for nothing? There is work to be done which you and only you can do. The ripe results of your long experience must be given to the world. The maturity of your judgment must be felt about you.

"'What can I do?' do you again ask? Much every way. Look about you. Sanctify yourself in the name of the Lord. Then go up to Ai. Your Ai is whatever you can do best. At eighty years old, Cato learned the Greek language. Plutarch, when nearly as old, learned Latin. Socrates learned to play on musical instruments when far advanced in life. Arnauld translated Josephus when eighty years of age. Until fifty years of age, Sir Henry Spelman was devoted to farming; then he began and afterwards mastered the sciences. Tellier, Chancellor of France, learned logic in order to dispute with his grandchildren. Chaucer commenced his Canterbury Tales in his fifty-fourth year. I might multiply such instances almost indefinitely.

"There is a beautiful device, invented by Michael Angelo, to be seen in Rome, of an old man in a go-cart, on which is an hour-glass, with the inscription, '*Yet I am learning.*'

"Of Fontenelle, who continued his literary labors to his ninety-ninth year, a friend wrote — 'Fontenelle, like our neighboring thorn, blossoms in the winter of his days.' Not all are made for this kind of going to Ai. Some go there for one object; some for another; but it matters not, so that all go, and possess the land — so that all work to some good purpose. * * * * *

"I beseech you, not to look back on your way. Do not say — 'If I only could live my life over again!' One life in this world, with so many chances of lying flat on your face, much of the time, is enough for any man. Only serpents are emblems of a mortal life without end. The wandering Jew is the most to be pitied of all men. Says Goethe — 'Nature knows no pause in progress and development, and attaches her curse on all inaction.'

\* \* \* \* \* \*

"There are things innumerable and indescribable for all of us, of whatever class or age, to do, after we obey the command, 'Get thee up.' A willing mind will make them plain to us — but one at a time. We are to live only one day in the twenty-four hours, and one hour in the sixty minutes. If God gives us strength for this, we have all we need. Let us acquire the habit, if we do not already possess it, of a calm and holy confidence in Him, who only can help us over our difficulties. Getting down on our faces, if ever so hard beset, is not to be thought of. We should teach our children that trials are the best part of life, because they make us men and women of holy valor;— they fit us for a higher order of angels; they whiten our robes as no fuller can whiten them, be none never so royal in his patent right.

"Anything short of this leads the way to despair and rebellion against God and man. It often ends in insanity. \* \*

"But O! the joyful hope, ever present to the vision of him who overcometh to the end! That hope which is an anchor to the soul, both sure and stedfast, and which entereth into that within the vail whither the forerunner is for us entered, even Jesus! \* \* \* \*

"Therefore, whosoever thou art that crieth in thy soul — 'Alas, O Lord God, wherefore hast thou at all brought us over Jordan to deliver us into the hand of our enemies, and to destroy us! hear the voice of the Lord saying — "Get thee up; wherefore liest thou thus upon thy face?"'

"From this hour, determine, in His strength, to obey his command. Sanctify yourselves for work — new work in the vineyard of the Lord, and go forward towards Ai with a joyful heart, and with a song of praise upon your lips.

# FINDING THE CITY.

#### A LETTER.

ISRAEL KNIGHT wrote to his former guardian this:—

"DEAR SIR:—

"I have given some attention to nine different denominations of Christians. Many others, more or less akin to some one of these, equally claim my investigation; but I now despair of finding what I seek, viz: the church which shall correspond to the City of the Prophet's vision, whose name deserves to be, *The Lord is there.*

"Though I find something by which to profit in all, there is no one free from my dissent in articles of faith or practice. What shall I do to be saved from my perplexity?
Respectfully yours,
ISRAEL KNIGHT."

#### REPLY.

"MY DEAR YOUNG FRIEND:—

"Read more carefully the Prophet's vision of that City with the name for which you look.

"There were gates on all sides. Every gate led to the city.

"Keep straight on any of the roads, the church-gate of which you have entered, and you will come to the place where the Lord is, provided you are right yourself. It is not the gate through which you go, but the heart which you carry through that gate. 'The kingdom of God cometh not with observation. Neither shall they say Lo here! or Lo there! for behold the kingdom of God is within you.' God is no respecter of persons; in every nation he that feareth Him and worketh righteousness, is accepted with Him.

"Every church has within it elements of truth and of error. There is no perfection this side of the City of God.

"Nothing is more to be deprecated than the prayer that all may come to think just like our own little clan. It would be the utmost misfortune to all Christendom to have only one church. The city to which only one gate led, would be another Babylon, full of the abominations of the earth.

"When Christ sent forth the seventy disciples into every city and place whither he himself would come, he gave them no creed, imposed no restrictions save of the merest practical import. To him who, wishing to tempt the Lord, asked him, 'What shall I do to inherit eternal life?' reference was given to the law which read, 'Thou shalt love the Lord thy God with all thy heart, and with all thy soul, and with all thy strength, and with all thy mind; and thy neighbor as thyself.'

"'Teaching them to observe all things whatsoever

I have commanded you,' were the words of Jesus to the twelve in his commission to them before his departure from their sight. The summary of these 'all things' was repentance and faith. This is the utmost simplicity consistent with any expression of doctrine.

"Different temperaments with different degrees of cultivation require varying modes of expansion of this central doctrine, in its two-fold expression. This is well. It is promotive of enterprise; it keeps the spiritual atmosphere of churches comparatively pure; it saves man from falling into the grossest error of his nature, which is tyranny.

"Doubtless God sees that this is good, or he would not repeat his signal manifestations of goodness to each and all of the churches.

"Therefore I say to him who prefers to journey by the gate of Joseph, toward the City whose name is *The Lord is there*, let him not turn coldly away from him who cometh by the gate of Dan, or Simeon, or Gad, or Napthali.

"This business is between you and God, and concerns no other so nearly.

"I enclose for you a branch broken from the palm-tree, under which once sat a great Heart.

Truly yours,

Ephraim Stearns."

This was what Israel found enclosed: —

"Truth indeed came once into the world with her Divine Master, and was a perfect shape most glorious to look on; but when he ascended, and his Apostles after him were laid asleep, then straight arose a wicked race of deceivers, who, as that story goes of the Egyptian Typhon with his conspirators, how they dealt with the good Osiris, took the virgin Truth, hewed her lovely form into a thousand pieces, and scattered them to the four winds. From that time ever since, the sad friends of Truth, such as durst appear, imitating the careful search that Isis made for the mangled body of Osiris, went up and down gathering up limb by limb still as they could find them. We have not yet found them all, lords and commons, nor ever shall do, till her master's second coming; he shall bring together every joint and member, and shall mould them into an immortal feature of loveliness and perfection." — *Milton's Areopagitica.*

## CONCLUSION.

After this, Israel Knight spent some time, chiefly alone. Among his possessions was a solitary estate managed by a tenant with a small family. Thither he betook himself, and sought to discover what manner of man he was.

By accident he read of Uriel Acosta, a Portuguese, who embraced so many religious opinions, he suffered many persecutions. Born a Christian, he became a pervert to Judaism, and ended by being a deist. In despair, he finally shot himself.

Then Israel said — " There is peril in my thus halting between opinions. Henceforth, I will seek to be a disciple of Christ. I shall love all men though they love me not. In whatever place I find a true worker for the good of his fellowmen, I will be to him a brother.

And with this simple yet sublime faith in his heart, he went forth again into the world, no longer seeking the city. He had found it; and over all the gates on either side, he read this inscription: —

"*Therefore thou art inexcusable, O man, whosoever thou art that judgest.*"

www.ingramcontent.com/pod-product-compliance
Lightning Source LLC
Chambersburg PA
CBHW030255240426
43673CB00040B/973